Careers in Social Work

Second Edition

WITHDRAWN

Leon H. Ginsberg
University of South Carolina

Allyn and Bacon
Boston • London • Toronto • Sydney • Tokyo • Singapore

Editor-in-Chief, Social Sciences: Karen Hanson
Editorial Assistant: Alyssa Pratt
Marketing Manager: Jackie Aaron
Production Editor: Christopher H. Rawlings
Editorial-Production Service: Omegatype Typography, Inc.
Composition and Prepress Buyer: Linda Cox
Manufacturing Buyer: Julie McNeill
Cover Administrator: Brian Gogolin
Electronic Composition: Omegatype Typography, Inc.

Library of Congress Cataloging-in-Publication Data

Ginsberg, Leon H.
    Careers in social work / Leon H. Ginsberg. — 2nd ed.
      p. cm.
    Includes bibliographical references.
    ISBN 0-205-33074-6 (alk. paper)
    1. Social service—Vocational guidance—United States.   I. Title.

HV10.5 .G55 2001
361.3'023'73—dc21

                                                    00-032277

Printed in the United States of America

10 9 8 7 6 5 4 3 2 1   05 04 03 02 01 00

Contents

Preface

This is the second edition of a book about becoming a social worker, being a social worker, and building a professional career in that exciting and growing field. It is also about finding social work jobs, choosing among the many kinds of work social workers do, and succeeding in the profession.

The need for this book is new because the social work profession was, until recently, much smaller, less formal, and much less diverse. As readers will see, social work has grown to become a large and influential profession that extends into every part of the United States and into every kind of human service.

The audience for this book is people who are considering social work careers or who are already studying for a professional career in the field. It is written from a practical perspective—where to go to find a job; how to evaluate a job; how to decide if the job, or even the field of social work, is for you. It describes the ways social workers work, what they know, and what they believe. It also deals with job applications, licenses, credentials, salaries, benefits, and working conditions—the information people need to decide about and begin working in social work.

Social work is different now than it was for much of its history. Although formal education for social work has been in existence for over 100 years, many social workers began their careers by practicing social work before they formally studied it in a college or university. If they liked what they did and seemed to have a talent for it, they might decide to go, or their agency might send them, to school to acquire the specialized knowledge and credentials of a social worker. Until the 1970s, social work was a fairly small occupation and workers came from and went to a relatively small range of agencies. Public assistance, child welfare, and voluntary agencies such as family service societies, Red Cross, and a variety of sectarian or religious programs absorbed large numbers of those who graduated from social work schools. The demand for social workers was great and the supply was small. Almost anyone who qualified for graduate social work education received financial support to pay for his or her education, with the understanding that upon graduation they would work for the agency or in the field that gave them support.

Although today many social work students still come directly from practice and large numbers receive financial support and assistance, the numbers of students are very different. Most students pay their own educational expenses with personal funds and student loans.

In 1998 there were more than 40,000 students in social work degree programs, many of whom chose social work as a major or their area of graduate study before they had experience in the field. For comparison, in 1978, only 9,476 accredited master of social work degrees were awarded compared to 13,660 in 1998. There were 11,435 bachelor of social work degrees awarded in 1998. One hundred and seventy-eight people were awarded social work doctorates in 1978, compared to 266 in 1998.

Much about social work has changed, as this book explains. There are now some 600,000 people in social work positions in the United States. Some 500 educational programs in every part of the United States and most of the nations of the world offer baccalaureate, doctorate, and master's degrees in social work. Whereas the master's degree was the primary professional degree until the 1970s, baccalaureate degrees began to be accredited for social work practice by the middle of that decade. Doctoral degrees in social work were once rare, but now there are more than fifty programs offering the Doctor of Social Work or the Ph.D. in social work. Licensing or legal regulation of social work was also rare until recently. Now all states have some arrangement for assuring that those who are called social workers are qualified to practice the profession. This book includes information about those licensing and other regulation programs.

Part of the reason for writing this book has been my interest, during a career of more than forty years in social work, in the ways the profession has changed—especially the ways social workers have worked. When I began studying social work at Tulane University in New Orleans in 1958, a few days after finishing my active service as an Army artillery officer, there were many more jobs for social workers than there were social workers. Although they were not able to recruit with very high salaries, agencies competed in any ways they could for professional social workers. It was a seller's market. Qualified social workers could find employment almost anywhere in the United States at the modest but middle-income salaries that social agencies paid.

Of course, numbers change. In 1961 I took my second social work job in Tulsa, Oklahoma. I couldn't turn it down because it paid $9,500 per year, which was then a grand salary. My employer was a community planning and services agency and the board of directors was heavily composed of prosperous oil executives. When I left there to become an assistant professor of social work at the University of Oklahoma, the salary was $8,750 per year, a little less than in Tulsa, but that was for only nine months. Those were good salaries at the time but they are below the minimum wage of the new millenium.

Social work salaries continue to change. In 2000 $35,000 was a good beginning salary but many graduates right out of school took jobs with much higher earnings. Generally, whatever the averages are at any time, our incomes are in the middle of all wage earners. There are not many very wealthy or very poor social workers whose incomes come primarily from their professional work.

I briefly explain what social work is and how it is structured—who pays for it, who controls it, where it has come from, and where it may be going. In some cases, I illustrate the information with examples from my own experiences and those of others. In a few cases, I provide fictional case examples to illustrate how something may be effective in social work. Readers should understand that social workers are involved in more activities than are described. The several introductory texts on social work, the *Encyclopedia of Social Work* (Edwards et al., 1995), and the 1997 Supplement (Edwards et al., 1997) are good sources for detailed information on the total field of social work. Also, not all social workers would handle all the case examples and ethical dilemmas discussed in this book in the same ways I do. There are usually several different ways to deal with any social work incident and all or most of them may be correct.

My top priority is for this book to be accurate, readable, and clear. There are some grand pieces of esoteric scholarship in social work that everyone should read, but I answer the practical questions readers have about social work and social work careers in ways they can use immediately.

I hope my explanations are simple and readily understood. However, the social work field is varied and complex. For the most part, social workers don't exactly teach; we don't usually direct other people; we don't exactly lead; we don't exactly counsel; but we do a little of all of that in the course of our work, no matter what the organization or service that employs us.

Social work is a profession like no other and parts of some of its tasks are so subtle that they are difficult to explain in writing and in teaching. A fully developed education in social work requires reading, class attendance, and, above all, actual practice experience under the direction of an accomplished social work practitioner. I hope this book will help give some practical direction to those personal developments and efforts.

Part 1 guides the reader through the development of social work as a profession, describing the personal and professional factors that build a social work career. The ethics that guide the profession, some of the rules and regulations that govern us, and the ways we can compete for the kinds of work we pursue are the basic subjects of this introductory portion of the book.

Part 2 deals with the nature of social work jobs. It describes what social workers do and how they do it in a few large, selected fields.

Part 3 discusses the skills and knowledge individuals should have, even if they were not learned in professional education, and guidance on how social work professionals are able to take care of themselves and their own needs, an important but often neglected component of any career guidance.

One of the rewarding realities of social work is the satisfaction our clients report with the services we provide. Those we try to help often think we succeed, which is gratifying. Few would want to be social workers if they did not believe they were helping others. After all, that is the essence of what we are about. As the book makes clear, people become social workers because they like social welfare and what it does and because they enjoy their work. Those who worked on this book, primarily the author and the editors, feel confident about its potential for helping future social workers and we hope our readers feel the same.

My thanks go to several who assisted in developing this project—Judy Fifer who saw the promise of this effort and helped conceptualize and develop it; Alyssa Pratt of

Allyn and Bacon who helped shepherd this edition through the editing and production processes; Omegatype Typography, Inc., especially Karla Walsh, for editorial services; Joyce Shaw of the University of South Carolina College of Social Work, who assisted with the early drafts; Dean Frank Raymond of the same College, for his continuous support of my research and writing; Lee Aanderud, also of the College, for his assistance with data processing; Kathleen C. Hoffman and Donna DeAngelis of the American Association of State Social Work Boards; and my wife, Connie Ginsberg, for tolerating my months in front of a computer. Writing about social work, unlike practicing it, is a lonely pastime. It would be much lonelier without the support and encouragement of those who have helped.

We will appreciate comments from readers. The book is designed to help with some critical decisions and choices of directions. We promise to listen and to respond.

L. G.

Part 1

Working in Social Work

Many books tell us how to be social workers—how to understand and evaluate clients, their families, and their larger environments; how to interview people; and how to understand and work to change social policy among other complicated and important subjects.

This book is different because its focus is on the employment issues that social workers, like people in any other profession, address throughout their careers. Practical matters such as finding and keeping a job; knowing what to look for in salary and benefits; seeking and obtaining proper credentials, such as social work licenses; and a number of other issues are the primary emphases of this book. These issues, which are not and perhaps should not be high on the list of concerns of new social workers, can ultimately make the difference between success and the lack of success in a professional career. Understanding these subjects before choosing social work as a profession, and especially before embarking on a professional career, is worth a great deal. I wish someone had told me more about them before I began working in this exciting and rewarding field. Many experienced social workers agree. But those who are often most eager for the kind of information presented in Part 1 are new graduates of baccalaureate and master's social work programs. Each year, several come to me and to other social work professors to seek our advice and to tell us about their often frustrating on-the-job learning about some of the subjects discussed here. Familiarity with the way social work jobs are organized, social work compensation and benefits, and the questions applicants need to ask before taking a job would have saved them much time and frustration.

The first chapter of Part 1 defines the social work profession and its history. It also details some of the major professional concerns of social workers and those preparing for social work careers such as their personal traits, attitudes, and values. The National Association of Social Workers Code of Ethics, which is Appendix 1, is discussed and explained.

1

In addition, some information on social work education at the baccalaureate, master's, and doctoral levels, is introduced. Chapter 3, which is included in Part 1, covers the subject of education for professional social work in much more detail and Appendix 2 lists the educational institutions that provide accredited social work education at the baccalaureate and master's levels as well as the schools that offer doctoral education in the field.

Chapter 2 deals with a question that is often of major importance to those considering or pursuing social work careers—the nature of employment in the field. It also offers some basic information on the structure of social work jobs and the practice methods used by social workers in carrying out their work with clients, organizations, and communities. It also covers the various kinds of agencies, both governmental (public) and nongovernmental (voluntary) in the United States. Of course, much more information on social work jobs is provided in later chapters.

Part 1 is the basic introduction to the book and its content. The balance of the book elaborates on these areas of interest for social workers and those interested in becoming social workers.

1

What Is Social Work?

What Being a Social Worker Means

Social work is unique in the helping or human service professions, which include many fields that are sometimes more familiar to the general public than social work. They include health care professions such as medicine and nursing, psychology, education, counseling, physical and vocational rehabilitation, and many others. Social work's similarities to, differences from, and relationships with those other professions are discussed later in this chapter.

More than anything else, this book is designed to help readers understand the social work profession; to help them determine whether they would like to be part of it; to become aware of the ways one becomes a social worker; and to help them find work and build a career in this large and growing profession.

Size and Scope of Social Work

The profession of social work is large and growing. There are some 600,000 people in the United States employed as social workers. Social workers serve in a wide variety of places in many different roles, which is much of what this book is about. According to Bernstein and Ma (1996), the federal government's Bureau of Labor Statistics (Bureau of Labor Statistics, 1998, 1999a, 1999b) predicts that social work and fields to which it is related will be in the top ten occupation growth areas through 2006. *Newsweek* magazine (Begun, 2000) shows that social work will grow by 74 percent between 1994 and 2005. The Bureau of Labor Statistics (1999a) says that social workers held 585,000 jobs in 1996. Another 178,000 people were employed as social and human service assistants—many of whom were educated as social workers—in 1996. Some 175,000 people were employed as counselors and many of them were social workers in 1996. Total employment in social work and its related fields was predicted to be more than one million by 2001. The increased portion of the population that is elderly, the needs of people with disabilities such as physical and mental illness and mental retardation, as well as the larger numbers of people who are imprisoned for long terms, all contribute to the need for more social workers. Many social workers and people with social work preparation hold jobs that are considered part of the human services field. The number of home health aides, workers in another field in which social work has some involvement, is projected to grow to over one million by 2005. The coming years appear to be promising for those who plan careers in social work and related fields.

The Social Work Profession

Social work, like the other disciplines discussed in this chapter, is a profession rather than a job or an occupation. Professions have three characteristics, all of which social work includes:

1. A profession has a body of knowledge that its members must know about.
2. Members of a profession believe in something or some set of things. They adhere to a set of shared ethics and values, such as the Code of Ethics in Appendix 1.
3. Professions have skills that their members use to serve others.

Social work's knowledge, values, and skills and how they are used in professional careers are a large part of the subject matter of this book.

Despite its size, social work is not as well known to most people as some other professions are. Many who have graduated from high school and even college have never heard of it. There are probably many reasons for social work's lack of recognition, which is often a source of frustration for those of us who are social workers and, especially, for students who choose to become social work majors and to pursue social work careers. Explaining the career choice to parents and friends is often difficult because they haven't heard of the field before. New social work undergraduate majors or graduate students may be asked, "Is that a major? Is that a real job? What will you do? Do they pay people for that?"

Yes, social work is a real major, a real job, and people are paid to be social workers. This book helps explain the work of social workers—their preparation, their pay, their career choices, and the variety of ways in which they help others. It also helps explain why social work is one of the largest single industries in the United States.

Social Work Is Not Well Known

I began studying social work and working as a social worker over forty years ago. It was difficult then to explain my chosen occupation to my family and friends, just as it is for many new social workers and social work students today. I am not sure my parents ever sufficiently understood what I did until I became a social work professor in the early 1960s. Being a college professor was something that they could explain to others, because everyone had heard of colleges and professors.

Things are not much different now. In the 1980s when I was in charge of a large social work agency in the state of West Virginia, my boss was the governor (he's now a U.S. Senator), John D. (Jay) Rockefeller IV. I wanted to bring more social workers into the Department of Human Services because I thought they could help our impoverished clients better than many of the other people we hired. One of the nonsocial workers in the agency called an investigative reporter for the local newspaper, who, in turn, called the governor's top assistant, a smart and successful lawyer. The assistant called me to ask, "What's a BSW; what's an MSW?" I explained it to him and we continued with our efforts to increase the numbers of professionally educated social workers in the agency. But it was clear then, and it is not much different now, that few outside the social work profession are as familiar with our work and our objectives as we would like.

Why Social Work Is Sometimes Poorly Understood

Several reasons and gaps in our educational system keep many people unaware of social work. Those who have heard of social work are likely to misunderstand the profession. Some of the reasons for the lack of knowledge of social work in the larger public and its being misunderstood are:

1. Social work sounds like other disciplines and may cause confusion. People who have heard of sociology, for example, may confuse that social science with social work, even though they are far from the same. In elementary school most people studied "social studies," another term with which social work can be confused. Mention social work and some are likely to think one means sociology or social studies.

2. People outside social work often view social workers by what they do or where they work, rather than by their profession, because social workers almost always have job titles in addition to the professional title of social worker. Many work with older people, so they and their families may consider social workers "senior center employees" rather than social workers. Those who work in mental health centers, hospitals, and prisons may be viewed as counselors within those facilities rather than as social workers. Social workers may work in camps and recreation programs as directors or counselors. They are more likely to be identified by these titles rather than as members of the social work profession. Most social workers are called something other than "social workers."

3. Social work is not a subject that is usually taught in elementary and secondary schools. Students learn about physicians, lawyers, soldiers, and teachers, but not often about social workers. Even in colleges and universities—where there are some 500 social work colleges, departments, or schools, with more than 40,000 undergraduate and graduate students—social work is not always well known (Lennon, 1998). Many colleges and universities offer *no* social work degrees—or even courses. Although the profession is large, we are only a small part of the much larger world of higher education.

4. Although there are many social workers and social work services, most people do not come into contact with social workers during the normal course of their lives. If they do, they do not recognize them as social workers. Many of the services that social workers provide are for people with special characteristics or problems, such as being elderly, being a child who is not able to be cared for by biological parents, having developmental disabilities, being poor, being seriously ill, or being in trouble with the law. People with those characteristics usually know more about social work and social workers than the general public. However, they are a minority of the total population.

5. The media do not cover social workers or social work programs as extensively as they do other fields such as education, health care, or law enforcement. Even when social workers are covered in newspapers and on radio and television, they may not be identified as social workers.

6. The social work profession has not spent as much time and money as it might to educate the public about its work. Most social agencies are part of the government, or are nonprofit, charitable organizations. Therefore, it seems wrong to many social workers to use their time and money for public relations when there are still unserved clients. Public education about the profession takes a secondary role in social workers' efforts.

7. Social work is not always a powerful profession although it has had fairly high degrees of success in influencing the laws and budgets that deal with those it serves. Therefore, social workers do not always have the resources to make themselves well-known or well-understood.

For such reasons, social workers often find it necessary to explain themselves to others. They are engaged in a career that is neither well-known nor well-understood. Despite their relative anonymity, however, most like to call themselves social workers. They are proud of their profession and their work. They want more people to know and care about them. Many resist other titles—such as therapist, planner, social science expert, or administrator—which are possibly better understood and may convey higher status.

According to the *Social Work Dictionary* (Barker, 1999, p. 455), social work is "the applied science of helping people achieve an effective level of psychosocial functioning and effecting societal changes to enhance the well-being of all people." Throughout this book, the ways in which social workers carry out those two intertwined kinds of work are explained.

Comparisons with Other Professions

Social work connects with and has some similarities to many other human services professions. However, it is also distinct from them and has its own characteristics. Part of social work's knowledge base is an understanding of how other professions operate and what they do, because social workers—probably more than many other professionals—collaborate with other professions. Interdisciplinary and team work are major elements of the role of social workers, especially in fields such as corrections, health, and mental health (Andrews, 1990). Addressing social problems often requires the knowledge and perspectives of a number of disciplines, whether the task is as large as revising the nation's welfare system, or as particular as helping one individual or family overcome some social or personal problems. Therefore, learning about other professions and learning to work together with other disciplines is a critical factor in the success of social workers.

Some of the ways social work compares to other fields of study and other disciplines follows.

Sociology

As discussed earlier in this chapter, many people confuse sociology with social work. Of course, they are quite different. Sociology is a field of study, a social science, that examines the ways human beings interact with one another and with the larger society and how organizations behave.

Social work makes extensive use of information from sociology, as well as other disciplines, but social work is a practice field. As its name implies, the social work profession does things with knowledge to help others. Social work does not emphasize knowledge for its own sake. Instead, it emphasizes the use of knowledge for application to the issues of helping others. Stated another way, sociology develops knowledge that social work and other human services professions put into practice.

Psychology

Psychologists are professionals who study behavior and mental processes (Barker, 1999). It has many specialties such as community psychology; experimental, clinical, and educational, psychology; and counseling. Many psychologists evaluate and treat mental illnesses. Consequently, social workers and psychologists often work together in the same agencies and serve the same clients from different perspectives. Many graduate social work students were undergraduate psychology majors. Social workers rely on extensive information from the field of psychology, just as they do on information and knowledge from sociology. Psychology also interacts with sociology, and in some ways the two sciences overlap. For example, there is a specialized field of social psychology, which studies issues similar to those studied by sociologists.

Psychology is also an applied or practice profession. The field of clinical psychology is one of its largest specializations. Clinical psychologists counsel clients, administer psychological tests and measurements, and diagnose and assess client conditions. When they collaborate on the same cases, psychologists and social workers often assess clients, with psychologists focusing on psychological issues, and social workers focusing on social concerns. In some states psychologists are legally authorized to prescribe drugs that affect the mind. The terminal or most advanced practice degree required for clinical psychologists is ordinarily a doctorate; in social work, it is ordinarily a master's.

Psychiatry

Psychiatrists are physicians who have completed special training and a residency in psychiatry after earning the degree in medicine. They are specialists in diagnosing and treating mental disorders. Social workers work closely with psychiatrists; there is a social work subdiscipline called psychiatric social work. Psychiatric social workers specialize in work with psychiatric or mental health patients in psychiatric settings.

Frequently, when social workers work with psychiatrists, the psychiatrist deals with the medical aspects of the patient's care and the social worker deals with the social elements of the patient's problems. Many social workers devote their efforts to helping the patient make adjustments and arrangements for living outside a mental institution, or for helping the patient and the family deal with the patient's mental or emotional difficulties in the community.

Of course, many social workers also provide counseling and problem-solving help to mental health clients, plus help them deal with the social and practical elements of mental illness.

Nursing

Nursing is a profession that shares some similarities with social work. The majority of its practitioners are women, it is primarily a baccalaureate and master's degree profession, and nurses often work in jobs that are under the direction of other professionals, as social workers often do. (Specially trained nurse practitioners perform some of the tasks that were once only the province of physicians.)

Although providing nursing care is the best-known responsibility of nurses, nursing, like social work, has many dimensions. Nurses work extensively in public health, education, and health care management. There are psychiatric nurses—parallel, in some ways, to psychiatric social workers—who work with the social and emotional problems of people with mental illness. Nurses also help patients with some of the social issues surrounding their illnesses and assist families in dealing with the health problems of patients.

Like social workers, nurses serve in community-based positions as well as in institutional settings. However, nursing services are always related to health in some way, whereas social work extends into a variety of nonhealth areas.

Counseling and Therapy

Counseling and therapy are terms used in a variety of professions, many of which are close to social work in their nature and function, and the credentials for which many social workers also hold.

Among the disciplines included in counseling and therapy are marital and family therapy, a field that is licensed in many states and for which there is professional preparation. Many social workers also hold credentials as marital and family thera-pists. Another subdiscipline is rehabilitation counseling, which focuses on helping people with various kinds of physical, mental, and social disabilities. The focus of this counseling is on helping clients become rehabilitated so they can become em-ployable or self-sufficient in other ways.

Guidance counseling is a discipline often taught in departments or schools of education. Its primary focus has traditionally been helping students with educational planning and problems, including designing curricula and selecting colleges and careers. School guidance counselors and school social workers often work closely to assist troubled students and their families. Many counselors with preparation in educational counseling are also qualified to counsel individuals and families who have emotional or social problems. In some states, counselors may qualify for psy-chology licenses. Some, like social workers, qualify for certification in marriage and family therapy. Many counselors also work in the personnel offices of businesses (Barker, 1999).

In general, social workers differ from counselors in an additional emphasis on working with larger systems, environmental issues, and for social and policy change. While many social workers work mostly with individual clients and their families, the field of social work has a broader goal: working with (and as) policy makers. As part of their professional responsibilities, social workers develop programs that as-sist people to prevent or solve problems, develop and promote legislation, and oth-erwise deal with larger, systemic concerns. These roles distinguish social work from many other human services.

Social and Human Service Assistants

Many social workers or people who want to become social workers serve as social and human service assistants. This is one of the top ten growth professions, accord-ing to the Bureau of Labor Statistics (1999b) but it is really a general kind of cate-gory that includes social service and social work assistants, case management aides, residential counselors in group facilities, drug and alcohol abuse counselors, mental health technicians, child care workers, gerontology aides, and outreach workers. Many social workers with bachelor's degrees fill these jobs. With some experience, these assistants may earn $20,000 to $30,000 per year, but that depends on where they work, the kind of work they do, and their other qualifications.

Medicine

Social workers in many settings deal frequently with physicians other than psychi-atrists in a variety of ways. In general, social workers help with the psychosocial needs of patients. Social workers help patients and their families arrange social so-lutions to illness or convalescence. Social workers help physicians understand the social issues associated with the health problems they treat. Social workers also help patients find the means to pay their doctor and hospital bills when their insurance or personal funds are insufficient.

Social workers serve in many specialized medical fields (such as renal dialysis, organ transplantation, and neonatal services) as well as in general medical practice, family practice, and internal medicine. Social workers in health care settings are sometimes called medical social workers.

Law

Social workers also collaborate with lawyers in a variety of ways, some of which are described in this book. They help lawyers serve clients who are involved in domestic conflicts and child custody issues. In child welfare or family service programs, social workers often work with attorneys in adoption cases. In the corrections field, social workers who are probation and parole workers frequently work with lawyers for the benefit of their mutual clients.

Although there are no supporting census figures, there are professionals who hold both law and social work degrees. Some have become judges. Others work as policy experts on laws governing social welfare issues.

Administration

Social workers are often administrators of social programs. Administration (or management, as this work is increasingly called) is one of social work's specialized areas. Some social workers are commissioners or directors of state government human services agencies, hospital administrators, directors of many kinds of institutions, and chief executives of national organizations. In those roles, they often direct and supervise the work of the other professionals mentioned here.

However, there are also many other fields of administration, especially business, hospital, and public administration, which are involved in human services. Social workers often work as consultants, colleagues, or employees of administrators in various governmental as well as voluntary agencies.

This list does not include all the disciplines with which social work interacts. There are many others—physical rehabilitation, teaching, theology, law enforcement and criminal justice, speech pathology—almost any field that deals with human issues and human problems.

Social Work's History

Social work students all learn about the history of the profession, but students in other fields are not likely to know very much about it. Standard history texts do not often cover much, if anything, about social work. Political science texts, which may discuss social programs, only rarely mention the social workers who operate those programs. The following is a quick review of social work's origins.

In some ways, social work is a fairly new profession when compared to law, medicine, nursing, and teaching, but it has a fairly long history. In the United States, social work is over one hundred years old. Most believe it began in the early 1900s, but it had even earlier origins.

Origins of Social Work

In many ways, social work and social workers are as old as civilization. For all of human history, people have shared their houses, their food, and their clothing with others who are less fortunate. They have cared for children and older people from the families of their relatives and neighbors when their families and neighbors were unable to care for them.

The Old and New Testaments of the Bible are filled with social work injunctions—to care for the poor, to provide for the widows and children of one's siblings, to honor one's parents, and many others. Social welfare, which is the general name for the programs and services in which social workers work, has always been a part of all the religions of the world—Christianity, Islam, Judaism, Buddhism, Hinduism, and every other religious persuasion. Part of the worship of God is providing help to others—providing social work services.

Although we do not know very much about early social work in cultures other than those that are close to our own, we think the tradition exists in every human culture. A book by Phyllis Day (2000) describes well the early social work in non-Western nations, as well as our own. A standard text by Axinn and Levin (1997) outlines the origins as well as much of the current information about American social welfare programs in the United States.

We know that in early English history church parishes took responsibility for helping the disadvantaged, such as the poor, widows, dependent children, people with disabilities, and the elderly. After the break with the Roman Catholic Church and the founding of the Church of England, the English religious institutions continued to provide social welfare services. The first social workers, although they were not known as such, were ministers and priests.

In the late 1500s and early 1600s, England began passing laws to deal formally with social welfare problems and services. The best known of those laws was the Elizabethan Poor Law of 1601, which pulled together a number of existing laws, defining the ways people were expected to care for their relatives and outlining how the government would provide help to those who could not be helped by their families.

Early English history is important to social work in the United States because much of what we do is based on the policies of England. The forerunners of social workers in the United States in the 1800s were "friendly visitors" for charity organizations in England. They went to the homes of disadvantaged people and helped them overcome their personal problems and their poverty through counseling as well as helping the families obtain food, clothing, shelter, and other necessities. These helpers usually had a degree of wealth and high community status. Their charge was to teach child care, housekeeping, budgeting, and shopping to others who were less fortunate than they.

Systematic and Scientific Help

In the process of serving others, some early helpers developed ideas about systematically and scientifically helping disadvantaged people in ways that would make them self-sufficient and prevent their becoming dependent on the larger society.

Some of those principles were adopted by the English Charity Organization Societies, forerunners of the American charity organizations. The Charity Organization Societies' approach was imported to the United States and began in Buffalo, New York, in 1877 (Alexander, 1995). The work of the friendly visitors was the forerunner of social work's direct services workers, whose skills are a major part of the efforts we see in mental health and health services and in work with disadvantaged people in both government and private social services programs, such as family service agencies.

Research and Administration

Many early predecessors to professional social workers also helped society understand social problems by organizing and conducting social research. Others focused on social administration, helping to ensure that funds were available and properly spent, as well as managing social services in ways that best helped clients. Another of the classic administrative functions was establishing registries of aid recipients, so help wasn't duplicated, and developing directories of services so clients would know where to go for help. These functions of studying, administering, and coordinating services arose from the charity organization movements.

As Chapter 3 on educational preparation shows, social research remains a major emphasis in social work. All social work students study and practice research as part of their educational program. Many social work agencies and schools of social work are deeply involved in carrying out research projects, and many social workers devote all or part of their working time to research studies, indicating there are many career opportunities for social workers in research.

Social administration also remains a major part of social work. All students study administration and management. Many social workers who show administrative talent in their jobs are promoted to management positions (Ginsberg & Keys, 1995; Weinbach, 1994).

Settlement Houses and Self-Help

Only about half of all social work should be traced to charity organizations. Another social service movement developed in England, and later in the United States. In 1884 a group of social reformers and university students developed the first "settlement house," Kingsley House in London (Alexander, 1995). The settlement house movement began in the United States with the development of the Neighborhood Guild in New York in 1886, followed in 1889 by Hull House, founded by Jane Addams in Chicago. These original settlements were soon followed throughout the United States by other settlement houses, such as the Henry Street Settlement in New York, Kingsley House in New Orleans, and many similar organizations.

The settlement movement also viewed its charge as helping the poor overcome their problems, but their approach was quite different. Whereas the Charity Organization Society movement sent its friendly visitors to the poor for short visits in order to help them, the settlement movement permanently located students and other successful, idealistic people in impoverished neighborhoods. The helpers settled and lived among the disadvantaged. The emphasis of the settlement movement was on helping people to help themselves. The neighborhood residents learned, especially in the United States, to deal with local governments to obtain adequate environmental and educational services. They also learned about art, drama, and music, as well as job skills, through the educational and cultural opportunities offered at the centralized settlement "house."

One of the primary functions of the early settlements (still a function today) is teaching English to immigrants. Immigrants to the United States have traditionally been among the poorest of American residents. To move up in the economy and qualify for citizenship requires knowledge of English. Settlements helped newcomers from places such as Italy, Poland, and Russia learn the language in an earlier time, just as many today help immigrants from Asia, Latin America, and the Caribbean learn the language. Settlements, then as well as now, focused on helping people through group approaches—groups of teenagers, groups of mothers, groups of fathers, and groups of families. Helping people to help one another, as well as themselves, was and is the predominant strategy. Settlement workers also sometimes helped organize the kind of political clout that was necessary to obtain better services from government for the neighborhood residents. Frank McCourt, the author of two popular autobiographical books, *Angela's Ashes* and *'Tis* (1996, 1999) describes his and his family's experiences as Irish-Americans in making the transition to citizenship and employment.

Modern Milestones

Many modern developments in social work history have led to the expansion of the social work profession. Such social welfare policies and programs as the Social Security Act of 1935, the various federal and state statutes dealing with mental health and disabilities, the Economic Opportunity Act of 1964, Medicare and Medicaid, and many others are the cornerstone of social services in the United States. The most far-reaching changes in the American social welfare system came with the passage of the federal government's Personal Responsibility and Work Opportunity Reconciliation Act of 1996, which was implemented in 1997. It gave more power to the states, established strict work requirements for recipients of aid, and set time limits for receiving aid (Ginsberg, 1999b). These government acts made the intentions and efforts of the early social work movements into laws and public policies. They are the basis for the agencies in which social workers work, and are discussed in detail throughout this book.

The Two Traditions

As this chapter makes clear, social work comes from two great historical traditions, the Charity Organization Societies and the settlement movement. Although they had many similarities, the charity movement was largely oriented to helping change individuals and their families—the source of social problems, according to its proponents. The settlements, on the other hand, took a more social perspective on human problems and wanted to change the larger society or the environment. Both groups understood that both strategies had their place.

It was out of these two great traditions that social work, as a single profession, began to emerge. Direct practice or casework was the contribution of the charity organizations. Group work, community organization, social planning, and social change emanate from the settlement movement. Social research and social work management have roots in both traditions.

Early Social Work Training Programs

In 1898 the first education or training programs for professional social workers were developed in New York to prepare people for work in the charity organization societies (Alexander, 1995). Mary Richmond, the primary organizer, became the first social work teacher and textbook writer, as well as the founder of social casework. Many of her principles are still part of the education of all social workers. Her training program became and remains the Columbia University School of Social Work in New York. In 1903 it was followed by the Chicago School of Civics and Philanthropy, which became the University of Chicago School of Social Service Administration (Alexander, 1995).

The Birth of a Profession

By the early twentieth century, social workers organized a number of professional organizations, often with a special focus for their own agencies and institutions. There were organizations for caseworkers, group workers, community organizers, psychiatric social workers, school social workers, and many of the other specialized places where social workers were employed.

In 1955, nearly 50 years ago, the American social work organizations came together as the National Association of Social Workers (NASW), which has remained the largest and most inclusive of all the profession's various entities.

The NASW developed and regularly updates the social work Code of Ethics (see Appendix 1), maintains information on the branches of social work, and lobbies (along with other groups) for better social welfare programs as well as for opportunities for social workers.

This simplified discussion of the highlights of social work's history shows its development and its characteristics—important background for much of what follows about the profession.

Social Work Education—Degrees, Levels, and Credentials

Social work education is monitored and accredited by the Council on Social Work Education, an association of social work education programs, educators, some social work students, and some social agencies that employ social workers. Chapter 3, the detailed chapter on educational preparation, describes some of what prospective and new social work students need to know about social work education.

Generally, education for social workers consists of the study of five curriculum areas: (1) human behavior and the social environment to understand human psychology, sociology, and biology; (2) social welfare policy and services to understand programs and services and the ways they are developed and changed; (3) social research to help social workers better evaluate better their work and contribute to new knowledge about people and the problems they face; (4) social work methods of practice, for information about skills and approaches social workers need for carrying out their responsibilities; and (5) field practicum, for practical experience in the profession under the supervision of experienced professional social workers.

There are three levels of professional social workers in the United States: (1) those with baccalaureate or bachelor's degrees in social work (BSWs); (2) people who hold master's degrees (MSWs); and (3) those who have doctoral degrees, either a Ph.D. in Social Work or a Doctor of Social Work (DSW).

In 1998 there were 11,435 social work bachelor's degrees, 13,660 MSWs, and 266 doctoral degrees awarded in the some 500 social work education programs in the United States (Lennon, 1999).

Recognition of Baccalaureate Education

For a long time the only accredited degree in social work was the master's. Bachelor's degrees were offered in many schools, but they were not well recognized by the profession or accredited by the Council on Social Work Education, the profession's accrediting organization. This is partly because so many people became social agency employees after they finished their bachelor's degree in a different discipline; the MSW was an added educational credential for people who were practicing social workers with little or no formal education about the profession.

The paradox of social work was that most of the jobs called social work positions were filled by people with a wide variety of bachelor's degrees, such as education, psychology, sociology, and history, while few were filled by social work degree holders. To remedy that situation, the federal government and the social work profession joined together in the 1970s to recognize and support the bachelor of social work (BSW) degree and to prepare bachelor's level students for social work jobs. In 1998 there were 358 accredited BSW degree programs. The National Association of Social Workers, which had limited membership to MSWs, now provides membership and board representation to BSWs. Most state licensing and regulation laws, which were primarily enacted in the 1970s and 1980s, give professional recognition to BSWs as well as those with graduate degrees.

For decades, before baccalaureate social work degrees were accredited, there were undergraduate degree programs throughout the United States that educated thousands of social workers. Many of the programs were distinguished by their high quality and many of their alumni continue to fill important positions in the social work profession. Several states provide social work licensing opportunities for graduates of certain unaccredited bachelor's social work degree programs. In addition, some states treat holders of bachelor's degrees in other fields as social workers and certain licensing laws recognize holders of those degrees depending on other requirements such as their passing licensing examinations, their employment in social work, and their professional experience.

Relationships among Education Levels

All three professional levels of social work connect with one another in some ways. The graduates of an accredited baccalaureate degree or BSW program can apply for and receive up to a year of credit toward their master's degree in many MSW programs. Those who teach in BSW programs, especially those who conduct the field experience component and teach practice courses, are required to hold MSW degrees. A large proportion of those who provide field supervision to BSW students hold MSWs.

Many of the over 5,000 people who hold the doctorate in social work also hold the BSW or MSW or both, and almost all have had some experience practicing social work. A large proportion of social work doctoral degree holders teach social work to bachelor's and master's students. Some other doctoral degree holders are directors of social work agencies or programs, or they are clinical social workers who provide counseling and other forms of therapy to people who have social or emotional problems. Others fill leadership roles in the many social work settings described in this book. Many also provide field practicum supervision to bachelor's and master's students.

In some areas of the United States and in some agencies, bachelor's level social workers perform the same tasks that master's level social workers perform in other places and agencies. Some agencies make careful distinctions between the two levels. In most cases, there are specific differences between the tasks the two levels can perform. Generally, MSWs are allowed to perform more complex and sensitive tasks, often with little or no direct supervision. MSWs are also more likely to be appointed to supervisory, consultative, and administrative positions in the human services. Although in some circumstances BSWs are able to fill such roles and carry out responsibilities ordinarily assigned to MSWs, those are idiosyncratic occurrences rather than the norm. In general, MSWs have larger roles and responsibilities than their BSW colleagues, which is why the MSW degree is often the target of BSW graduates.

Social work education is more fully described in Chapter 3, Education for Social Work Careers.

Licensing and Regulation

All the states license or regulate social workers in some way (see Chapter 6 on social work licensing and credentials for details on the state systems). Each state has some way of legally defining the use of the title of social worker and of providing credentials for social workers. Each state has a different licensing or regulation arrangement, but all are designed to restrict the title of social worker to those who meet the state requirements. As mentioned earlier, some states recognize bachelor's degree holders through licensing, while others do not. There are also variations in the ways the states treat the licensing of doctoral degree holders, as discussed in Chapter 6.

Traits, Attitudes, and Values

Being an effective social worker requires certain traits and attitudes. Most academic social work programs look for those traits and attitudes in their applicants. Educational programs interview applicants, solicit references for them, and try to make sure that students begin studying social work with the right approaches to the problems people face. The following are some prerequisites to consider before choosing social work as a career.

Be a People Person

Social workers ought to be empathetic. Good social workers care about people, are curious about people, like to be around other people, and have a desire to understand and to help others. Although not all social workers have to be as gregarious and friendly as some, most people cannot be effective social workers if they are overly shy, unable to talk to others, or unsociable.

Social workers should make people feel welcome, be able to communicate that they accept and care about people, be able to look people in the eye, shake their hands, and generally respond warmly to them. Social work is based on positive relationships between client and worker. The ability to build and sustain positive relationships is central to being a social worker.

Do Not Judge Others

Social workers don't judge other people—they try to be nonjudgmental. Although social workers are often put in a position of diagnosing or assessing other people for a variety of purposes, such as determining the state of their mental health or the likelihood that they will be good probation or parole clients, they generally try to avoid making personal judgments about other people. They accept people as they are and they do not try to impose their own moral standards or their own values. Therefore, social workers—most of whom never are, and never want to be personally involved in criminal acts—have to be able to accept even the worst criminal offenders as human beings who have potential and who are worth the efforts of society to help them.

There are both ethical and practical reasons for such nonjudgmental attitudes. It probably is not possible to help someone whose life and values one rejects. Moreover, no one who feels hated or rejected by others wants to accept help or believes there is any help coming from someone who is negative about them.

The other reasons are ethical. Social workers believe that all people are worthwhile, that all people have rights, and that all people deserve to have what they need to become the very best that they can be.

Social workers try to understand behavior and they try to help people change their behavior so that they can get along better in the world. However, they don't make moral or ethical judgments about clients or evaluate people on the basis of their own beliefs.

For example, Wendy is a child protective services social worker. She is assigned to visit a home in which the father has been accused of sexually abusing his eleven-year-old daughter, who told her teacher about the problem. She told her teacher, "Daddy touches me in places that I don't like to be touched."

Wendy makes the visit, meets the mother and the father, and asks about the father's behavior. She tries to evaluate, through her interview, the extent of the problem and whether the father's reputed sexual abuse was innocent or might go beyond occasional touching. She asks questions, observes the interactions between the father and the child, and tries to determine whether the child will be punished for having made the report.

On the basis of her interview with the family, Wendy is able to prepare a recommendation to her supervisor and, if the case seems to be extreme, to law enforcement authorities. If the situation seems dangerous to the child, she may recommend that the child be immediately removed from the home.

However, Wendy, who has normal relationships with her own family and would be repulsed by sexual abuse in her personal life, does not make a moral judgment of the father. She doesn't think about whether he is bad, despicable, understandable, or anything else. Rather than judge him, she wants to understand him so she can work with him and the family to resolve the problem. She evaluates objectively and clinically for the best interest of the family and the child. Judging the father might make it impossible for her to work with him.

A good illustration of nonjudgmental behavior is the 1995 movie *Dead Man Walking*. The story is about a man convicted of murder who is about to be executed. He is helped and counseled by a Roman Catholic nun who clearly opposes murder but is able to help the convicted man. She tries to understand rather than judge him.

Nonjudgmental behavior is one of the ways social workers differ from the general public. Many people are quick to judge other people and their situations. Social workers try to understand others in their professional work and do their best to avoid making judgments about those they serve.

Avoid Quick Decisions about People

Social workers also reserve their judgment when assessment is their task. They do not make up their minds about other people without having all the facts and without giving the benefit of the doubt, as well as giving them a chance to explain. Social workers do not operate on hearsay and rumors, though they may consider them. They try to make decisions solely on the basis of facts.

Maintain Confidentiality

Social workers need to be confidential. Like attorneys and physicians, social workers view confidentiality as a crucial ethical concern. Because they deal with people who are involved in all sorts of deeds, some hated by the larger society, social workers have to be able to keep what they know to themselves or confine what they know to conversations with their supervisors or others who have a right to the information. When dealing with couples who are in the midst of marital disputes, social workers cannot divulge to one partner information that was given by the other partner. When dealing with problems such as child abuse or other crimes, social workers cannot pass that information along to others who have no right to know about it.

Social workers can't be gossips. They shouldn't tell even their closest friends or relatives confidential information about their clients.

Clients Come First

Social workers always have to keep their clients uppermost in their minds. Their primary concern is the client's well-being. Self-improvement or gratification through serving clients cannot be a social worker's motive. For example, social workers can't take money or other valuable gifts from clients, except as part of a preunderstood fee arrangement. They cannot exploit their clients for money or sex or any other kind of gratification.

Social workers are not permitted to have dual relationships. They cannot be a client's social worker and also enter into economic or business arrangements with that client, even if that business arrangement may be quite ethical and fair to the client.

For example, George is working with Mandy. He learns in the course of their discussions that Mandy's car needs extensive repairs and she has decided to replace it with a newer used car. George's three-year-old car is for sale because he has replaced it with a current model. He can't offer to sell his car to Mandy because that would violate the prohibitions on dual relationships. His professional relationship with the client might influence the business relationship, or Mandy might feel uncomfortable turning down George's offer because of the close, helpful relationship they have developed. Therefore, George doesn't mention that his car is for sale—though he knows it might be a good one for Mandy.

Another example of dual relationships is perhaps a more common and complex problem. George, who is unmarried, has finished his work with Mandy, who has been divorced for five years. His last appointment with her was two months earlier and she has resolved the problem that brought her to him. The two find each other romantically attractive. When, if ever, is it appropriate for George to invite Mandy out to dinner?

George's situation involves a close call, ethically. Ideally, he would not become involved in a second relationship with his former client. Ideally, he would talk it over with a supervisor or a trusted colleague. If he does, however, become involved he should be reasonably sure that the ethical principle is not likely to be violated. "Social workers should not engage in dual or multiple relationships with clients or former clients in which there is a risk of exploitation or potential harm to the client. In instances when dual or multiple relationships are unavoidable, social workers should take steps to protect clients and are responsible for setting clear, appropriate, and culturally sensitive boundaries." (National Association of Social Workers, 1999, section 1.03)

For another example, William has worked closely with his client Marsha for six months on her personal problems at work and with her family. William is thirty-five and Marsha is almost thirty. Marsha is grateful to William for the help he has given her, and the relationship between the worker and the client is close and positive. She tells William that she has an extra ticket for a popular band's concert. The friend she had bought the ticket for cannot attend and she doesn't want the ticket to be wasted. She asks William if he would like to join her.

Although William might want to go to the concert, it would be potentially unethical and improper if he accepted Marsha's offer and accompanied her to the concert. The situation has potential for becoming a personal rather than a professional relationship between the two and could constitute a dual relationship. Therefore, William thanks Marsha for the offer but declines it.

When serving a client professionally, a social worker does not become engaged with that client in another kind of relationship. If William's wife sells cosmetics for Avon or Mary Kay, he avoids introducing Marsha to his wife for purposes of helping them connect and make a sale, even if Marsha uses the kinds of products his wife sells. It is best to keep the relationships separate.

Some social workers in rural areas think it is difficult, if not impossible, to avoid dual relationships with clients. Clients and workers may go to the same church, have children in the same schools, or see each other at the same social functions. It is true that such dual relationships are more difficult to avoid in smaller communities than in big cities. (See Chapter 11 on rural social work for a more extensive discussion of these issues.) In those circumstances, the social worker tries hard not to let the relationship become so personal that it interferes with or in any way affects the professional relationship with the client. A good rule for most social workers anywhere is to avoid having any connections outside the professional relationship, especially if they involve money or sex.

Separate Personal and Professional Lives and Values

Much of what social workers do looks like the everyday activities of all human beings. We talk to other people, we listen, we try to understand. However, it is critical for social workers to keep their personal lives and attitudes separate from their professional lives and their work with their clients. Social workers must be careful to avoid imposing their own beliefs and values on their clients.

For example, Susan is a counselor in a community mental health center. Bob and Lois, a couple in their late twenties with two young children, come to Susan with concerns about their marriage. For a variety of reasons, they are thinking about divorce. Lois is particularly anxious for the divorce. Bob is not sure he wants to split the family but he is not happy in the marriage. Susan is deeply opposed to divorce on personal and religious grounds. No one in her family has ever divorced and she would rather never marry again if her marriage dissolved. However, her job is to listen to Bob and Lois, try to understand them, and try to help them clarify what they want. Her job is also to help them decide what steps they might take before deciding that divorce is the best answer for them. Never in her dealings with them does she state her opinion or try to persuade them that her feelings about divorce are correct. She recognizes that divorce is a legal alternative for couples and that couples have the right to choose divorce. She respects their freedom to determine their own course of action. Her goal is to help them make the decision they believe is best for them, rather than the decision that best fits her personal moral code.

Be a Loyal Employee
In most cases, social workers are employees. Few are self-employed or private practitioners. (Private practice is discussed in another chapter.) As employees, social workers are expected to perform ethically on the job. That means providing a full day of work for each day of pay, complying with agency regulations, respecting and responding to their supervisor or boss, and being generally loyal to their work. It is unethical to neglect their duties or otherwise give less than their best efforts to the job.

Maintain a Private Personal Life
Finding places other than work for personal needs is an important mandate. For example, Wilma is director of the local department of social services office in her community of 15,000 people. Everyone knows her and everyone has questions about economic assistance, such as food stamps, cash assistance for families, and Medicaid. At parties, at church, and in the grocery store people ask her questions, such as "How is it that Barry Smith is able to get food stamps when everyone knows he has a good job and plenty of money?" Wilma always responds, with good humor and friendliness, that she cannot talk about cases or even say who does or who does not receive assistance. She is bound by rules of confidentiality. Because her office also deals with foster care and adoption, people ask her whether they can adopt a child, whether their niece will be removed from her home and placed in foster care, whether a local man will be charged with child abuse, and many other kinds of issues. Wilma always refuses to answer because she legally is not able to do so and because her ethics as a social worker make her keep personal client information confidential.

At least one weekend a month, and often two, Wilma spends time in a nearby city with friends. She takes mini-vacations, has extensive social contacts in other places, and generally tries to keep her personal and social life strictly separate from her work.

Establish Emotional Privacy
Social workers are people. They become angry, happy, depressed, and thrilled, just as anyone else does. However, in their professional lives, when dealing with clients or the

community, they keep their feelings to themselves. They can react warmly and posi-
tively to what they hear or see but they do not take their joys or their upsets from their
work or satisfy their personal social or emotional needs with their work and their clients.

For example, George is director of a youth recreation program. The organization has been given fifteen free tickets to a basketball game played by the local
professional team. The group goes to the game but one of the teenage boys in the
group is very upset. He separates himself from the group and sits in a different
section of the fieldhouse where the game is taking place. He wants to leave and
threatens to do so on his own, though he came with the group in an agency van.
George spends much of his time monitoring the boy's behavior and making sure
that he comes to no harm. George loves basketball and would prefer seeing the
game, but he can't. He remembers that his job is to help the members of the group
use and enjoy the experience of being at the game rather than enjoy it himself. If
he wants to see a basketball game, his best chance is to go alone or with friends
on his free time and with a ticket he purchased by himself. The purpose of the trip
to the game is not to bring pleasure to George but to expose the young members
of his group to professional basketball.

Identify with the Profession

Professionals involve themselves in their professional associations; NASW has
memberships for students, as well as full membership for those who have completed
their educations. Being a member of NASW and the several other related professional groups helps members stay current with the field by receiving publications
and by keeping them involved in public policy issues through the professional association's work. Attending meetings and assuming leadership when asked to do so
are also viewed as professional obligations. Some social workers do not bother or
do not care to spend the money for dues that NASW membership requires. However,
most of the profession's leadership believes that it is an obligation for professionals
to associate with their professional groups.

NASW Code of Ethics

The 1999 Social Work Code of Ethics is reproduced in Appendix 1. Social workers
need to understand that professional ethics and conduct are *much* more than platitudes.

Sanctions for Ethics Violations

Ignoring or violating professional ethics may have consequences. Members of the
National Association of Social Workers who violate the Code of Ethics (see Appendix 1) may be sanctioned or punished through an inquiry and adjudication process
operated by NASW, beginning at the chapter level. Members may be denied continued membership and may also find their names and cases listed in publications because of their violations. Those who violate the codes of other professional
associations are subject to similar actions. Violating a licensing board's code of con-

duct or ethics may lead to a number of actions, including license revocation and the loss of the privilege to practice social work.

Habits of Effective People

Social workers who want to be successful professionally may benefit from the wisdom of S. R. Covey's (1990) concepts of the habits of effective people. His work has been highly regarded and heavily used in U.S. life for several years. The habits he identifies are:

1. Be proactive.
2. Begin with the end in mind. (Know where you want to end up—your goals, the mission when you begin.)
3. Put first things first. (Know how to set priorities and stick to them.)
4. Think win–win. (Don't look for ways to defeat others. Instead, work to find ways in which all sides win.)
5. Seek first to understand, then to be understood. (Your emphasis should be on understanding the other person, not on making sure the other person understands you.)
6. Synergize. (Put things together so that one factor builds on another and the combination is better than the sum of the two parts.)
7. "Sharpen the saw." (Improve your skills and abilities. Don't neglect self-improvement.)

These habits will improve your ability to function as a social worker and as an employee of a social welfare or services program.

Conclusion

This chapter has introduced and covered some of the basics of social work—what it is, its history, a summary of the preparation required for it through education, and some of the practical and ethical issues that social workers face on the job. Many of these subjects are covered in greater detail in other chapters. However, some of the fundamental information necessary for deciding about whether you want to pursue a professional career in social work, as well as some of the demands that face those who choose a social work career, are provided here. Starting out on a social work career is a major step, just as any other career decision is. This chapter has summarized some of the considerations that aspiring professionals ought to give before entering this field of study and work.

2

Where the Jobs Are

How Social Work Jobs Are Organized

As Chapter 1 showed, there are many different kinds of work and, therefore, many kinds of jobs in social work. Social work employment opportunities are organized in many different ways, and because of that the maze of the social work job market is sometimes difficult for new social workers to understand. It is often even more difficult for new social work professionals to understand how to find information about those jobs.

Because the social work field is so diverse and specialized and the kinds of work so varied, few people know the whole employment picture. Even experienced social work professors and high-level social agency executives do not always know all that they might about the broad range of jobs. One purpose of this book is to help explain the ways to find information on social work jobs, the qualifications for employment and how to meet them, and how to apply for jobs. Chapter 4 on job searches provides detailed information on some of the routes for locating social work positions of all kinds. This chapter provides general information on the ways in which social work jobs are organized, as well as some of the means for finding out about them and filling them.

The Structure of Social Work Employment

Jobs in social work can be organized in several categories. One category is by sponsorship—where the money comes from to operate the organization and to pay the salaries of those who work in it. Social work jobs are also organized according to the kinds of clients or populations the jobs deal with, the kinds of services that are provided, their locations, and the kinds of social or personal problems they address. Some of these concepts are discussed later in this chapter.

Sponsorship and Financing

Despite their broad range, there are only a few large categories of social work jobs. Social work positions are in public agencies; private or, as they are sometimes called, voluntary agencies; mixed public and private or voluntary agencies; and agencies or programs that are financed by fees paid by the clients, either with their own funds or with payments by third parties such as insurance companies or government programs such as Medicaid and Medicare. The last category includes the private practice of social work, which is discussed in more detail later in this book.

Another way to categorize or classify social work jobs is by their kind of funding or auspices. Agencies may be public, which means they are part of government; or private, which means they are nongovernmental and owned by organizations as well as governed by a board of directors. In some cases, such groups are called NGOs for nongovernmental organizations. Agencies can also be classified as profit-making or proprietary, which means they are businesses that deliver social services. Some nursing homes, hospitals, day care centers, and mental health organizations are proprietary. As such, they may have stockholders, try to earn profits, and pay taxes. Other organizations are nonprofit. That is, they do not have stockholders, do not pay taxes, and use any money they obtain over their costs for the purposes of the organization, rather than treating such earnings as profit.

In the United States, the trend is away from government owning and operating social welfare programs. It is more common, when governments develop new priorities and objectives, for those new services to be operated by private organizations with funds provided by government through grants or contracts. The last several presidents have endorsed a reduction in the size of government. Therefore, it is less common to see government expansion and more common for governments to finance their new goals through nongovernmental organizations and programs.

Public Social Work Employment

Public social work jobs are those that are in government programs and services. Most and sometimes all of the money that supports government agencies comes from tax revenues. The funds are appropriated by legislative bodies such as state legislatures, city councils, or the federal government, usually on the recommendation and with the agreement of the chief executive, such as the governor of a state, the mayor of a city, or the president of the United States.

The Bureau of Labor Statistics (1999a) believes social work employment in government will grow faster than other employment until at least 2006. However, some of the jobs that social workers might do in government might be contracted out to private and voluntary agencies. About 40 percent of social workers and large numbers of social work assistants are employed by governments (Bureau of Labor Statistics, 1999a). In the United States, there are three levels of government—federal, state, and local (city and county)—each of which has different rules and regulations for filling jobs. Each state and locality is different from every other state and locality. The types of work done within the various levels of government are also different. Federal agencies and programs do not do the same work with the same people that state and local agencies do.

Almost all public social work jobs are located in the executive branch of government and are responsible to the chief government executive, such as the mayor or city manager, governor, or president. There is typically a cabinet officer, such as a secretary of health and human services, or a director or commissioner of a department, such as social services, mental health, or corrections between the social work program and the mayor, governor, or president. In the executive branch, social workers are responsible for carrying out and implementing public social welfare programs of many kinds.

A few social workers are employed by legislative branches of government such as state legislatures and the U.S. Congress. In those positions, social workers analyze social welfare policies, help write legislation, organize and help conduct public hearings on social issues, and otherwise assist with the work of legislators.

Some social workers are also employed in the judicial branch. In those jobs, social workers serve as probation and parole officers, investigate people who come before the court for trial, and make investigations of those convicted of crimes. The social worker in the judicial system often recommends sentences to the judge.

In probation and parole, which are discussed in more detail in Chapter 10, the social worker supervises people convicted of crimes who are on probation or prisoners who are paroled from prison and are living in the community.

Some 20 percent of social workers work for state governments, 19 percent for local governments, such as cities and counties, and 1 percent for the federal government (U.S. Department of Labor, Bureau of Statistics, 1993). Many of them are in the military or in organizations such as the Veterans Administration or in the federal prison system.

Applying for Government Jobs

Generally, there are clear rules, regulations, and procedures for filling government jobs. Social workers who want to be considered for government jobs have access to definitive information on existing vacancies and the means for being considered for them.

In most cases, there is some formal announcement of the job and some formal application is required. In many cases an examination is given by the agency or by a central personnel or merit system office. By law, people are employed on the basis of their qualifications, not their politics or their connections with important people in the government. Those qualifications are determined by systematic examination. The announcement of the job or jobs will also contain information on the application and selection process.

Detailed discussions of the kinds of work social workers do in public social service agencies are provided in Chapter 7 on government jobs for social workers.

Equal Employment Opportunity and Affirmative Action

Almost all government organizations are required to practice equal employment opportunity and most say, on their letterheads and other official documents, that they are equal opportunity employers. That means they do not discriminate against anyone because of color, religion, national origin, age, gender, or physical condition. In every local, state, and federal government program, discrimination on those grounds is prohibited by law. Therefore, people who are physically disabled, members of a minority group, seeking a job traditionally held by the opposite gender, or older than most other employees must be given equal consideration for a job vacancy with all other applicants. This does not mean that the older applicant, the minority group member, or the female applicant will be appointed to the job. Agencies are free to select the best qualified applicant (more about the designation of best qualified later). They are not permitted to use personal characteristics such as those mentioned above as the basis for denying a job to someone.

Some government personnel policies also prohibit discrimination on the basis of sexual orientation, such as denying jobs to qualified people such as gays, lesbians, and bisexuals. However, some governments allow rejection of applicants who identify themselves, or are identified, as having a sexual orientation other than heterosexual.

Equal employment opportunity is not absolute. There are physical requirements for some jobs that not all people with disabilities can meet. A job may require someone with a driver's license and a car, which excludes persons with a vision impairment. The position may require someone who is bilingual in English and Spanish, a qualification that not all applicants can meet. Special qualifications that are built into job descriptions and job announcements, in a practical sense, may mean that not all applicants have equal access to all jobs.

Affirmative Action

Affirmative action is different than equal employment opportunity. Under affirmative action, which the federal government and most state and local governments follow, employers are required to make special efforts to hire people from groups that have been discriminated against in the past. Organizations are required to have affirmative action plans that include statements of their efforts to recruit and select people from protected minority groups. In most cases, those groups are women, African Americans, Hispanic Americans, Asian Americans, and Native Americans.

Some observers express concern that affirmative action programs set up hiring quotas for the protected groups. However, that is not the case and organizations that treat their affirmative action plans as quota systems make an error. In fact, establishing and enforcing specific hiring quotas violates the law. Organizations have affirmative action goals and they have timetables, which are substantially different.

In all cases, government organizations are required to hire the best qualified candidates for their vacancies. However, when there are equally qualified candidates—

candidates who equally meet the job's qualifications—and one is a member of a protected group, the agency hires the minority group or other protected class member
rather than, perhaps, a white candidate.

Under affirmative action rules, employers are also forbidden from setting higher
qualifications than are needed for the job and from hiring people whose qualifications may be greater than required in ways that discriminate against other applicants.
For example, a job is announced that requires someone who holds a BSW. One of
the applicants holds a Ph.D. Just because one applicant has the higher degree does
not mean that the agency can select the Ph.D. over a BSW who has the required
knowledge, values, and skill. A bachelor's degree in social work was all that was
required. Although one candidate might have higher credentials, if they are not required for the job, that candidate cannot be given greater consideration than the
bachelor's degree holder.

Most social work jobs are not filled by affirmative action decisions. However,
affirmative action rules have created circumstances in which some groups of applicants, which had been treated less than fairly by employers in the past, are now
treated more fairly. Affirmative action rules are unpopular with some who think that
they allow for quota hiring or reverse discrimination. However, that is not the intent
of affirmative action, and should not be the result.

Affirmative action information is collected to guarantee that an agency is recruiting and considering people of all groups, but color, ethnicity, and gender are not
considered in the application to determine one's qualifications.

Nepotism

Some governments have special rules that limit or prohibit nepotism, which means
hiring one's relatives or employing people who are supervised by or otherwise under
the jurisdiction of relatives. The goal of antinepotism rules is to prevent government
staff with the power to hire people from using that power to employ their relatives.
In times of high unemployment, there is also public resentment of many people from
the same family filling the scarce government jobs.

It is not only public or government organizations that follow equal employment
opportunity and affirmative action guidelines. Many private or voluntary organizations and mixed public and private agencies also have such policies, especially social
work organizations. Throughout its history, social work has stood in strong opposi-
tion to discrimination against minority people and those who are disadvantaged.
Therefore, even when they are not required by law to do so, many social agencies
follow the kinds of rules and procedures that are required of government groups.

Determining the Best Qualified

For much of the twentieth century, the trend in filling government jobs, including social work jobs, was to hire people on the basis of merit or qualifications, rather than
political affiliation or other nonmerit characteristics. In the spoils system, which merit
hiring replaced, government employees changed with the political party or official who
won the election. Today, only the highest level, policy-making positions such as cabi-

net officials and those near them in the organizational hierarchy, are political appointees who serve at the pleasure of the mayor, governor, or president. Some of them, such as human services commissioners, education superintendents, and law enforcement officials, are protected from political dismissal so they can do their jobs and make decisions without worrying about the political implications of their actions.

Another consequence of the selection of government employees on the basis of merit is that public employees give up some of their rights to become involved in politics. Laws called Hatch acts (the name of the federal statute) limit, on some bases, the right of public workers to be active in politics and political campaigns.

Determining Merit

What is merit and how do governments determine who is best qualified for the jobs that they fill? In most cases, they do so through government personnel offices or merit system departments that set up procedures for hiring and firing employees and that devise schemes for evaluating applicants so that those who are best qualified can be identified.

Usually, the first step in applying for and being considered for a government job is the completion of an application. The goal is to be listed on a specific register, a listing of people certified as qualified for specific jobs. The officials who choose employees do so from a register for the job they are trying to fill. Being placed on the register requires the applicant to qualify for the classification from which the job is to be filled. For example, someone may be on the Social Worker I or the Social Services Worker II register. Each government organization has its own set of job classifications and its own registers that interested persons may learn about from the merit or civil service systems. Each system has its own rules but, ordinarily, an applicant's name stays on the register for a period of time—until a job is offered and accepted, or until a specific period of time expires.

The important step is to make the application and be listed on a register. An applicant has to be certified as eligible for the job, as well as qualified, before being considered by the hiring authority.

Applications

Obtaining information on government jobs is not difficult. A visit to a state Job Opportunities in the Business Sector (JOBS) service office, which is discussed in more detail later, can be the source of good information on vacancies, application forms, and guidance about making application. Simply visiting any government office will often yield detailed job information. On any day, announcements of government job vacancies are available in most government offices. Visiting the personnel office of a Veterans Administration Hospital or office, a state department of social services, a mental hospital, or almost any other public services program is often another good way to begin a job search.

Job announcements are made available to interested people. They specify the vacancies and the qualifications. For federal jobs, there are published telephone numbers and e-mail addresses. The numbers, which vary by location, can be found on the federal job announcements forms. Detailed information on jobs, including application forms, is on federal and state government web sites.

A sample job application for federal government jobs is included in Appendix 4. Standard Form (SF) 171 is generally required for federal employment along with a more specific application for the job being sought.

Current federal government application forms and extensive information on federal jobs are available at the Internet site http://federaljobs.net. Two of the basic forms used in government employment, the SF-171 and the OF (optional form) 612 are provided in Appendix 4. However, it always important to check with potential employing agencies' personnel offices for the most current forms and procedures because they change periodically. The forms are also available from the employing agency. The OF-612 form provides only two spaces to describe the most current work experiences. Applicants are advised by the government to include additional work experience, using continuation sheets, back at least ten years and including military experiences if applicable. There is a software program available at the same site that expands the OF-612 form or the SF-171 federal application to accommodate all past work experience. The site provides three download versions of the forms; text, Microsoft Word, and an HTML format. These downloads are helpful, of course, to those who use computers for such work.

Information on preparing resumes, when those are required for jobs, as well as information on obtaining help in preparing them is also provided at the site mentioned above.

The instructions for the form instruct the applicant to read the announcement and other materials; to be sure that the applicant has the qualifications required for the position; to ensure that the job is open in the area where one lives or wants to work; to be sure one is allowed to apply (some jobs are open only to certain categories of people); to complete the Standard Form 171, as well as other application forms; and to be ready to take an examination, if required.

Note that SF 171 asks for general, personal information and for specific background information on one's connection or family connections with government work; military service; and criminal as well as other potentially problematic personal behavior. Applicants are asked if they have defaulted on federal debts, such as student loans, whether they have been convicted of crimes, and whether they have been fired or forced to resign from a job.

The typical social work job application for placement on one or more registers asks for details about the applicant's residence, educational background, work history, and other data on the applicant's past. Some applications also request references, as well as signed permission to contact former employers and personal references for appraisals of the applicant's abilities and personality.

Applicants must submit the appropriate forms. Sending a resumé instead is not acceptable; the evaluating authorities want to evaluate all candidates comparably and equally.

An application form for the South Carolina Department of Social Services is found in Appendix 3. It is noteworthy that some special conditions prevail. For example, clients of the department may be given special consideration for jobs. This application functions as a kind of examination, because the credentials of the applicant are carefully considered and rated for suitability for vacancies. It is something of an unassembled examination, as described below.

Merit Examinations

The primary means for determining qualifications for some jobs is an examination, not terribly different than the kinds of examinations students take in colleges and universities, or those that are required for social work credentials, such as licenses. For several kinds of social work and other professional jobs, the application and the applicant's qualifications are the examination, as described below.

In some cases, the examination is objective (multiple choice). Less commonly, it is an essay examination. Ideally, the questions are developed by teams of people who perform work that is the same as, or similar to, that which the job involves. In the best cases, the tests measure the applicant's ability to do the job. In some cases, however, more general tests of knowledge—of government, general information, mathematics, and other subjects—are used to determine the applicant's qualifications.

The test scores are compiled and the applicants are rated according to a number of additional criteria, which are discussed later. Then the results are sent to the organization that is filling the job, in the form of a register of qualified candidates. Usually, the top-rated candidates' names are forwarded and the employer chooses someone to fill the vacancy from among those names.

When to Apply

It is critical in most merit systems to apply for appropriate jobs as soon as possible. That is, when a student graduates, applications ought to be made immediately for all the possibly appropriate position descriptions. Then, when a vacancy occurs, the applicant will be on the proper register, available to be selected for the job.

Unassembled Applications or Examinations

For some jobs, there is an "unassembled examination" which requires the applicant to complete an application form. The application is then graded by a formal checklist used by the merit system or personnel office. Some elements are required in the resumé; other elements earn the applicant additional points.

For example, the applicant's relevant work experience is evaluated from the application. Successful performance of similar work in another organization or position is given credence in the application. An applicant who has performed effectively as a social welfare supervisor in another agency is given greater credit than someone who has never performed a similar job.

The application is also evaluated for educational level and specific educational achievements. If the job requires an MSW, for example, applicants are given a higher rating than they would receive if the resumé did not show such credentials. Similarly, if candidates do not have the desired educational credentials, applications are graded down or rejected. A candidate's references are also a factor in rating the application. Positive references add to the rating and, of course, negative references have the opposite effect.

In some government employment, formal interviews are part of the procedure. Specific checklists may be used to analyze the ways in which the candidate's responses to questions make the candidate appear to be more or less qualified to fill the vacancy. The interviewing process and preparing for interviews are covered in greater detail in Chapter 4.

Bonus Points

Specific characteristics may earn a candidate extra points in merit system rating. For example, in many systems being a veteran of the military gives a person extra credit on their score. (Note the military service section on Optional Form 612 in Appendix 4.) Sometimes, age affects the score if the vacancy is in an organization of senior citizens. Some systems give extra points for people who live in the area where the job is to be filled, such as the same county or city. Such bonuses give some candidates additional opportunities to be successful in their pursuit of a government job. But note that military retirees, unless they are disabled, cannot be appointed to federal positions (because they're already "retired" in the federal system).

Probationary Periods

Public jobs usually have a specific probationary period, as do many jobs in private organizations. The most common length of probation is six months, but it is sometimes one year, and, in some cases, the probation can be extended to eighteen months.

After the probationary period in a public job, the employee usually has a relatively permanent appointment, unless there is a major reduction in the budget or unless the employee violates the rules of the organization. In recent years, budget cuts and errors in some government organizations have resulted in employees being laid off, temporarily or permanently.

Government employees may also lose their positions when a particular job or classification is eliminated for some organizational reason. And, as has been mentioned, if the employee performs unsatisfactorily or unethically on the job, such as not serving clients properly, failing to report to work, or otherwise failing to perform required duties, the employee may be dismissed for cause. Grievance and appeals procedures in government organizations help protect employees from unfair dismissal. However, even after the probationary period is over, it is still possible for government employees to lose their jobs for failing to perform properly or for violating agency laws or rules.

Social workers who work for the government are employees of their city, county, or state, or of the federal government. They become public employees. Chapter 7 on government positions describes the work in all levels of government—federal, state, and local. It discusses what social workers do in government jobs.

Evaluations

Most public employees receive periodic evaluations from a supervisor. These are ordinarily conducted at least annually. Positive evaluations can help an employee receive salary increases and promotions. Negative evaluations can stifle a career and prevent the employee from moving up in the organization.

Private or Voluntary Agency Employment

Over half of social work employment is in voluntary or private organizations. In some parts of the world, especially the United Kingdom, these organizations are called nongovernmental organizations or NGOs, as mentioned earlier. The term has not fully caught on in the United States; however, NGO is an efficient term. These organizations are distinguished from public agencies because they are not part of government. One of the primary differences between these organizations and government agencies is their control by boards of directors rather than government officials. Boards of directors are usually composed of citizens who are active in their community and who care about the services offered by the agency.

One of the growing roles of social workers in voluntary agencies is performing work under contract with government that might have once been performed by the government agencies. Government organizations often find that it is less expensive and provides greater flexibility to contract with voluntary agencies than to carry out those programs themselves.

Employment for Doctoral Degree Candidates

The emphasis of this book is careers in social work at the predoctoral level. However, there is a growing number of doctoral students and positions for which they are sought by employers. Large numbers of doctoral students aspire to careers in higher education, management, or research. Information about such jobs is available in some of the same ways and through the same kinds of resources mentioned for other work in this chapter.

Another important resource for those seeking higher education positions is the *Chronicle of Higher Education,* a national weekly newspaper about colleges and universities, which carries extensive information about employment. College and university openings are also regularly announced to other colleges and universities and posted on bulletin boards. The Council on Social Work Education also helps aspiring professors and schools find one another, especially at their Annual Program Meetings usually held in the spring, when extensive interviewing and employment discussions take place. College Internet sites also provide data on employment opportunities.

Many doctoral students seek and find positions in higher education while they continue to work on their degrees. Many are at the stage of completing their dissertations before assuming employment and they continue to work to complete their degrees while they are employees of colleges or universities.

Evaluations, probationary periods, and tenure are complicated and are quite different in higher education than they are in social work practice and are beyond the scope of this book. However, doctoral faculty and a number of other resources can provide information and these sources can help doctoral students interested in higher education to evaluate faculty positions and chart their academic careers.

Some private or voluntary organizations are affiliated with churches or religious bodies such as the Roman Catholic Church, as in the case of Catholic Charities. There are also Protestant and Jewish agencies. The Church of Jesus Christ of Latter Day Saints (Mormons) and Seventh Day Adventists also have extensive social programs. However, many voluntary or private programs are nonsectarian—not affiliated with any religious group.

The money that is used to support voluntary or private agencies comes from contributions, either directly solicited from individuals, families, private foundations, and corporations, or as part of a centralized fund-raising and allocating system such as the United Way. In some states, funds raised through government-sponsored or approved lotteries and other gambling activities are given to these organizations. In many organizations, fees and dues from those who participate in the organization help support it. YMCAs and YWCAs, for example, obtain large portions of their revenues from membership dues. Some family service and other counseling agencies receive substantial portions of their incomes from fees, some of which are paid directly from clients' personal funds, and some from their insurance policies or government programs such as Medicaid or Medicare. Some voluntary agencies also receive funds from corporations as contracts for employee assistance programs, which are discussed in Chapter 11.

Increasingly, voluntary agencies receive part of their money from government contracts and grants. In turn, they provide services that the government would like to provide to citizens. Instead of organizing and providing those services themselves, the government may allocate money to voluntary organizations to provide them on the government's behalf.

What Are Voluntary Agencies?

The range of voluntary or private agencies in the United States is so great that it is impossible to generalize about them. They serve the diverse needs of all population groups in every corner of the nation. Many voluntary or private agencies are described in later chapters, but such organizations are so common in the United States and come into existence so quickly, it is likely that many new voluntary agencies were developed while this book was being printed.

Voluntary agencies help children, older adults, people with terminal illnesses, people with HIV and AIDS, people with mental retardation and mental illness, released offenders against the law, crime victims, children involved in recreation and leisure-time programs, sexual assault survivors, arts students, and essentially every other group of people in the nation that may need or want social services. Some are very large, with hundreds of employees and multi-million dollar budgets. Others are small, with one or two part-time employees who work from borrowed, shared, or donated office space.

Finding Voluntary and Private Organization Employment

Jobs in the voluntary sector are much less centralized or organized than are the government jobs described earlier. Employees are hired in as many different ways as there are organizations, though some use standardized procedures that mirror those of government.

For example, most voluntary organizations and agencies require a written application and references. The application may be as informal as a letter, or as detailed as those reproduced in the appendixes. There are usually interviews with the agency or organization staff, the board, or a committee of the board.

Jobs in voluntary organizations may be advertised in the daily newspapers or in professional newsletters such as those published by chapters of the National Association of Social Workers. The monthly social work newspaper, *NASW News,* carries state-by-state job listings in each issue. NASW took over that function from the Social Work Vocational Service, a former national organization that was devoted to matching social workers with social work employers. Sometimes jobs are posted on bulletin boards in social work education programs, or in other frequently visited agency settings. The local office of the JOBS service, the state employment agency, is also a good source for all social work jobs.

The World Wide Web is also a good source of information about social work positions. Searching under key words such as "social work jobs," "social work employment," or specific fields such as "mental health" and "corrections" sometimes provides information. The George Warren Brown School of Social Work at Washington University in St. Louis, Missouri, operates a World Wide Web social work job information resource and service called Social Work and Social Services Jobs Online. Information can be obtained at (314)935-4245 or by searching under http://gwbweb.wusl.edu.

Some of the best and most challenging social work jobs are found in voluntary or private agencies. Those that are new and not yet tightly structured are often the best for people who want to work independently and exercise leadership. Ambitious social workers who seek administrative responsibility often find that minimally defined jobs in developing private organizations are the best available.

Personnel Policies

Many voluntary organizations, even those that are new, have detailed personnel policies. Those are often similar to the policies of established government organizations— specified probationary periods, permanent employment after six months, fringe benefits, specified working hours and work weeks, vacation benefits, and statements of work expectations—all of which are described later.

Private or voluntary organizations may also have affirmative action and equal employment opportunity policies. Some are required to do so by their funding organizations, such as the United Way. Others do so, without any external influence, because they believe such policies are correct. When organizations have such policies, they operate in approximately the same ways as are described for government organizations earlier in this chapter.

Mixed Organizations—Government and Nongovernmental

For over twenty years, the typical social work or social welfare organization has become mixed. It may officially be private or voluntary but may receive much of its financing from government contracts or fees. Community hospitals, for example, most of which are nongovernmental, receive the largest proportions of their finances from the two giant government medical assistance programs, Medicare and Medicaid. Other private agencies receive contract funds and fees for their services from programs such as the federal social services block grant, or various other units of the U.S. Departments of Agriculture, Education, Health and Human Services, Housing and Urban Development, and Labor.

These organizations follow job placement and screening patterns that are similar to those of the voluntary and private agencies described previously because they are technically voluntary. However, their reliance on government funds may have some special influences, depending upon the sources of the funds and the requirements of the funding agencies. They may be required to operate in specific ways because of the government support.

Private, For-Profit Employment

In a 1995 survey of NASW members, Gibelman and Schervish (1996) found that private, for-profit employment was a growing area for social workers. There was an increase of 8 percent in such employment and a decline of 8 percent in not-for-profit or voluntary and government work. That growth included the social workers engaged in private or independent practice, as well as those who work for profit-making organizations. This includes many, but not all, nursing homes; some hospitals; and a variety of services that are provided to the government under contract. For example, the juvenile institutions in South Carolina were operated for some time by a private corporation, instead of state government, which is again operating them. That trend toward private nonprofit organizations delivering services under contract with the government that had been operated directly by the government in the past is likely to continue. An increasing number of social workers will be employed by corporations that organize client work training and placement programs, corporations that manage institutions, corporations that provide child welfare, and even corporations that provide economic assistance programs with government funds.

Patterns of Employment

In their study of NASW members, Gibelman and Schervish found that in 1995 fewer (18.1 percent) BSW-level workers were in the for-profit sector than MSWs and those with doctorates. In contrast, there were more BSWs in state and local governments than MSWs. Over one-fourth of doctoral level social workers were in state government employment, but many of them were professors at state colleges and universities. Gibelman and Schervish also found that 2.7 percent of BSWs and MSWs and 2.4 percent of doctoral level social workers were employed by the federal government, more than twice as many as the Bureau of Labor Statistics reported.

Social Work Employment and Programs

In human services work, the largest expenditures are for personnel—for people who perform social work jobs. The personnel budgets of most social agencies are about 80 percent of the total, with only 20 percent for essentials such as office rent, transportation, telephones, and other functions that support the people who are employed in the program.

One of the exceptions in human services organizations is, of course, the public assistance or public welfare agency which provides cash assistance, food stamps, and Medicaid for low-income people. In those agencies, the largest portion of the budget is for those assistance services.

Part 2 describes social work employment in a variety of different kinds of circumstances. There is an excellent current book on the work of social workers, *What Social Workers Do* (Gibelman, 1995). A few other books have been published on the subject and the *Encyclopedia of Social Work: 19th Edition* (Edwards, 1995) provides current information on a variety of agencies and fields of practice. It is always a good source of information for those seeking employment in the human services. The other two books in the National Association of Social Workers' Reference Library, *Social Work Dictionary* (Barker, 1999), and *Social Work Almanac* (Ginsberg, 1995) provide, respectively, definitions of social work fields and data on social issues and social work employment. Gibelman and Schervish's two books (listed in the references) on social work employment and social work earnings were valuable references for this book and will be helpful to anyone examining social work employment and earnings patterns.

Principles of Organizing Social Work Programs and Jobs

Social work, social welfare, and social services jobs, themselves, are organized according to several varied principles.

There are distinctions between the terms *social welfare, social work,* and *social services.* The following are some definitions from *Social Work Dictionary* (Barker, 1999), which should help readers distinguish among these various concepts.

Social welfare is "a nation's system of programs, benefits, and services that help people meet those social, economic, educational, and health needs that are fundamental to the maintenance of society" (Barker, 1999, p. 455).

Social work is "the applied science of helping people achieve an effective level of psychosocial functioning and effecting societal changes to enhance the well-being of all people" (Barker, 1999, p. 455).

Social services are "the activities of social workers and others in promoting the health and well-being of people and in helping people become more self-sufficient; preventing dependency; strengthening family relationships; and restoring individuals, families, groups, or communities to successful social functioning" (Barker, 1999, p. 453).

Social welfare is the most comprehensive concept; it includes economic assistance, health care, rehabilitation programs, public housing, and a large number of other activities of which social work is only a part. There is a social work component to most elements of social welfare, but social work is only one cog in a larger system that includes other professionals such as public administrators, health care providers, teachers, and many others. *Social services* are also larger than the social work profession, and include many functions that are not social work, and many people that are not trained social workers.

Social welfare and social services are organized into social programs and social agencies in accord with some of the concepts that follow. Their organization affects the structuring of social work jobs.

Service Provided
One of the criteria by which social work jobs are organized is the function of the organization in which the social worker works. Some examples of functional organization include agencies and services such as public welfare, mental health, public health, corrections, social planning, and public housing.

Social Problem
Some social work jobs and social agencies are organized to focus on a social problem that society has determined it wants to overcome. These include such familiar problems as crime and delinquency, child abuse, poverty, and homelessness. Agencies may be organized to deal with these problems in a variety of ways; the agency strategy is to find and implement the most effective means for reducing or overcoming the problem.

Diagnosis
Some programs are organized around a diagnosis or condition. Programs such as alcohol and drug addiction treatment, services to people with HIV/AIDS, and organizations for people who are developmentally disabled are examples of organizations on the basis of a diagnosis or a personal problem.

Clientele or Auspices
Some social programs are structured according to the clientele who are served, or the auspices under which the services are provided. For example, the national and local associations for mental health are voluntary organizations of people who are concerned with improving the care and treatment of people with mental illness. The

Alliance for the Mentally Ill is composed, in large measure, of friends, relatives, and advocates for people with mental illness. There are also, within these categories, self-help groups, person-to-person programs, and family support groups. Self-help groups are those such as Alcoholics Anonymous—but there are growing numbers of others that deal with other kinds of problems—that help people in similar circumstances come together and assist each other in overcoming those problems. Family support groups provide vehicles for families that have concerns about special conditions to come together and assist each other in dealing with those special concerns or conditions. An example is a program that brings together families of children with disabilities for mutual advice and support. The person-to-person program is exemplified by groups such as Big Brothers and Big Sisters of America. In those programs, individuals who want to help young people are matched with children or adolescents who need an adult who can substitute for an absent parent, or who can help them with personal situations they might be encountering.

Personal Enhancement
Many social services and social programs do not deal with people who have identified problems but, instead, are organized to help enhance the lives of a client or a client group. Personal enhancement groups tend to call their clients members or participants rather than clients.

For example, YMCA and YWCA, Boy Scouts, Girl Scouts, Jewish Community Centers, Catholic Youth Organizations, and other groups help individuals grow, learn leadership skills, and develop their potential for more fully satisfying lives. Social workers helped found some of those services and continue to be employed in those kinds of programs.

Indirect Services
Most of what has been described above deals with direct services by social workers to people who are facing social or emotional problems and need personal help. However, there are also many indirect services in which social workers are employed. Those services do not work directly with individuals or their families, but work on planning and developing services and service programs designed to establish or improve the larger community. These programs include organizations such as the United Way, a body that plans for meeting the community's social service needs, helps the community set priorities for those needs, helps raise resources through contributions for meeting those needs, and helps support the community's larger service needs through their fund-raising activities. The essential effort is to balance community needs and community resources so that social concerns of all kinds are effectively addressed.

Community housing boards, community planning councils, community action organizations that work to alleviate poverty, and a variety of other organizations and programs provide these kinds of help. Social workers are actively involved in such groups.

These indirect services, which are sometimes called macro-social work or community organization, are modern versions of the social change and social development traditions which began with both the settlement movement and the charity organization societies. These macro-services are also discussed in Chapter 12.

In many situations, social workers combine indirect services with group services, which are described later in this chapter. The following example illustrates a typical kind of service and the strategies that social workers employ in helping clients.

George Cartwright is director of an agency that helps families who live in low-cost public housing organize themselves for education about child rearing, family relations, and work opportunities. A group of women residents decides to have a picnic for their spouses and children. The staff member in charge of the picnic, who is not a trained social worker, decides that these low-income women's kitchens are not clean enough for them to cook the food. She plans to hire a catering service for part of the meal and ask staff members to contribute the rest. George insists that there be committees of members to plan the menu and decide on the best ways to obtain the food and organize the activities. He wants the members to be involved and says that learning how to organize the picnic is as valuable as the picnic.

This illustrates some of the ways in which trained social workers think differently about activities and the ways in which social workers are interested in finding ways to make every activity a learning and growth experience for clients, rather than simply being concerned about activities.

Population Groups

Some human services are organized to provide services to specific population groups. These include organizations that serve older adults, groups that serve children and adolescents, agencies that serve discharged mental patients, and programs that deal with offenders against the law who are released from correctional institutions and returned to their communities. Other groups are those who are disadvantaged, those who live in public housing, and those who have disabilities.

Combinations of Programs

Many social welfare agencies and social services programs provide a combination of services. They may be heavily involved in planning social services, in providing direct services to clients, and in seeking solutions to social problems.

Those agencies are, therefore, multi-functional and have opportunities for employment for social workers with many different skills and interests as well as those who do not want to limit their careers to only one service or one approach to practicing social work.

The Social Work Practice Methods

Some social work jobs are classified solely or in part by the helping method they use. Social workers have long been identified with their principal method of practice. For much of its history, the profession defined those as social casework, social group work, and community organization. Although some programs and many practitioners continue to view the field as divided into those three methods, they have been reconceptualized by others into micro- or direct practice; macro- or indirect practice, which combines community organization with administration and adds emphases on social planning and related processes; and work with groups (which actually can also fall into the other two methods). In some cases, administration and research are conceptualized as separate practice methods parallel with social casework, group work, and community organization. The following sections comment briefly on these three approaches or methods. The majority of social workers are direct practitioners. The other methods have traditionally been smaller. Both direct and indirect practitioners employ group methods in their professional work, which has made work with groups more important than ever, but has somewhat blurred work with groups as a distinct and separate method. All social work students study all of the methods.

What Is Social Work Direct Practice?

Direct practice is the major method of helping in social work—at least, it is the approach used by the largest proportion of social workers. Barker (1999) says it is the professional activity social workers use through personal contact with their clients. However, several different approaches to helping people comprise direct practice.

Perhaps the best known is clinical social work, in which social workers help clients with "treatment and prevention of psychosocial dysfunction, disability, or impairment, including emotional and mental disorders" (Barker, 1999, p. 82). That is counseling of the best known sort, though social workers place more emphasis on dealing with the environment of the client than some other clinical approaches might. Long-term clinical work has been one of the characteristics of various kinds of therapy.

However, the trend in clinical services is toward short-term treatment for specific problems. There is also a tendency toward group treatment and family treatment. And, for social workers, there is a heavy emphasis on concrete help for people facing problems, such as having enough money for basic needs, finding an affordable place to live, finding a job, staying out of trouble with the law, avoiding the use of drugs and alcohol, and otherwise dealing with social rather than internal or family difficulties. Concrete help has long been one of the traditions of social work and it continues to be the pattern of practice for many social workers.

Many clients of social workers come to them involuntarily. They see the social worker, as well as other clinicians, because they are required to do so by courts or other agencies that seek assessments and treatment of problems, such as child abuse, substance abuse, or illegal conduct.

Some direct practice social work is case management, in which the social worker helps the client by coordinating a variety of services and helping bring them to bear on the client's problem situation.

Social casework is the traditional name for direct practice and continues to be used by many social workers and social work schools. Some social workers consider the term to be synonymous with clinical social work practice, while others believe it also includes the various approaches mentioned here.

Whatever the definitions, it is important for newcomers to the profession to know that direct practice means more than counseling, for many practitioners. It means working with the realities of the client situation, intervening with other agencies on behalf of the client and his or her family, and serving people who may not be willing participants in the direct practice provided by the worker. It also often means working with more than one person at a time—with couples, with families, and with groups—services that are described below.

Services to People in Groups

For much of its history, social work has provided services to people in groups. That method or approach, historically called social group work, originally focused on helping people help each other through group activities in settlement houses, community centers, and informal leisure-time groups. The focus was originally on groups of young people in the community but, over the years, theories about social group work were enlarged to include services to people in correctional institutions, people with mental illness, services to older adults, and programs for people experiencing specific personal and social problems. A growing emphasis on group therapy, which implied treatment for mental illness, became a major treatment focus for many who experience personal problems.

Although social group work is a distinct method of social work practice, with its own body of literature and knowledge, in some parts of the profession and in some educational institutions it has become almost totally defined as group therapy and is organizationally and conceptually placed in the micro- or direct practice area of the curriculum.

Although all BSW and MSW students study group work, a minority of social work education programs continues to sponsor concentrations of study in social group work. Social group work includes a range of approaches to helping people, from direct to indirect services. Social group workers serve people with problems, as well as those engaged in life enhancement programs and services such as those described above. Some writers about social work practice refer to social group work and services to groups as mezzo social work practice.

Community, Macro-, or Larger System Work

Indirect social work has a long tradition, as do the direct services of social casework and social group work. However, indirect or, as it is often called, macro-social work is designed to help organizations function more adequately and to help the larger systems such as the community, the state, or the nation in developing social policies and carrying out social programs to address social problems. The macro- or indirect services social worker may be an aide to a legislative group that is working on the budget or new legislation for social work services. The worker may be an administrator of a social work program who is responsible for making the program work and for helping the direct services workers carry out their responsibilities.

Administrators have a variety of responsibilities. One writer conceptualized those functions as planning, staffing, organizing, controlling, and leading (Weinbach, 1994.) Many social workers become managers or supervisors in the human services field.

Another common kind of indirect social work practice is in community planning and development. Many social workers in these fields are employed by United Way or other organizations and their primary task is to help plan for and organize the raising of funds for financing social programs. Another function of the indirect social worker is to organize and direct studies of community issues so social welfare programs can be organized and planned in ways that will provide the services that people need.

Cross-Referencing among Approaches

Although these various functions may sound as if they are mutually exclusive, in reality they are not. Many social workers, especially those in smaller agencies or in smaller communities, carry out a number of these functions. They counsel individuals and families, they direct and plan social services, and they work with groups of individuals. They function as generalists.

Because so many social workers are called on to carry out such a broad variety of tasks, social work education programs require that baccalaureate and master's graduates have backgrounds in generalist social work practice. Graduates must understand and be able to carry out a number of different functions which they may be called upon to discharge during their professional careers. Although most social work jobs are relatively specialized, all social work graduates are prepared, at least in part, as generalists so they will have the ability to carry out a variety of tasks during their careers.

Conclusion

Taking a position as a social worker requires learning about the sources of jobs—the places where social workers work. This chapter has described the organization and structure of the social work job market—where the jobs are located, where they are announced, and how to apply and qualify for them.

Much of the balance of this book deals with handling an interview, choosing among job opportunities, sizing up job offers, and other practical issues that concern all social workers at some points in their professional lives.

3

Education for Social Work Careers

Baccalaureate, Master's, and Doctoral

As Chapter 1 indicates, being a social worker requires professional education. In some places people with education in fields other than social work can apply for and be appointed to social work or social work–type jobs, though that practice is becoming increasingly rare.

For many years, those who worked in social work positions—especially in public social services such as financial assistance, income maintenance, and child welfare—were, in the majority, not professionally educated as social workers. Most had undifferentiated baccalaureate degrees perhaps in other professions or in the social sciences.

Although there are many professions engaged in human services work, it is becoming the law in most states that persons may not refer to themselves as social workers or hold a position designated as a social work job unless they have a social work degree. State licensing and regulation laws (see Chapter 6 on licensing and credentials) provide legal protection for the title of social worker. But even without legal regulation, many social work employers want employees with social work preparation because they understand the social services system and have developed some of the skills needed to practice social work.

Accreditation of Social Work Education

As Chapter 1 points out, there are three levels of social work education, the baccalaureate or Bachelor of Social Work, which it is called in most colleges and universities that offer it; the Master of Social Work, or MSW; and the doctorate, either the Doctor of Social Work or the Doctor of Philosophy in Social Work.

Accreditation is an important issue in professional education, including social work. In the United States, there are two kinds of accreditation—regional and specialized, or professional. Each state is affiliated for accreditation purposes with one of the regional accrediting bodies, which evaluate their higher education institutions every several years. Several professional programs such as education, law, medicine, and nursing, may also seek accreditation from a specialized or professional accrediting body, such as social work's Council on Social Work Education. However, most professional accrediting bodies require a program to be affiliated with a college or university that is accredited by its regional body.

The Council on Social Work Education is an organization of social work education programs, faculty, and practitioners. It is controlled by a board of directors, who are predominantly social work education administrators and faculty but also practitioners, community leaders, and students. Bachelor's and master's social work education may be accredited by the Council. Doctoral programs are not accredited by that Council. The fact that social work's doctoral and associate degree programs, which are described in this chapter, are not accredited does not imply that they are not worthwhile. The Council has simply chosen not to evaluate them for accreditation, just as it did not accredit baccalaureate programs until the 1970s. Similarly, the community college associate degree programs and the doctoral programs have not placed a high priority on developing accreditation procedures for their levels of education.

There are also some social work education programs that do not seek accreditation, especially at the bachelor's level. Some states allow graduates of unaccredited social work programs, especially those in their own states, to take the licensing examinations and grant licenses to graduates of both accredited or unaccredited social work education programs while many grant licenses only to those who hold degrees from accredited schools.

It is always advisable to investigate the accreditation of an education program. If it is accredited, the school catalog or bulletin will say so. Students and their parents may also check the program's accreditation status with the college or university administration, or with the professors in the social work program. Some students may want to study in an unaccredited undergraduate social work program, of which there are several. The convenience of attending the school where the program is offered may outweigh its lack of accreditation. Even an unaccredited program may provide sound preparation for the MSW, though it would not qualify the student for advanced standing. Some state agencies may recognize degrees from unaccredited programs in their own states.

A listing of colleges and universities in the United States that offer accredited BSW and MSW programs is provided in Appendix 2. Programs that are listed as being in candidacy in Appendix 2 are working toward accreditation. The individual program can inform potential students about its accreditation status.

Some states allow people with degrees other than social work to take the social work licensing examination and carry the title of social worker, especially at the beginning social work level. That is another issue that should be checked with the state licensing board or with the faculty. A listing of all state licensing boards is included in Appendix 5.

Some community colleges offer two-year associate degrees in human services or, in some cases, social work or social work assistant work. Graduates of those programs, in some states, work in some social agency jobs. However, as mentioned, two-year social work degrees are not accredited by the Council. A few states grant social work technician or social work associate licenses to those who hold two-year degrees.

In addition, some baccalaureate and graduate social work programs offer parts of their degrees in the form of extension or off-campus programs on community college campuses to reach more people in areas that are distant from their primary locations.

Financial Assistance and Scholarships

Students in social work may qualify for one or more forms of financial assistance including assistanceships, scholarships, work-study plans, and student loans.

For bachelor's students, the best source of information is the college or university's student financial aid office. Those units of universities provide comprehensive and central information for students seeking assistance. An application can be taken and the student screened for and referred to a number of different sources of help. Work-study arrangements are possible through many colleges and universities in social welfare agencies. For a periodic paycheck, students work for the agency and provide a range of administrative, clerical, and professional social work services under the supervision of the agency staff. The agency pays part of the cost and federal funds, allocated to the educational institution, pays the balance. Scholarships, which are based on both financial need and academic ability, are provided on a competitive basis. Student loans are available to both graduate and undergraduate students. They are also based on need and must be repaid, with interest, once the student graduates. The student financial aid office provides advice on applications for student loans for both graduate and undergraduate students.

For MSW and doctoral students, the graduate social work program often administers many kinds of student aid including scholarships and graduate assistantships, which require a prescribed number of hours of work each day for a periodic paycheck.

In addition, some governmental agencies, including federal agencies, provide stipends for students in social work education programs, primarily graduate programs. Students are often required to study in a specialized social area, such as child welfare or mental health, and perform their field practicum in that specialization. The Veterans Administration is a large provider of training assistance for social work students. In return for studying in the field and for their specialized field instruction, students may receive a financial stipend, paid tuition, or both. Interested student applicants should not contact the federal government for these kinds of assistance because the aid is given directly to local agencies or college and university social work programs, which administer the stipends.

In some cases, agencies provide stipends, more commonly to graduate students than undergraduate, who are willing to sign an agreement to work for the agency for a period of time after they graduate. Such stipends often include tuition for the students selected.

Graduate students may also be eligible for graduate assistantships, which require work in the college, university, or an agency that contracts with the college or university and, in turn, provide payments to students for their work. In some cases, they also provide reduced or waived tuition. In the case of public universities, which charge significantly greater tuition for out-of-state students than for in-state students, a reduction of a nonresident's tuition to the in-state rate can make a large difference in his or her educational expenses. Many graduate assistantships involve helping professors with their classes or research, which is a beneficial and educational experience for the students.

Educational Costs

Costs of education at all colleges and universities are spelled out in their bulletins. Fundamentally, the cost of social work education is not significantly different in most institutions than it is for any other kind of graduate or undergraduate study. Many social work programs require students to pay a small charge for insurance in connection with their field instruction placements. The costs of having transportation in the field placement are an additional cost in some programs.

Living expenses are highly individualistic, as most students come to understand. Many social work students, especially graduate students, earn part of their educational costs by serving as resident assistants or counselors in student residential halls, which usually includes free housing and sometimes free meals. However, students who live in dormitories, apartments, or other individual or shared arrangements pay the required costs, which vary significantly by areas of the country.

Tuition is a major expense in social work studies but it, too, varies significantly by areas of the country. In some colleges and universities, social work tuition is slightly greater than tuition for other programs because social work education—with its field instruction, smaller classes, and greater administrative expenses—is more expensive than some other programs.

In general, private or nongovernmental schools are more expensive than state colleges or universities. However, even that may vary. For example, nonresident tuition at some state universities may be more than tuition at some private institutions that do not make distinctions based on residence.

Baccalaureate Social Work Education

Social work is a major degree program in many colleges and universities in the United States. Earning the social work degree, which is usually called the Bachelor of Social Work, but which may also be called the Bachelor of Arts or the Bachelor of Science in Social Work, is similar to earning any other bachelor's degree. Core courses, which vary with the college or university, are required. Several additional courses or sequences of courses are part of the major. A large portion of the major involves social work courses, at least one of which is the field practicum—supervised, professional experience as a social worker.

Some BSW programs offer their degrees at branches away from the main campus. Still others operate under consortium arrangements in which two or more schools join together to offer the BSW degree. A student may take courses at any of the participating institutions, but receives the degree from the home campus, where most of the student's studies have been completed.

Pre-Social Work Courses

In most colleges and universities that offer social work majors, students may enroll in one or two courses that orient them to the field so they will be familiar with social work. Because they are usually open to both first and second year (freshman and sophomore) students, those courses also help students determine whether they want to become social work majors later in their college careers. You may be reading this book as a student in such a course. The courses usually describe the history of social work, the social welfare system, and social work careers or jobs. Usually, these courses meet some of the requirements for the social work major. When students decide that social work is not their preferred major, the courses can be used for electives as part of other majors.

Admission to the Social Work Major

In all accredited social work majors, students have to be formally admitted for study. An application must be completed and submitted to the program's faculty. Many admissions processes require a personal statement indicating the reasons the student would like to be a social worker. In some programs, personal references from former and current employers, professors, and others who know the student's character and work are also required. Personal interviews with the faculty or admissions committee may also be required. Of course, grades already earned in college are also evaluated by the program's admissions committee, which may include faculty, social workers in the community, and others, before it decides on the student's admission.

Students who want to be admitted to social work majors need to earn good grades and exhibit good personal behavior as well as a concern for people. Admissions committees look for some of the kinds of qualities and commitments in their applicants that were discussed in Chapter 1.

The Course of Study

Once admitted, bachelor's social work students embark upon a course of study that is determined by their college or university. In accredited programs, some guidelines for the curriculum are provided by the Council on Social Work Education. Generally, one or more introductory courses, as discussed above, are required for majors.

Liberal Arts Base

Social work programs also require students to complete a series of courses in the liberal arts and the sciences, many of which are also required by most college or university core curricula. Social workers need to understand some of the content taught in these courses in order to more fully comprehend the content of social work courses, most of which include materials from other fields of study. Social workers also need skill in communicating with other people and need to understand others around them, which is knowledge that comes from many sources, such as the social and behavioral sciences, history, and literature. They should have some familiarity with the politics and government of their state and nation, and must also have some comprehension of subjects such as economics, human biology, and mathematics, to understand social problems, social research, social welfare policy and services, human behavior, and the administration of social programs.

Each program defines its own liberal arts base and its rationale for selecting it. But most social work programs require some of the following liberal arts content and courses:

Anthropology
Sociology
Psychology
Economics
English (both composition and literature)
Government or political science
History
Human biology
Mathematics, especially statistics
Philosophy

The specific required courses and the amounts of content vary from program to program, but most include some of these areas of study in some way.

The Professional Foundation

The social work major courses are divided into five areas (Council on Social Work Education, 1994), which were discussed in Chapter 1. Taken together, these sequences of courses are called the professional foundation. Its objective is to prepare the student to become a generalist, a social worker who is able to work anywhere and with any kind of client group in any setting, with appropriate supervision after an orientation to the job.

The professional foundation is offered for all BSW and MSW students, and all accredited programs have to show that they provide the required generalist professional foundation to all students. The ways in which the professional foundation is incorporated into MSW programs are described later. The foundation courses and some of the content they usually entail as well as the ways in which they are organized for the bachelor's social work student in each of the foundation areas are described below.

Human Behavior and the Social Environment

These are the courses that provide the background information about human institutions and people that is crucial for understanding those with whom social workers work. When the program offers one or two courses of its own, they are usually a combination of knowledge from anthropology, psychology, and sociology. Some courses also include information from economics and political science. The emphasis in the psychological content is often on developmental psychology. Many programs emphasize human growth, development, and behavior, from birth through death, in this content area or sequence, as these subjects are sometimes called in social work education. Programs also provide information on families, groups and group behavior, communities, institutions, and organizations. Students must become aware of human behavior at all levels because social workers are called on to help people in a variety of circumstances and through a variety of social situations.

Some social work programs provide the Human Behavior and the Social Environment (HBSE) content through specially designed social work courses mentioned earlier. In those programs, one or two courses cover this content. Other programs design a sequence of HBSE content from courses offered throughout the college or university—a sociology course, one or two in psychology, some study of human biology, perhaps another in anthropology, and, in some cases, a course in economics.

Social Welfare Policy and Services

One of the unique elements of social work education is its teaching about social welfare policy. Social workers need to learn about the history of social welfare to be familiar with the origins of their own efforts. In order to be knowledgeable professionals, they must also know the sources and rationales for the social welfare programs and services so they can be aware of the significance and roots of what they do. In addition, they should be aware of how services are developed and brought into operation by legislative bodies and executive actions, partly to understand their work and partly so they will be able to influence the enactment of policies that best fit with the values and ethics of social work. They must also know about both the origin and nature of social problems, as well as the extent of those problems in a given state, locality, the whole nation, or the world. Social workers also need the ability to systematically analyze social policies in order to implement them correctly or to work for their change, when that seems more appropriate. In most bachelor's degree curricula, the program offers one or two courses in this content area or sequence.

Social Research

In line with social work's history of conducting research and basing its programs on facts and ideas that come from scientifically developed information, all social workers must be familiar with research concepts. In most social work majors, the emphasis is on two areas of research—understanding the scientific research method, especially as it applies to evaluating social work practice, and understanding and being able to use and interpret social statistics. As in the HBSE sequence, some social work programs rely on courses in sociology or psychology to get across the research methods material and the statistics. Others teach social research content as social work courses with their own faculty. Still others use a combination of courses from other departments and social work courses to achieve their social research teaching objectives. Much of social work's content on social research is the same as that taught in psychology and sociology so it is relatively easy to adapt social and behavioral science courses to social work objectives. However, one distinct area of social work research teaching objectives may not be covered in the social and behavioral science research courses. That area is the systematic evaluation of a social worker's own social work practice. The social work profession believes that the main objective for teaching social research is to enable social workers to better determine how well they are serving their clients, whether those clients are individuals or larger systems, such as communities. They do so through the methods of "single subject design" (Tripodi, 1994) in which individual cases are studied, services provided, and evaluations performed to determine the extent to which those cases have improved, or failed to improve, because of the services that were provided. Another useful source on single system design is Bloom, Fischer, and Orme (1999). In the case of larger systems such as programs, agencies, and communities, social workers are taught to use "program evaluation" (Gabor & Grinnell, Jr., 1994; Royse & Thyer, 1996) methods to help determine the effectiveness of the social work services provided to those larger systems. This author's text, *Social Work Evaluation* (Ginsberg, 2001), discusses and provides evaluation and single system design.

In some social work majors, the sociology or psychology professors add content on single subject design and program evaluation to the sections that include social work students so the social work majors can master those dimensions of research. In others, social work courses are taught which emphasize those subjects. In still others, content on program evaluation and evaluation of one's practice with clients is added to other courses in the curriculum such as social work practice or methods courses, as a way of ensuring that the information is provided.

Social work students are also usually required to learn about social statistics. Again, the content can be taught through statistics courses offered by other departments or as part of the social work curriculum, through a specific course offered by the department.

Social Work Practice

Social workers believe that the most important content for students is social work practice or, as some term the subject, social work methods, because social work is about *doing* something with and for people. Unlike the social science and policy or political science material that forms the bases of the other sequences of content, the social work practice sequence is geared to helping students learn how to perform the work of a social worker with the help of the background provided by the other three areas.

Most bachelor's programs have two and many have three practice courses. The total sequence is required to teach about work with individuals, couples, families, groups, organizations, institutions, and communities because social workers are called upon to help (in some cases) and to know about (in all cases) clients and systems of all sizes and with all kinds of problems. Students learn to interview, to assess client problems, to write records or notes about their clients, to make referrals, to participate in and help conduct meetings of community groups, to work with groups of people of various ages, and to plan for future steps in the helping process with those they serve.

Bachelor's programs use a variety of teaching techniques in these courses including watching videotapes and films of practitioners at work, role playing, videotaping their own role-played interviews, discussions with practitioners, visits to social agencies, analysis of case records, applying social work practice methods to examples from literature, and many others.

Usually, it is the sequence of social work practice courses that captures the greatest student interest and helps the social work student understand the processes of serving others. Those courses are also effective in helping students begin thinking about the kinds of social work jobs they might want to pursue.

Field Practicum

The field practicum is another required sequence of content for bachelor's students. The accreditation standard is a minimum of 400 clock hours of actual work in a social work program under the supervision of a professional social worker. It is also a popular part of the social work curriculum because it provides opportunities for students to do what they majored in social work to do—serve people and help them overcome the problems they are facing.

Field practica are organized differently in different programs. Some extend over a whole year, with students working enough hours each week to meet or exceed the requirements. Others assign students for just a semester or two quarters, but students work every day or almost every day at their field practica placements.

The supervisors or field instructors have to be well-qualified social workers who hold BSW or MSW degrees. Sometimes, the student may work under the daily direction of a non–social worker but a BSW or MSW consults with that person and meets periodically with the student to ensure that the student is learning social work content.

A field liaison faculty member or a field coordinator from the educational program meets with the student and the field instructor and visits the agency periodically to assess the student's progress and ensure that the educational experience is sound. Some programs also have periodic field seminars in which students come to the campus for classes with a faculty member and to discuss their experiences in the field practicum.

Although the primary emphasis of the field practicum is on social work practice, some emphasis is also placed on carrying out research, learning more about social policy, and dealing with human behavior and the social environment issues that are part of that sequence. In the area of social work practice, students are also provided with the whole range of generalist skills. Even if the focus of the agency's services is help for individuals, arrangements are also made for the student to be exposed to work with larger systems such as groups and communities. If the placement is with a community-focused agency, the student is also provided opportunities to work with and better understand individuals and families. Taken together, these courses and experiences constitute the educational preparation for the bachelor's level social worker.

Master of Social Work Education

The largest social work education degree, in terms of student enrollments, is the Master of Social Work (MSW), which requires two years of full-time study. It was developed in the early part of the twentieth century, when the social work profession began to define itself. Much of social work education began with the master's degree because many people became interested in social work employment and began social work practice after they had already completed their bachelor's degrees. Therefore, many who wanted to become professionals in the field did so with advanced, post-bachelor's studies. It is still true that many master's of social work students are people who entered the social work field after college and decided to continue in it with graduate education.

In some social agencies, employees who want to continue in their work or advance in the organization are required to complete the MSW, sometimes with the help of an agency stipend or scholarship and a commitment to return to the agency's employment after graduation.

In most schools, MSW student bodies are diverse. They consist of a smaller number of relatively young people, including recent BSWs, and a larger number of people older than traditional college age. The ages of students range into the 60s. All have college degrees, many of which are in psychology but others run the gamut—business, education, religion, the biological and natural sciences, and sociology, among others. Many have completed BSW degrees. The largest proportion of graduate social work students are women, although the gender balance in social work changes from time to time.

A large number of master's students are pursuing second careers. Many are women whose children have completed school or are otherwise old enough to require less parenting. Others have divorced and are seeking a career to help them become more self-sufficient. Some MSW students have doctoral degrees in other fields and still others have had educational preparation and careers in fields such as law and medicine.

Graduate Admissions

Accredited MSW programs (almost all MSW programs are accredited or are new programs seeking to become accredited) all require relatively complicated admissions processes, including some of the kinds of documents and actions mentioned for BSW admission.

The application procedures and deadlines vary among the graduate programs. Some set deadlines and evaluate all applications after the deadline dates have passed. Others accept and evaluate applications all year long and admit students until their complement is completed. Most allow students to begin their studies only in the fall, but others have mid-year admissions and still others accept students in the summer.

Almost all programs require a written statement of some kind which is used partly to assess the applicant's motivation for admission and partly to evaluate the applicant's ability to express thoughts in writing. References are ordinarily requested, usually from teachers, employers, and others who can appraise the applicant's suitability for the field. Many schools also require applicants to complete and achieve specific scores on either the Graduate Record Examination or the Miller's Analogies Test.

The Graduate Record Examination general test and a writing assessment are given in two ways: by computer and by test papers (Educational Testing Service, 1999). The computer-based exams are given year-round and the paper tests are given some three times each year. Complete details on the examination process, dates, costs, and other information, can be obtained online with the address *www.gre.org*. The telephone number for people wanting to inquire about the examination is (609) 771–7670. The Educational Testing Service e-mail address is *gre-info@ets.org*. Their mailing address is GRE Program, Educational Testing Service, P. O. Box 6000, Princeton, NJ 08541–6000. The fax number is (609) 771-7906. They also provide a practice examination (Educational Testing Service, 1997), which is available through the same addresses and telephone numbers.

Most colleges and universities have information and booklets available on the Graduate Record Examination. Some also administer the Miller's Analogies Test. So the first place to seek information on examinations for social work admission is usually in one's own educational institution.

Admission is not limited to those with bachelor's degrees in social work. MSW students come from many different disciplines. However, most admissions committees want their applicants to show completion of courses in human biology. They also want to be sure that students have some course work in the liberal arts and the social and behavioral sciences, no matter what their undergraduate major might be. Some MSW programs insist that students have basic courses in social statistics before they enroll. Some applicants are admitted conditionally with the understanding that they will complete any deficiencies of these kinds before they begin their graduate studies.

All of the information is evaluated by an admissions committee, which makes a determination to admit or not admit the applicant. In some schools or programs, students are admitted conditionally. If they succeed in a few introductory courses, they are given full admission. Others are required to complete additional prerequisite courses, often in the liberal arts, before entering graduate education. Others are placed on waiting lists for admission, especially if there are larger numbers of applicants than the program can accommodate.

Admission to graduate social work education is competitive but, as in all higher education admissions, more competitive at some schools than others. Some schools receive as many as ten times the number of applications they can admit while others are able to accommodate all or most of their qualified applicants. Therefore, some potential master's students apply to several schools rather than just one. Of course, many potential MSW students are unable to relocate and, therefore, apply only to the school or schools in their geographic areas.

Although all master's programs offer a full-time, two-year course of studies, many schools also offer other learning arrangements. For example, the program may be offered for part-time study over four years or less. Several offer at least part of the program at off-campus sites such as community colleges located at some distance from the main campus. Faculty members travel to the distant sites and conduct classes in person for part of the graduate curriculum. A growing number of master's programs are offering at least part of their studies by distance television education to sites removed from the campus. Most distance education arrangements require some study on and some visits to the main campus. Although arrangements are always made for some library resources, sometimes they do not match the social work library materials on the main campus. Therefore, visits to the campus provide opportunities to complete research for papers and to otherwise extend the students' exposure to the professional literature. These part-time and special distance education arrangements make it possible for people who are interested in graduate social work to complete their degrees without having to relocate or leave their jobs, which are often with social work agencies, for two full years.

Advanced Standing Admission

Because the foundation educational program, which is discussed under the previous section on BSW education, has the same requirements for both the BSW and MSW, some students who have completed accredited bachelor's degrees in social work may seek advanced standing in MSW programs. Admission to advanced standing is selective. Not all students who have completed accredited baccalaureate programs are admitted with advanced standing, even if the MSW program has advanced standing provisions for some BSW graduates. For example, some MSW admissions committees give preference to those who have high grade-point averages as undergraduates. Others prefer students who have worked in a social agency prior to applying for the MSW.

Each MSW program that has advanced standing admissions, which not all do, defines for itself how much of the MSW program BSW graduates have completed. In some, it is as much as a full year of studies, but for others it is only a semester or a defined group of courses. Many advanced standing programs require students to complete some preliminary studies, often during the summer, before joining advanced students who are beginning their second year of graduate work in the fall.

Most MSW programs, including those that do not offer advanced standing, provide waiver arrangements for students who have completed content that is taught in the graduate curriculum. The waiver is given for a specific course. Usually the waiver requires passage of an examination, which may be written or oral. In some programs, those who pass the waiver examination graduate with fewer credit hours than their fellow students. In others, students who are granted waivers must make up for the waived courses with electives.

The Council on Social Work Education (1996) booklet on graduate programs, *Summary Information on Master of Social Work Programs,* published annually, provides information on the arrangements of advanced standing admission in each MSW program. The Council's address is 1725 Duke St., Alexandria, VA 22314-3457, telephone (703) 683-8080. Applicants who have BSWs can also find out about advanced standing from the programs in their admissions information.

The Graduate Curriculum

MSW programs are built upon the liberal arts, just as BSW programs are. Every program defines its liberal arts requirements and assures that its students have completed them prior to beginning their graduate studies, similar to the process described above for BSW programs. The rationale behind the liberal arts perspective in MSW study is the same as in baccalaureate study. That is, the knowledge of social work and skill in performing social work tasks is built upon a grounding in and understanding of the liberal arts.

The Professional Foundation

For the MSW, students complete the professional foundation just as BSW students do. The difference is that the study of the foundation is usually spread over at least two years in the BSW programs. For the MSW, the five professional foundation sequences are completed, in most schools, during the first year of a two-year program. Some schools spread their foundation learnings through the whole two years, but the majority complete the foundation in the first year and use the second for advanced studies. However, in all cases the MSW program must achieve the same objectives and convey the same content—although they may offer more than the minimum requirements—as BSW programs do in their professional foundations.

Of course, the professional foundation is not always exactly the same in all programs, or even in the BSW and MSW degrees in the same program. For example, among the many schools of social work that offer both the BSW and the MSW, many use different texts and course syllabi for the professional foundations in the two programs. In any case, BSW students who have completed the degree and MSW students who have completed the professional foundation should have the same fundamental knowledge of and skill in social work.

Field Practicum

Master of social work degree programs offer field instruction in either block or concurrent arrangements. In the block field placement, the student works full time in a social agency setting for a specified period of time; in the concurrent system, students work in a field education setting for two or three days per week and attend classes, concurrently with their field work, on the other days. Block placements can extend for a whole semester, two quarters, during a summer, or in some other combination of time blocks.

For the total MSW, a minimum of 900 clock hours of field education is required. Graduate programs use a variety of arrangements to meet that requirement, though the most common pattern is for half the time to be spent in field practicum during the first, or foundation, year while the other half is completed during the second, or advanced concentration, year. The plan is to provide generalist field experience first, in line with the foundation generalist curriculum, followed by more specialized field experience coordinated with the advanced program.

The most common pattern among the schools offering the master's is concurrent field instruction. A minority arrange the field practicum in blocks. Some routinely use the concurrent arrangement but offer the block option for some students. Others offer one year in a concurrent pattern and a second year in a block placement. At least one program provides classroom instruction in the summers and block field placements throughout both academic years. Each program will provide applicants with detailed information on its field practicum. That information is also provided in the Council on Social Work Education's annually published informational book on graduate social work education programs.

The Advanced Program

For the second half of their MSW studies, social work schools are required to offer an advanced, specialized concentration that builds upon the generalist studies of the first half of the program. These advanced concentrations are based upon the program's location and region, its special mission or missions, or the kinds of interests its faculty and students develop. Some programs organize their advanced programs around an advanced generalist concentration that is designed to prepare students for work as generalists with more advanced leadership skills.

There are several other concepts of organizing the advanced program: by population groups (older adults, minority group members, inner-city disadvantaged people, children, people with disabilities, and others); by social problems (poverty, crime and violence, mental illness, homelessness, and others); and by methods of practice (micro-practice—work with individuals, couples, and families; and macro-practice—work with organizations, institutions, communities, casework, group work, community organization, clinical social work practice, social work administration, social work research, as well as others).

For the advanced concentration chosen, the school must also offer advanced course content on human behavior and the social environment, social welfare policy and services, social research, and social work practice courses, to provide information for effective teaching of the advanced concentration.

Every MSW program is, by design, different from every other. Before applying to a program, potential students should learn what they can about the program's advanced concentration, its curriculum design, the structure of its field practicum, its educational format, and other details. To explain all the accredited graduate social work programs, the Council on Social Work Education booklet summarizes the emphases of each program and the ways in which each program operates, as mentioned earlier. It can be obtained from the social work faculty or in the social work library or directly from the Council.

Joint or Dual Degrees
Many MSW programs, in addition to their own specialized content, offer joint studies with other fields so that students can earn certification in both social work and, for example, law, public administration, public health, gerontology, or education. Each school can provide details on the way it handles its joint or dual degree programs.

Realistic Job-Seeking for MSWs

Although graduate programs, with their advanced concentrations, are highly specialized, it is not always true that graduates of MSW programs find jobs only in the areas in which they specialized. There are not always jobs available in those fields in the geographic area where a graduate seeks employment. Many employing agencies are willing to consider MSWs no matter what their area of concentration. In other words, employers think of MSWs as skilled social workers who can fill a variety of jobs. They are correct because all students have had a foundation of learning about the whole field as well as their specialized, concentration study.

For example, when I was dean of a school of social work that focused on preparing people for work in rural areas, many of the MSW graduates took jobs in big cities and did very good work. In another school where I taught, which had two concentrations, one in micro-work and another in macro-work, many of the macro-students took their first jobs in direct service or micro-agencies and programs, in which there are more positions available for new workers. Within a few years of graduation, many of the macro-students were holding macro-jobs as administrators, community workers, and social planners. However, they began their careers in direct services to clients. Some of the micro-students eventually took jobs as managers of agencies, which are more macro-oriented jobs.

In other words, the decisions about a course of study and an area of specialization are not as important as being a good student, learning about the whole field, and earning good grades. Most students in professional programs have careers that are quite different than those they anticipated when they were students. Professional education—whether it is in social work, medicine, law, nursing, or many other fields—provides a background from which people can move in a number of directions. It is usually not advisable for students to prepare for one job or for work in one agency. Students should keep their options open. The profession changes regularly and a good opportunity could be lost if a student is too fully locked into a specific career.

Doctoral Study in Social Work

Doctoral degrees with two different names are offered by schools of social work in the United States. One is the Ph.D. in Social Work and the other is the Doctor of Social Work (DSW) degree. Originally, in some educational programs, the Doctor of Social Work degree was earned by practitioners who would carry on extensive, sophisticated work with clients or who would manage agencies. Ph.D.s in Social Work were earned by practitioners who wished to become researchers and teachers, which are the roles of Ph.D.s in other fields. In the academic tradition, the Ph.D. is a research and teaching credential more than a practice certification. However, the distinction between those two degrees has blurred and much now depends on tradition or on the name chosen for the doctorate by each educational program. Some schools that have long offered doctoral social work degrees (DSWs) continue to do so. Some universities prefer granting the Ph.D. in social work.

Most of the doctoral degrees offered in social work are Ph.D.s. Generally, it doesn't make any practical difference whether one earns the Ph.D. or the DSW, though there may have been, in an earlier time, a distinction between the two in terms of courses students took and other educational or research requirements. Many times, the degree designation is a function of internal university or college decision making. Both degrees are well-respected in the human services field and both can lead to sound employment.

People who hold doctoral degrees in social work fill some of the kinds of jobs named above. Some choose to become skilled and specialized psychotherapists. Others become agency managers. Some become social work researchers. Some seek jobs in the higher levels of government social welfare agencies. Most pursue academic careers and become social work teachers in baccalaureate and master's programs in the United States or in other countries.

Doctoral studies in social work are all different. Each program is unique in its requirements and in its emphases. A few focus on preparing people for education. A few others prepare people for clinical work. All require between one and two academic years of classroom work. They also require some kinds of comprehensive examinations, which test student knowledge on all the areas of social work they have studied. All programs also require the completion of a doctoral dissertation, which is a major piece of original research on a topic related to social work. Whereas the Master of Social Work degree is usually a nonthesis degree, because very few programs require students to complete a thesis for the MSW, all doctoral degree programs require a dissertation.

A dissertation is a unique study that requires a student to develop a topic and conduct research and write about that topic in an extensive study. Some dissertations are based on survey or laboratory research. Others are based on studies of the literature. The dissertation, which comes after the student has finished courses and comprehensive examinations, must be approved and supervised by a four- or five-person committee of faculty members who approve the topic, the dissertation plan, and the final dissertation product. The committee members, who have special knowledge of the student's area of study, are appointed by the social work dean, director, or some other university official, often in consultation with the student.

Completing the doctoral degree takes, in most cases, a minimum of two years after the master's degree. The maximum can be much longer. Many doctoral students in all fields never complete the degree. They may finish the courses but not take or pass the comprehensive examination. More commonly, they may start but never finish the doctoral dissertation. Most universities have a time limit for completing the degree—usually seven or eight years from start to finish.

Before starting a doctoral program, students should find out about the completion rates and should also talk to some students who are in the program or have completed it about the unique characteristics of the program. Information on doctoral programs is available in most social work programs, based on data compiled by the Group for the Advancement of Doctoral Education, an association of doctoral social work programs. A current list of social work doctoral programs is in Appendix 2.

Admissions and Financial Aid for Doctoral Work
There is extensive financial aid for students in Ph.D. programs, including classroom teaching assignments and research project work.

Admission to doctoral programs is competitive. A good academic record is a major criterion. In addition, references and personal interviews as well as personal statements are usually required. Many admissions committees also require the Graduate Record Examination or the Miller's Analogies Test.

Some schools offer a joint Master of Social Work and doctorate in social work. Students may begin the program, complete the MSW, and move right into the Ph.D. so that study for both degrees is continuous. Several programs also offer a doctorate in social work combined with a doctorate in another field such as anthropology, law, political science, psychology, or sociology.

Conclusion

Fundamental to understanding social work is understanding its educational requirements. All professions, and social work is not an exception, require some formal education of those who want to enter into professional practice.

For those who know early in their college careers that they want to become social workers, a bachelor's degree in social work is an excellent choice. Through advanced standing, it can lead to the completion of a master's in as little as half the time one would spend in the full two-year MSW studies. However, deciding after the bachelor's that one wants to pursue a graduate social work degree is both reasonable and achievable. Most master of social work degree holders were not baccalaureate social work students and neither are most MSW students. For many, the decision to become a social worker comes later in life, a pattern that has been part of the profession for much of its history.

A social work career, now that there are more than fifty doctoral programs spread into every region, can include advanced education through the doctorate. In addition, following a long tradition, many MSWs pursue doctoral degrees in related fields such as education, public administration, law, and political science.

Social work education and the social work profession offer varied preparation at many levels. Education is available at every educational level from the community college through the doctorate. Therefore, social work includes many opportunities in education and, as the balance of this book shows, in employment.

4

<hr />

Guidelines for Finding Social Work Employment

Social work graduates find their jobs in many different ways. A large number are recruited by social service agencies or programs that know them or about them. Some have commitments to work for agencies that helped finance their educations. Others answer advertisements in professional or community newspapers. Some job listings for social workers can now be found on the Internet or World Wide Web. This chapter is about the various ways in which social workers locate professional employment.

Many people with social work backgrounds are hired almost immediately after they graduate from their degree programs. In some cases, they arrange employment before they graduate, and a job is waiting for them when they finish their degrees.

Some students have fewer opportunities to obtain jobs right away or find it impossible to find the kind of job they want in the location they want without a great deal of searching. In those cases, looking for a job should become a person's job for a while. Some people who are seeking work make specific efforts to explore three or four jobs every day. Others mail or drop off resumés to at least five agencies every working day. Finding a job takes time and effort and a good systematic attempt is ideal for most people. Most social workers eventually find a job that satisfies their needs and interests within a few months of beginning their search.

Finding employment in social work is diverse and the information and placement resources are not as well-developed as they may be in other fields. That is a result of the fact that social work has been a relatively small field for much of its history. In some ways, social work and social welfare operate as they did when the field was much smaller.

One of the consequences of that diverse set of patterns is that aspiring employees often find they must make multiple contacts in many different places as well as in many different ways. Some of those ways are discussed in this chapter. But aspiring employees often have to learn that newspaper advertisements and bulletin board announcements alone will not provide all the information on the available jobs. A thorough job search often requires conversations with some of the people mentioned later, attendance at professional meetings (which often provide placement services), reading *NASW News* as well as state NASW newsletters, checking many web sites, and making calls to all possible contacts. As previously stated, at times, locating the right job is a job in itself—perhaps the most important job one has at the beginning of a social work career.

The following are some other basic resources for finding a good job and being appointed to it.

Sources of Job Information

College and University Placement Services and Writing Centers

An excellent way to locate job possibilities is through the college and university a student attends or has attended. Virtually every institution of higher education has a placement service. Those services receive information about jobs that their students and alumni might fill. Some social agencies come to the placement services with vacancies and seek help in finding employees. Even if they do not have very much information about social work jobs, placement offices are still a useful resource. Many help prepare resumés, offer advice on interviewing, and generally assist with job searches.

College or university writing centers, which assist students in preparing papers and in correcting written work, also often are available to assist students in preparing resumés for career purposes.

School or Department Placement Resources

In some colleges and universities, social work has more specialized and different placement processes than one finds for positions in other fields. Therefore, it is useful for students to check not only their campus placement offices but also their own social work departments or schools. Social agencies frequently send letters or make calls to educational programs seeking employees. They may tell the dean, department chair, or a few professors about their needs for employees. Depending on the educational program, students often find it useful to:

1. Periodically check departmental or school bulletin boards. Many have special sections announcing job opportunities.

2. Talk to the chair or other person in charge of the program. They may have been asked to help find candidates for a job only hours earlier—for work that you especially want to do.

3. Talk to other faculty, as well. Most have regular contacts with agencies and may know about possibilities that would be ideal.

4. Some social work programs have organized placement services directed by placement officers or assigned as a responsibility to another faculty member or administrator.

It is important to learn about such resources and to use them. Those services may help with resumés and references as well as job information. Some programs sponsor job fairs, where employers come to the campus to interview potential social work employees.

The JOBS Service

One of the most reliable and useful resources for finding jobs in social work is the Job Opportunities in the Business Sector (JOBS) service, a publicly supported employment service that is located in every state. Most large cities as well as many smaller communities have JOBS service offices. These organizations are usually part of the state employment service, which deals with unemployment compensation for people who are out of work and also helps those people find jobs. It also serves as a way to locate employees for public and private employers and as a way for people who are looking for all kinds of work to become employed.

Although not all jobs are listed with the JOBS service, many are. Government jobs are almost always known to the JOBS service. The staff members of the organization are also well-informed about all kinds of employment opportunities, including work for social workers.

Wherever and however job applicants look for social work positions, they should keep in mind that employers have as much difficulty finding qualified personnel as those seeking work have in finding it. For many agencies, and especially for agency directors, finding qualified and congenial employees who are willing to work is their greatest challenge. Bringing oneself to their attention is as much a favor to them as being interviewed for work is a favor to the applicant. Social agencies need people— people and their skills are what the agency provides to the public—so applicants have many reasons to feel confident when they seek work as social workers.

Field Instruction Placements

One of the best ways to become known to an employing agency is through the field instruction placement. Many field instruction placements develop vacancies in positions during the year, and many of them like to hire those who have been in the agency as field practicum students. They know the skills of the worker—they know that the social worker has some knowledge of the agency; some relationship with the people who work there; and some idea of, and the ability to understand and carry out, the agency's objectives.

If the field instruction placement has no vacancies at the time the student graduates and is looking for work, the agency may refer students to another agency in which there is a vacancy. The field instruction placement is one of the best sources of jobs.

Networking

Before discussing the formal means students use in locating and qualifying for social work jobs, readers need to know that large numbers of jobs are found through networking. Barker (1999) defines networking as "the relationships professionals cultivate with other professionals to expedite action through the social system" (p. 325). Just as social workers are able to help those they serve through their relationships with one another, they help each other locate job information through personal contacts. They tell each other about available job sources, sometimes because employers have asked them to help find employees to fill vacancies. In some ways, the informal job location network is the most productive and commonly used system for filling vacancies and finding jobs. As part of staying in touch with those who have common interests and skills, social workers network with one another by mail, e-mail, and telephone, and at professional conferences and meetings.

Advertisements

Advertisements also provide information on jobs. Many social welfare organizations advertise their vacancies in community newspapers. People who are looking for work check the appropriate classified section daily to see if anything has opened that might be available for them. However, newspaper listings are not often the best source of information about jobs. Agencies often want to recruit people who know about the job through word of mouth or networking in the community, or who have applied to the agency on earlier occasions and expressed an interest in working for it.

National Registers and Meetings

Another source of jobs is national registers and national advertisements. As mentioned earlier, *NASW News,* which is published almost every month, has a state-by-state listing of job vacancies that may match the skills and interests of the social worker looking for employment.

Many social workers find the kinds of jobs they want at regional or national meetings of professional organizations. The annual national and statewide NASW conferences are excellent sources of information about possible employment. The Annual Program Meeting of the Council on Social Work Education, which meets in a different city each year, is also a source of job leads, though much of the employment discussed at those meetings is geared to positions in higher education.

Agency Visits

Information on jobs can also be obtained by visiting agencies, especially their personnel officers. The personnel or human resources office (they go by both names) will often have detailed information on openings for social workers.

Resumés

Every professional, and every job seeker at any level, should have a resumé, sometimes called a curriculum vita (CV) or vita. It should be as complete as possible and it should be kept up-to-date. A good resumé is well designed and attractive, typed, and duplicated clearly.

Some people like to have a one-page vita and think that is the best way to design one. Others believe that longer statements of two or three pages are appropriate. The correct length is discussed below. A resumé should include information about the applicant's educational background, degrees earned, and subjects studied at all the schools attended. A complete resumé provides information on every job the applicant has held, including jobs held while a social work student. Scholarships, awards, and other recognition should also be provided in the resumé.

References
A list of references is a useful component of a resumé, so potential employers can contact references without asking the applicant for a list. Employers want to know as much as possible about a candidate for a job. They also want to make sure the candidate has good references. Some people think that good references do not help very much because they assume any qualified candidate will be able to get a list of positive references. On the other hand, a negative reference can hurt the applicant badly.

References should be people who know something about the applicant's professional work and qualifications. They should also be contacted by the applicant before they are listed as a reference to be sure they agree to provide the reference. Be sure to include the person's title, office mailing address, fax number, telephone, and e-mail address.

Time Gaps
On a resumé, applicants should try to be sure that all the time periods of their adult life are covered by work, school, homemaking, raising children, or otherwise clearly occupied. Employers may become suspicious when they see an unexplained gap of six months or a year in which the candidate was, so far as the resumé shows, unemployed, not in school, and not discharging family responsibilities.

Some career issues counselors (Lyles & Mosley, 1996) suggest two ways of handling gaps in employment but note that they must always be explained. Their two techniques are (1) discuss the situation in a cover letter and explain that it was necessary to take a leave from work for a family medical emergency that has been resolved, or (2) list the leave of absence after the list of jobs one has held.

If the gap resulted from personal health problems, whether mental or physical, that can be stated in one of those two ways as a health emergency. If the employer wants to make more detailed inquiries, individuals can agree to provide statements from physicians attesting to their current good health.

Length of the Resumé
The length of the resumé is an issue that often raises questions, as mentioned above. Some experts think a resumé should be brief—only a page or two. Others believe it is important to list everything one has done—education, work, travel, special skills,

and work objectives. I suggest the longer resumé that includes a great deal of information. It is also useful to have a one-page brief biography or summary based on the more extensive resumé. Then those who only want a few facts about previous work and education will have them, while someone who wants all the information about the candidate for a job will have it in detail.

A Resumé Outline

Resumés are prepared in many different ways. As suggested earlier, college and university placement services often help graduates prepare them. Professional services will, for a fee, prepare attractive resumés. However, a simple and effective resumé can be prepared on a word processor by anyone who has a bit of time and an interest in completing the document.

These are the elements that may be included in any resumé:

1. Heading—name, address, telephone (both office and home), fax number, and e-mail address.

2. A statement of career or occupational objectives is sometimes effective. However, it is not essential to include such a statement.

3. Educational background—beginning with the highest degree: the name of the degree, the name and address of the institution where it was awarded, the years attended, and the year the degree was awarded. It is essential to include all higher education and, in some cases, the graduating high school should also be listed, especially when applying for a position in the same city as the high school.

4. Work experience—beginning with the current job and going back to the first professional work. Information on the job title, the dates of employment, the duties performed, and the name of the supervisor may all be included. If there were nonprofessional jobs mingled with the professional, those should be included, too, to show there were no breaks in employment or, if there were, to show what they were. Military service, maternity leave, illness, or any number of other explanations should be included. Include nonprofessional work that is related to a social work career, such as working as a legal aide, a law enforcement specialist, a retail worker, or in most other positions that provide the potential employer information about job experience and skills. For example, someone who has worked in a bank might impress an employer who favors precision and the ability to handle details.

5. Awards and honors—these may include leadership positions in civic and religious services or youth organizations, scholarships, and other forms of special recognition.

6. Affiliations and memberships—it is important to list professional memberships as well as civic and service club affiliations. Offices held and responsibilities discharged, such as chairing a committee, should be listed. Social work organizations are often more interested in people who are involved in community life. Many employers are favorably impressed by social workers who are members of and active in their professional organizations.

7. References—although they may be requested on the application form, it is also often useful to include a list of three or four references who can attest to the applicant's character, reputation, and professional skills.

Effective Employment Interviews

Getting to the job interview is an important step in finding a satisfactory position in social work. If the organization has chosen to interview you, it probably has some real interest in your abilities and your potential contribution to the organization. Of course, that is not always true. Some organizations make it a policy to interview a certain number of people for every opening, even though an internal candidate is their first choice or they feel that another external candidate is preferable to all others. In some situations, organizations want to interview specified numbers of men, women, and members of minority groups, to demonstrate their equal opportunity policies and their commitment to affirmative action. However, their choice may have been tentatively made long before the interviews take place. Potential employees should be enthusiastic about interviews and should feel positive about the opportunity to be interviewed for a job. On the other hand, applicants should not be discouraged when a job offer does not follow an interview. There are other uses for the interview besides simply selecting someone for a position; keep that reality in mind.

Interviews are always important. Treat them with a high degree of preparation and enthusiasm. Even if the job is not forthcoming, the interviewer may be impressed with the interview and with your abilities. The interviewer may have connections with other agencies and employers and may recommend the unsuccessful interviewee for a job in another organization, or the interviewer may call the interviewee back for another appointment when another vacancy opens. Therefore, an interview is definitely a positive and often pivotal element in building one's career and should always be treated that way.

Preparing for the Interview

Getting ready is one of the main components of an effective interview. Perhaps most important in the process of preparation is to learn as much as possible about the organization and its functions. Most interviewers are impressed with people who have taken the time to learn something about the agency—its philosophy, budget, and program—prior to the interview. It should be relatively easy to learn about the program from agency brochures, newspaper articles (which can be found in local library newspaper files), and conversations with agency employees or others who know about the organization and its program. Knowing about the organization will suggest ways you can further the agency's mission and activities. That kind of knowledge helps the potential employee connect directly with the work of the organization.

Knowledge about the board or other governing body, its functions, structure, history, salary situation, and some of its most notable achievements, will also help you in the interview.

If the interview is with an agency in a location other than your place of residence, it is often effective to know something about the community—its population, its special problems and achievements, and its history. Again, that kind of information helps you connect with the organization, and it also helps the interviewer know that you cared enough to conduct some research before arriving. However, because it is often difficult for the job applicant to know all the answers before arriving, some interviews involve questions that are difficult to answer.

I recall once being interviewed for the presidency of a small college. I thought well of the college and knew about its social work program, but not a great deal more. I was asked by the interviewing committee if I knew what the college was most proud of and what its greatest achievements were. I spoke generally about quality education, able students, and a top faculty. But the interview, which was conducted by its board members, would have been improved if I had known that they were proud of the number of teachers who taught in the surrounding counties and who had a reputation, the interviewing committee thought, for excellence. I didn't know that. I didn't get the job, either.

Identify the Interviewer

It is helpful to know who will conduct the interview. As mentioned in the example above, some interviews are conducted by groups or committees, and others by individual employers or staff members. In some cases, a candidate for a job is interviewed by several different groups or by several different individuals. Knowing who they are, their interests, and their responsibilities in the organization is helpful in preparing for the interview.

In higher education jobs, faculty candidates are usually interviewed by all of the faculty, either individually or in groups, by students, and by administrators in the upper levels of the university or college hierarchy. Faculty candidates are also often required to make a presentation to the faculty and students about a topic of special interest or, in some cases, on a topic that is assigned to them by a recruitment committee. Some social agencies are using similar systems and require presentations to the staff or to the board, in addition to individual interviews. Being able to prepare and deliver a good presentation is critical. In many cases, the organization places great emphasis on the content and quality of the presentation, so the opportunity to present information can never be taken lightly by the applicant.

Dressing for the Interview

Most people who write about job interviews say that it is wise to dress like the people with whom one is interviewing. That's a good idea but it is probably not possible in all situations. A man interviewing with an organization that works primarily with business people should wear a conservative business suit, white shirt, and tie for the interview. A woman would wear the dress or suit equivalent of a man's business suit. When not much is known about the dress of the agency staff, it is generally advisable to dress as you would for work in a professional organization with high dress standards. That would mean men should wear suits or sport jackets and slacks, dress shirts, and ties. Women should wear dresses or suits—usually not trousers, sweaters, or knit blouses. Even if the organization's staff does not ordinarily dress in typical business outfits, dressing well for the interview is a sign of respect to potential employers. Unless the organization is totally informal or wears uniforms or has other special kinds of garb, business suits, business dresses, and the like are almost always appropriate attire.

Some religious organizations, military employers, and other specialized groups have more specific dress expectations which should be respected and met. If the interview is with an agency that has religious objections to using makeup, for example, then it is probably wise for a woman applicant not to wear makeup and to be prepared to avoid wearing makeup on the job.

There are other exceptions to the general rule of "dress conservatively." Some radical and grassroots organizations prefer very informal clothing such as jeans and tee shirts. Coming to such an organization dressed in a business outfit may bring the interview to a rapid end.

Some commonsense criteria also have merit. For example, when interviewing for a youth camp job at the camp site, a coat and tie or high heels and hose would be inappropriate. In this case, neat and clean sportswear such as shirt and slacks or even shorts would be appropriate attire. Knowing the audience for an interview is critical.

Often, it is advisable for men to shave mustaches or beards before they interview for jobs. Interviewers may have facial hair, but that does not always mean they will feel comfortable with a job applicant who is bearded. Many employers have negative reactions to beards and mustaches; therefore, it is often advisable to avoid them when seeking work. The same is true for ear studs on men. Because many employers react negatively to them, it is wise not to wear them for interviews. Sandals are usually not appropriate for men being interviewed. Neither are suits that are green, or sports coats of very loud colors. Generally, modest and conservative attire will make a better impression.

Of course, some alternative agencies that serve special population groups may prefer that applicants wear longer hair and beards as well as casual clothing. In some situations, tattoos, which would raise concerns in more traditional agencies may even give an applicant an edge over others. That is not to suggest obtaining tattoos as a way to secure a desired job. They, like other less than conventional appearance factors, may limit access to some employment.

For women, many consultants suggest that long and elaborate earrings are not advisable on job interviews. Neither are large purses. Briefcases are a better way to carry personal articles and papers to an interview. Some interviewers suggest that women who are seeking jobs avoid wearing vests, sweaters, or tightly fitting outfits. Interviewers may consider them too provocative or suggestive.

Both men and women usually come across better without flashy jewelry and with a minimum of jewelry of any kind. One ring, including a wedding band, and a watch are enough. In most situations, nose and tongue rings often present a problem.

The applicant's appearance at an interview may have a great deal to do with the success of the interview in helping to secure the job.

During the Interview

Looking good is only the first part of participating effectively in an interview. The rest requires correct interview behavior, which can make a significant difference in the success of the encounter with the interviewer or the interviewing committee.

It is important to greet the interviewer or the committee properly. Make eye contact with those who are evaluating your credentials. Shake hands firmly and with some enthusiasm to make a positive impression.

Being interested in what the interviewer says is also critical. Interviewers for organizations are enthusiastic about their work and about the virtues of their agency. They will expect a potential employee to be equally enthusiastic and interested. Listening with interest, which is communicated through eye contact, head nodding, and posture, suggests that you want to hear more. Slouching, yawning, looking around the room, and otherwise seeming distracted or unconcerned are self-defeating behaviors.

Wilkes-Hull and Crosswait (1996) offer other practical suggestions. They say that one should not light a cigarette unless invited to do so, nor should the interviewee chew gum or eat candy during the interview. They also suggest it is a bad idea to bring a friend along to the interview. The interview is not a social occasion and applicants should stand on their own when seeking a job. Wilkes-Hull and Crosswait (1996) suggest that the interviewee not wear too much fragrance— cologne or aftershave for men or perfume or cologne for women. It is probably a good idea not to wear any fragrances at all in an interview situation. Reactions to fragrances are quite varied and some people have severe allergies to colognes and perfumes. I have seen situations in which people did not buy houses that were attractive to them because the seller was wearing a heavy overlay of a perfume to which the potential buyer was allergic.

Wilkes-Hull and Crosswait (1996) also advise against touching objects on the interviewer's desk. People are quite personal and protective about the items on their desks or in their offices. On the other hand, there is nothing wrong with admiring diplomas or art works on the interviewer's walls. These are posted for display and the interviewer obviously thinks well of them. The interviewee who enjoys them is likely to make a good impression—at least about taste in wall decorations.

Follow the Interviewer's Lead

The interviewer or interviewers are in charge of the conversation, and the interviewee ought to follow their lead. Asking questions or following up with a request for more detail is useful in the interview situation. However, interrupting the interviewer or changing the subject to one of greater interest to the interviewee is not a good idea. And the interviewer should be the one who ends the conversation. Glancing at one's watch frequently and communicating, even without words, that the session is taking too long may ruin the situation for the interviewee.

There are some other basic behaviors that can make a difference in an interview situation. For example, it is almost always a good idea to smile often during an interview. Of course, if the subject is something tragic, which it may well be in social work, then a smile is inappropriate. Do not smile when the subject of the interview turns to the tragedy of child abuse, serious illness, or disability; but when the interviewer is talking enthusiastically about the organization and its mission, a smile is appropriate and welcome. Posture also makes a difference. Sitting erect in a chair, standing at appropriate times, and not becoming too relaxed are all useful in an interview situation.

Permissible questions in interviews are limited by good taste and, in some cases, by legal limitations. Interviewers normally do not and cannot ask personal questions about marital status, religion, political affiliation, or sexual orientation. However, many interviewees voluntarily reveal some personal information during the course of the interview, such as their family situation. In larger cities, such topics are more likely to be avoidable than in smaller communities, where family issues are important and quickly become common knowledge anyway. It is a violation of most laws and most agency policies to discriminate on the basis of religion, health problems, political affiliation, marital status, or age.

Following Up after the Interview

It is important to send the interviewer any additional information or documents that may have been requested. It is also a good idea to send a courteous note thanking the interviewer for the time spent and letting the interviewer know that you are available for and interested in the job.

Ordinarily, the job applicant doesn't call promptly to see if a position is going to be offered. However, after two or three weeks, it is often appropriate to call and inquire about the status, especially if the interviewer has said that some information would be forthcoming within that period of time. And, as is often the case, if you receive a competing offer, it is courteous to call the interviewer and explain that you are considering another offer and may no longer be available within a few days.

Again, simple courtesy and common sense apply. Do not pester a potential employer. On the other hand, it is critical to let potential employers know if you are either still interested or on the verge of accepting another position.

Conclusion

Looking for and finding a job is work in itself. Applicants often must devote intensive efforts to locating the kind of job they want and that also will help them meet their professional goals and build their professional careers.

Even if you have a job you like, it is important to develop and maintain a resumé. Such documents are frequently requested by potential new employers, by persons seeking consultation, and by those considering social workers for memberships on boards or in other professional leadership positions. Follow the outline proposed in this chapter or use the help of a professional resumé service, a college or university writing laboratory, or placement office.

This chapter suggests a variety of mechanisms for locating jobs. Ideally, social workers follow a number of different routes to finding the kind of employment they want. Although a person may have an ideal job in mind, it is frequently not possible to find that ideal position and, therefore, it is necessary to take one of the jobs that is offered. However, that should not be discouraging. Much about work is a compromise, and taking a job that is not your first or perfect choice is a common experience. It is possible to make the job offered the job you most wanted. And it is always possible, after an appropriate period of time on the job and if the opportunity arises, to relocate to another position. Your first social work job is not likely to be your only job. Many professional social workers change jobs several times during their careers.

Interviewing is a crucial step in becoming an employee. I summarize interview behavior by suggesting that interviewers want people who want the job. Seeming eager to take the job, even you are privately considering something else or are less than enthusiastic about it, can make a large difference. No one wants reluctant or ambivalent employees. Organizations want their prospective employees to be as enthusiastic about the organization and its work as they are. Follow the chapter's other suggestions for performing effectively as an interviewee to have the best possible chance of obtaining the position you most want and that you can most effectively fulfill.

5

Salaries and Benefits

What to Expect, What to Request

Some think when they enter the labor market that there is nothing quite so important as how much they will earn. Those who have spent long careers working, including those who are social workers, learn that there are a number of other variables that are equally important.

Of course, intangibles make a difference. For example, social workers come to care greatly about enjoying their work. That is not to say that all work and all working hours must be exciting or even pleasant. As discussed, there are bad as well as good times in any job or any career. No one pays employees simply to provide them with opportunities to enjoy themselves. However, depending upon people's life's objectives and ambitions and the ways in which they prefer spending their time, some parts of life's work are simply more pleasant than others.

I personally so greatly enjoy social work—practicing it in many different ways, teaching about it, and writing about it—that I am always astonished (at least briefly) to hear people whose work is foreign to me say that they could never do what I do. Stockbrokers, retail store managers, sales people, carpenters, and construction supervisors have all said that to me. Of course, I feel the same way. I could never imagine doing their jobs for very long, unless I could not otherwise survive. But it is hard for me to believe that they are not envious or jealous of my good fortune—being a social work professor. Obviously, they aren't. There are differences in what we care about or, in the colloquial terms, "different strokes for different folks"; "whatever floats your boat"; and "to each his own."

Being satisfied in their work and doing what they care about are important considerations to many workers and may, in the larger picture, have greater importance than salary or fringe benefits. I have personally taught engineers, business people, people with doctorates in the arts and sciences, lawyers, and others who are not happy in their work and who have chosen social work as an alternative. I have known able medical students, in the process of pursuing the most prestigious and most highly paid career in the nation, who have switched to social work because they liked it better than medicine. Considering that most waking hours are spent working, job satisfaction takes on special and lasting importance.

Perhaps for social workers, the real issue is the ability to make a difference. Few who are successful in social work careers choose social work because of the compensation or the working hours or the fringe benefits. They become social workers because they have a passion to build a society that will eradicate injustice, provide help to those who need it, bring compassion to those who are victimized by the lack of it, and improve lives. When choosing social work as a career, salary and benefits are usually secondary considerations.

The Realities of Social Work Compensation

Despite our idealism, it is important to avoid discouragement about choosing social work because of the low opinions others may have of social work salaries. Those who need social workers and social work services deserve the help of talented people. Therefore, we do not want to discourage able individuals from becoming social workers because of misinformation about the earnings.

It is often heard that no one chooses a social work career for the money. That is probably true because social workers are usually motivated by a number of noneconomic factors such as feeling that they are making a difference in the world and enjoying their work. As a college senior at the age of twenty-one, I told my colleagues in the news department of the television station where I was employed that I planned to pursue a master of social work degree. A co-worker said, "Well, you have to love that kind of work because the salaries are so low, you will almost work for nothing." The comment stayed with me and I wondered if I were making an error. Social work seemed to be what I wanted to do, but I also wanted a family, a car, a place to live, and all the other things in life that cost money and require decent earnings.

My fellow workers' comments were simply misguided and not based on facts. Before long I learned my earnings were greater than a beginning television reporter's, which would have been my salary if I had returned to the TV station after serving in the Army.

My own discoveries were similar to those of people exploring social work careers today. The profession does not require great sacrifices (nor offer the occasional great financial successes) of vocations such as the arts and athletics. Careers in those fields require total commitment, and many who pursue them often earn only marginal incomes. Many have to survive on part-time or occasional employment supplemented by the day job, or work in another field. Actors, novelists and short-story writers, dancers, musicians, painters, and most professional athletes face much more difficult financial circumstances than social workers. Of course, social workers, from the practice of social work alone, never attain the wealth of hugely successful movie actors, best-selling authors, or the few highly successful professional athletes.

Parenthetically, professionals in other fields tend to agree that great wealth is beyond their reach from the sole practice of their professions. That is something of an axiom in understanding employment and earnings. Attorneys and physicians who, as groups, are among the highest earners in the United States, simply do not have enough hours available to earn great wealth. Most of those who become financially successful do so by investing their earnings in stocks, real estate, or businesses. In effect, their money can make big money, but their professional work cannot always do so.

Social work provides livable incomes for most of its professionals who are able to carry out their responsibilities adequately. It is not a hugely lucrative profession, but earning a large income is usually not the social worker's highest priority. Social work is certainly not as lucrative as successful business careers may be. Neither, however, does it entail the sacrifices encountered in some occupations.

Social Work Salaries

According to a study of salaries of NASW members (Gibelman & Schervish, 1996) three-fifths (76.5 percent) of social workers with BSW degrees had salaries that ranged from less than $15,000 up to $29,999 per year (all salaries in this section are for one year or twelve months) in 1995. Among that group roughly half earned more than $20,000. Nearly a quarter of the total number of BSW workers earned more than $29,999.

It should be noted that the study cited, which is one of the largest and most reliable ever done about social work earnings, may be affected by the fact that it studied members of NASW. NASW membership does not include all people who have finished social work education programs or who are employed in social work jobs. NASW members may be different than the average person who has completed social work education or taken a social work job.

The study showed that MSWs earned more, as would be expected, than BSWs. Ninety-five percent of MSWs earned between $20,000 and more than $40,000 in 1995. Thirty-one percent earned more than $40,000. One may assume that the MSW provides significantly greater earnings than the BSW, though age and experience are also factors. Most BSWs are younger and less experienced than their MSW counterparts.

The number of years of experience also makes a major difference. Social workers with eleven to fifteen years of experience, according to Gibelman and Schervish (1996), earn median incomes of $35,000–$39,999 and those with sixteen to twenty years of experience earn a median income of $40,000–$44,999. Therefore, one can assume that successful social work careers for the long term yield increasingly adequate incomes.

According to the Gibelman and Schervish study (1996) men earn higher salaries than women—a median of $37,503 for men and a median of $34,135 for women.

Part of the differential may be due to the larger proportion of men in administrative positions, who also enter such positions at an earlier age. According to Gibelman and Schervish (1996) administrative–management positions for NASW members in 1995 had a median income of $47,499. Minority group NASW members from the African American, Asian, Puerto Rican, and mixed heritage populations included in the study appeared to have higher median salaries than White social workers. However, 86.9 percent of the respondents were White.

Salary information provided by the Bureau of Labor Statistics (1998, 1999a, 1999b) says, based on what the Bureau calls limited information, that in 1997 MSWs had median earnings of $35,000 per year while BSWs had median earnings of about $25,000. In acute care hospitals, MSWs earned median salaries of $35,000. The middle 50 percent earned between $32,500 and $38,700. In the federal government, all social workers who had supervisory, managerial, and nonsupervisory positions, as well, earned average salaries of $46,900.

People with the title of counselor, some of whom hold social work degrees, in vocational and educational positions had median earnings in 1996 of $35,800. The middle 50 percent had salaries between $25,600 and $48,500. The average salary of public school counselors was about $44,100.

Social and human service assistants, many of whom are social work degree holders, had earnings in 1997 between $15,000 and $24,000. Depending on their experience, education, and specific employment, experienced workers earned $20,000 to $30,000.

Variations by Type of Work

Salaries vary significantly among social work jobs and it is important to ask the amount of salaries in the process of job exploration. Even more importantly, job applicants need to know what salary the job may bring in the future. In many large agencies, people enter at a low salary but after six months of probation they are routinely promoted to a higher classification and, therefore, a higher salary. In other agencies, people earn about the same, with incremental increases associated with inflation and occasional promotions, throughout their careers. In some smaller agencies, salaries are negotiable based upon how much money the organization has and the qualifications of the applicant. People who are experienced in social work or who have other exceptional records may find that they can ask for and receive a little more than the agency was initially willing to pay them.

It is all right and usually not considered bad judgment for an applicant to ask for a better salary or at least to inquire about the propriety of asking for a better salary. Agency executives realize that potential employees are interested in their incomes and that everyone wants to earn as much as possible.

If the answer is, "No, the salary is as high as we can make it," applicants have to decide whether the salary is adequate and whether they might do better somewhere else. If the salary is open to negotiation, the applicant may have another figure in mind—for example, $1,000 or $1,500 or 20 percent more than the initial offer. If the employment is given with an understanding that there will be a significant salary increase after the probationary period, that may be satisfactory to the applicant.

It is all right to ask but it is best not to make salary a condition of employment. If the employer says, "We can pay you $23,000 per year," the applicant ought to be careful about saying, "I want $25,000 a year or I will not take the job." Asking for salary information, negotiating, and discussing are very different than issuing ultimatums. Many employers react badly to demands that sound like ultimatums.

Salaries are not always described on a yearly basis, as they are in this discussion. Sometimes jobs are described on the basis of the amount earned during a month or a pay period, which is often two weeks or half a month. It is always wise to convert whatever the salary is to an annual salary to make comparisons easier.

Variations by Type of Employment
According to Gibelman and Schervish (1996) the highest median incomes, $37,499, were earned by those in private, for-profit settings, federal employees, and military employees. Less than 3 percent were federal employees and only 1 percent were military employees. Median salaries for private, not-for-profit and for state and local employees were $32,499.

Median salaries, however, are not always valid indicators of the best paid employment for those who are beginning social work careers. Many social workers have excellent, lengthy, and productive careers in the nonprofit field, where close to half of all social workers are employed, and have salaries commensurate with well-compensated careers. Others in various kinds of government service may earn less than they might in nongovernment work. Perhaps the key decision is to seek employment that is challenging and in which the social worker feels comfortable and competent. When those conditions are met, salaries tend to take care of themselves. As is evident from the salary figures reported here, the range of social work incomes is not very great. There are not vast differences among fields of practice for people with similar credentials and experience. Some jobs pay more than others but not usually a great deal more.

Benefits and Total Compensation Packages

A potential employee is usually able to find out about the details of the salary structure and the employee benefits, which are discussed below, in an agency's personnel policies booklet or manual. In some cases, there is no printed document, and questions such as those suggested in this chapter have to be asked in interviews with the employer or the employer representative.

Salary is only part of the overall compensation package of all employees, including social work employees. There are other factors that may make a lower salary financially more attractive in some jobs than a higher salary in another job. Fringe benefits are those additions to an employee's compensation that help meet health, retirement, and other needs. They are paid to or paid for an employee. The benefits an employee is likely to encounter are described later in this chapter. The whole package of fringe benefits should be evaluated when a social worker explores a job offer. As has been mentioned, it is sometimes true that the salary plus the benefits in one job are worth more than the total compensation in another job that may initially appear to be more generous.

Although many of the people who will read this book are young and may not think they need to be concerned about employee benefits, these benefits make a difference to everyone and they ought to be considered by anyone looking for a job. The most important and most common benefits should be discussed in any job interview. The following sections discuss some of the most important employee benefits.

Social Security

The keystone of benefits is Social Security or, as it is technically known, Old Age, Survivors, and Disability Insurance. Available as a benefit in almost all social agencies, it provides the worker and the family with basic benefits such as monthly payments to widows and children (until the youngest child is eighteen) if a worker dies; monthly payments to the worker and the family if the worker becomes disabled; and retirement benefits for spouses and for employees when the worker retires at age sixty-two or later, depending on the year of birth. It provides medical insurance, Medicare, for persons over sixty-five and for people with disabilities.

Contrary to what readers may have read or heard, the Social Security system is viable and will be of benefit into the middle of the new century and beyond. The U.S. Congress has always corrected any deficiencies in the system and ensured that benefits are available. However, Social Security is only part of an adequate package of benefits. It provides an important base but the other benefits discussed in this chapter are also important to combine with Social Security. Social Security is an important benefit; however, by itself, it is rarely adequate to provide for workers and their families.

Retirement

It sometimes seems odd for a twenty-two-year-old beginning social worker to ask about retirement that is thirty to fifty years away. However, retirement plans are simply money in another form, and having a good retirement program is comparable to having a better salary.

Retirement plans come in two kinds—portable and nonportable. The best plan for a new worker is usually the portable plan, which the employee can keep and transfer to another job. Most social workers do not stay in the same job for their whole careers. Many social workers hold three or four or more jobs between the beginning of their work and their retirement. Creating a retirement plan early that can be taken from job to job is an important benefit. Nonportable plans are part of the agency program only and are more common. The worker in the agency may retire at some point with the money that has built up in the retirement plan. However, if they leave, employees often lose all the money that the employer has put into their retirement account, taking with them only their contribution.

Most retirement plans require a payment by the worker and a matching payment by the organization. For example, many agencies take 4, 5, or 6 percent out of the worker's salary every year and put it in the retirement plan. The agency may match that plan at the same amount for the employee. That is true of portable as well as nonportable plans. Ordinarily, if workers leave the agency, they are reimbursed for their contributions to retirement, plus interest. However, the employer contribution is ordinarily returned to the agency.

Some plans are vested after a period of years. Workers can leave their money in the plan when moving to a different job. The money will build up over a period of time and workers will, upon reaching a specified age, be able to retire with benefits from the retirement plan. Often, a person has to work five years or more in the organization for the retirement to be vested. Frequently those vested retirement plans have other features. For example, workers can retire as disabled if they become injured or ill while they participate in the plan. So staying part of a retirement plan is a good thing, unless the money that has been put in it is needed immediately. In the portable plans, and in some more generous situations, both the worker's and the agency's contribution are given to the worker upon leaving employment. That amount builds up and provides retirement benefits for the worker who is moving to a new job. In some rare situations, the worker can cash in the entire plan before retirement, both the employer's and the employee's portions. However, retirement contributions are often made in a way that exempts them from taxes until the time of retirement. Withdrawing the funds early can trigger a tax penalty and the employee forfeits part of the funds.

It should be clear that being young is not a reason to be unconcerned about retirement. A retirement policy on the job is often a good way to start a savings account and build up some money, not only for eventual retirement but for a house, car, and many other kinds of eventual investments. The employee contribution is often nearly $1,000 per year, even for a low salary. That is an amount of savings that is difficult to achieve without the compulsion of a retirement plan.

Portable retirement plans are often those that are part of national organizations rather than the specific agency or the state. The plans are transferable from one agency to another. These are especially useful for agencies in which people move from one to another of a similar kind such as family service agencies, United Ways, Jewish Community Centers, and others.

If given the choice, most people are better off with a portable policy that they can take with them if they change employment. It is also advantageous to have a policy to which employees can contribute extra money when they want to. The retirement policy constitutes an excellent and convenient savings account for many workers.

Insurance

Health Insurance

In the United States, health insurance is an important employment benefit. In fact, for most U.S. citizens, health care insurance is paid through the workplace rather than through government, which is the arrangement in Canada and much of the Western world. Sometimes it is more valuable than any other benefit. Employees should always ask if health insurance is provided and if it covers only the employee or the employee and the family. They should also ask how much the employee pays and how much the employer pays towards health insurance. Agencies have varying policies on paying for employee health insurance. Some pay the whole cost for the employee and the family; others pay the cost for the employee, but not the employee's family. Usually, the agency deducts the employee's health insurance contributions directly from the employee's salary each pay period.

It is also important to look at the health insurance policies offered by the agency to learn what they cover. In some agencies employees are given the opportunity to select a variety of health services in a "cafeteria" plan. Employees may have spouses who receive some health benefits and, therefore, the new employees may not want the usual health insurance policy. Instead, they may prefer having vision care insurance, dental care, or a life insurance policy.

Looking very carefully at a health policy is important. Policies can vary. Some have large deductibles—the portion that the employee must pay before the insurance starts paying—while others have small deductibles. Some cover more services than others. Some have special limits on mental health care. Some cover full emergency room care in hospitals, while others cover none. Some require clearance with a central planning or managed care group before surgery or other procedures or services can be covered under the policy. Other policies allow the worker's own physician to arrange for and approve the same procedures without any other consultation or approval.

Increasing numbers of health insurance policies are provided through Health Maintenance Organizations (HMOs). Some agencies give their workers a choice between the HMO and the more open, standard policy, where the worker chooses a physician. Many insurers have negotiated contracts with health care providers. They encourage the insured to utilize these so-called preferred providers as a way of controlling costs.

The Health Maintenance Organization has a number of advantages for many workers. HMOs agree, for a specific amount of money every year, to care for workers and their families. They provide all the care that is needed, including doctor's visits, annual physical exams, maternity care, inoculations, and surgery. Some also include dental and vision care. An advantage to the worker is that HMOs provide health care and preventive health services for people who are healthy or ill, whereas traditional health insurance programs only treat people who are ill.

One disadvantage of the HMO is that the workers and their families are limited to a panel of doctors, hospitals, and pharmacies. If employees want to use different services, they may not be able to do so. As indicated, some more traditional health insurance policies also restrict policyholders to specific panels of health care providers.

The HMO has a gatekeeper doctor or primary care physician, and people in the HMO see that physician before being referred to other physicians or treatment facilities. All of the health care for the family is managed; that is why HMO arrangements are called managed care services.

In evaluating traditional health insurance policies, workers need to know what the policy covers. Some experts say the most important coverage is for major medical costs—for care that costs in the hundreds of thousands to millions of dollars to treat medical events such as auto accidents, heart disease, cancer, and organ transplants. Therefore, it is always critical to know the limits of health insurance coverage. Full coverage that stops at $50,000, for example, is not extensive coverage. Employees may want to locate private policies that extend their coverage to higher limits. In any case, health insurance is one of the most important employee compensation variables.

Disability Insurance

It is usually prudent for employees, especially younger workers, to obtain a disability insurance policy and to maintain it even if it isn't offered by the agency. Some agencies pay all or part of the cost of disability coverage or make a low-cost group policy available for employees. Younger workers are more likely to be victims of accidents and illnesses which leave them disabled than they are to die. That is why life insurance does not always provide the most important kind of protection for one's family and, of course, it does not provide aid to disabled people. A disability policy will cover them with at least partial income and some services until they recover or, in extreme cases, for the rest of their lives. A disability policy, combined with Social Security disability, can help a worker survive even under terrible circumstances. If the agency provides it, it is a valuable fringe benefit.

For a younger social worker, disability insurance is second in importance to adequate health insurance and more important than life insurance which, as suggested, is important and useful, but the chances are greater that a younger worker will become disabled than die. Therefore, disability coverage is more important than coverage which only becomes available if the worker dies.

Liability Insurance

It is advisable for social workers to be ensured against malpractice or liability. Some agencies provide such coverage and it is important to know the circumstances and the extent of the coverage. The subjects of malpractice coverage and liability are discussed in a later chapter.

Accident Insurance

Many agencies provide accident insurance to their employees or offer low-cost group policies. It is usually inexpensive because most people do not collect from accident insurance for the events it covers such as losing a limb, becoming blind, or being killed in an accident. It is useful to have accident insurance but it is not ordinarily a particularly relevant part of an overall fringe benefits package because so few social workers suffer serious accidents.

Life Insurance

Many agencies provide life insurance coverage for their employees. Life insurance is always good protection for a worker and the worker's family. There are two basic kinds of life insurance—term and cash value (which may also be called ordinary, universal, or whole life insurance).

Term life insurance is relatively inexpensive, especially for younger people. The price increases as people grow older. It usually provides a great deal of life insurance protection that is paid in cash to the survivors of the worker in the case of death, for relatively small annual payments.

Cash value life insurance provides death benefits, too, usually less benefits for more money than term insurance. However, it is also a form of savings. The policy not only pays in case of death but over the years builds up cash value. The growth is greater for policies that have been kept for a long time and on which regular premiums have been paid. It, too, costs less for younger people than for older people. However, the cost does not increase with age. A twenty-five-year-old's cash value life insurance annual premium will be the same when that person is fifty.

People who own cash value life insurance policies can take the cash at some point for a major investment such as a house; they may use the money as part of a retirement plan; or they can borrow some of the cash value at low interest rates when they want to make a purchase or need some extra money for a short period of time.

Most agency-provided insurance policies are term life, and the insurance may be ended if the employee moves to another job.

It is always wise to ask about the kinds of life insurance available and to also ask if it can be taken to another job—if it is portable like the retirement plans discussed above. It is also a good idea to have an individual life insurance policy to cover a spouse, children, or other dependents in the family. Single people usually do not have any great need for life insurance and they may decide to spend their money on disability insurance, for example.

Life insurance purchasers also need to know the viability of the company that issues the policy. Although most life insurance companies have enormous assets and careful management, a few have failed in recent years. In those cases, policyholders lost their investments. Therefore, finding the company's rating in the public library or from the state government insurance department is worth the effort.

Long-Term Care Insurance

A relatively new form of insurance coverage is long-term care insurance that provides payments for nursing home or other extended care for people who need it. Policies are often available at group rates through employers. If employees purchase such insurance for themselves and their family while young, the premiums are lower than they would have been if the insurance were purchased at an older age. In some policies, an employee is able to provide coverage for parents and in-laws as well as for the employer and the spouse. A variety of social changes have made long-term care a necessity for increasing numbers of people. This kind of insurance is becoming increasingly popular. In 2000, Congress considered tax breaks for those who buy long-term care insurance.

Dental and Visual Insurance

Many agencies provide or offer dental insurance and visual insurance as employee benefits or as employee-paid options. These policies cover varying degrees of routine care by dentists, orthodontists, ophthalmologists, and optometrists. The cost of braces, as well as prescription eyeglasses or contact lenses, may be entirely or partially covered. Such insurance can be useful and as a fringe benefit is especially worth having. It may also be worth purchasing, though the typical family's annual expenditures for dental and optical services are often approximately equal to the premiums. Therefore, some people consider these policies prepaid care arrangements rather than insurance.

Spending Accounts

Some organizations make provisions for people to authorize money to be deducted from their salaries to use for the care of elderly parents or other dependents, for child day care, or for unreimbursed health expenses. These accounts have the value of being pre-tax payments. The employee does not pay tax on the money that is put aside for these purposes—purposes that are going to be carried out anyway. Spending accounts are usually a good thing to have, if the agency makes them available. Federal tax laws dictate the kinds of organizations and employees that can use these kinds of accounts, as well as the maximum amount that can be set aside.

For example, you might authorize $100 per month to be deducted from your salary to go toward a day care bill. After you paid the day care fee, you would submit payment evidence to the spending account manager, who would reimburse you for the full amount you had set aside. The money in your spending account is sheltered from federal income tax liability. That has an effect similar to deducting the costs from your income tax. However, some of the expenses that can be paid from spending accounts cannot ordinarily be deducted from taxes. Therefore, if you deduct no more than you are going to spend on these necessary expenditures, the spending account provides for tax savings. The negative side is that if you set aside more than you actually spend, you forfeit the difference between the deductions and the expenditures.

Spending accounts are well worth exploring with the agency personnel office. When properly handled, they can increase an employee's disposable income.

Other Benefits

Vacation.   The normal vacation for social workers who have been on the job for a few years is twenty working days, or one month of vacation every year. They may start out with only five or ten days of vacation per year but the vacation time may increase with length of service. Some agencies have arrangements in which vacation time is earned at a specified rate. For each month of employment, for example, a specified number of vacation days are earned.

It is important to know whether vacation accrues and, if so, how much can accrue. If an employee has a three-week vacation in one year but only uses one week of it, can the two weeks of extra vacation be carried over until the next year? If someone wants to go on vacation for four weeks during the following year, can the time carried over be used? Also, if workers leave the agency with accrued vacation time can they be paid for that accrued time after leaving? Some agencies say yes and some say no. Those who say no justify their position by asserting that the purpose of a vacation is not to give the worker more compensation but to refresh workers so that they can do a better job. Vacation is not only a pleasant benefit, it may also involve cash value. Therefore, it is one of the areas a social worker should explore with a potential employer.

Sick Leave.   Sick leave accrues much like vacation leave in most agencies. When an employee has an illness, the accrued sick leave can be used so the employee continues to be paid, even though he or she is not at work. There may be limits on the amount of sick leave employees can accrue, just as there are limits on the amount of vacation that can be accrued.

Sick leave can be a very valuable fringe benefit, especially in cases of long-term illness. It also keeps people from having their salaries or accrued vacation time reduced when they have to spend a day or two at home or in the hospital because of illness.

Family Leave.   Federal law requires employers to grant employees family leave when they have family health problems. Although that leave is not always with pay, the employee cannot be terminated for taking it. In the case of a new child in the family, whether from childbirth or adoption, fathers as well as mothers are eligible for leave under the family leave regulations. Caring for sick children or parents are other examples for which family leave may be taken. A potential employer's family leave policy should be explored.

Workers' Compensation.   Most organizations are required to have workers' compensation, which provides benefits to a worker's family in the case of death connected with the job, or care and benefits to the worker if a worker is injured on the job or in connection with the job.

Additional Benefits.   There are other benefits that agencies pay. These can be part of a general personnel policy, or they can be part of a negotiation between the worker and the employer, especially in a smaller agency. They include:

1. Agency payment of professional dues, such as NASW dues, for the worker.
2. Paid travel to professional conferences.
3. Agency-paid book purchases and professional journal subscriptions.

In some cases, agencies pay for parking for workers. Some agencies provide company cars that the worker can use for personal purposes, for a fee, in addition to free use for work.

Conclusion

There are many kinds of benefits that can be sought by the social worker or offered by the agency, and they make a great difference. Generous fringe benefits may make a smaller salary larger than it might otherwise seem. And a solid package of fringe benefits may make a job more attractive than it would be without them. Knowing about salary alone doesn't tell very much about the value or quality of the job. Knowing about both the fringe benefits and the salary provides much better and more complete information. It is the total compensation package that ought to be of interest to the employee. Examining the whole thing is an important step to take prior to accepting a job.

6

Licensing, Credentials, and Legal Regulation for Social Work Practice

Those who have the title of social worker are subject to a number of voluntary and legally required credentials and certifying procedures. Credentials reflect the professional's educational preparation and knowledge of the field. There are also specialized certifications and requirements for various fields of social work practice. Licensing or other certification regulates social work in every state but it is not necessarily required for all work. Some agencies and other types of social work do not require licensing—for example, social work professors. Some of the variations are discussed in the chapter.

Most occupations of significance in the United States require credentials, whether for trades such as plumbing and electrical work, or for professions such as law, medicine, and, more recently, social work. These regulations are designed to protect the public—to guarantee that a person who practices a profession or trade knows the field, will be effective and not harmful, and is bound by a code of ethical conduct. Those who do not meet and maintain the standards and criteria for legal regulation are suspended or removed from the legal practice of their disciplines.

Legal Regulation

Legal regulation of social workers is required in all fifty states, the District of Columbia, Puerto Rico, and the Virgin Islands. The procedures and forms of legal regulation vary from jurisdiction to jurisdiction. In Appendix 6 there is a list of all the licensing regulations used in the United States.

Some states provide for *reciprocity*. If social workers are licensed in one place, they can be licensed in another without re-taking the examination or providing information on experience, education, and supervision. State laws also provide for what the Association of Social Work Boards (ASWB, formerly the American Association of State Social Work Boards) calls *endorsement,* which means that one state will accept a passing score from another state on a licensure exam. However, it has to be the same examination used by the state offering the reciprocal license.

Licensing and regulation is the government's way of protecting the public against people who might call themselves social workers or who try to perform social work jobs but do not have the proper training or experience. Licensing regulates the use of the title and protects the title of social worker.

Types of Legal Regulation

There are several types of state legal regulation for professions, according to the ASWB, which prepares examinations and study guides and assists the states in carrying out their regulatory functions. Each state establishes its own passing score levels. Regulation is carried out by a state board, either an independent board solely for social work, or a composite board that covers several disciplines, all of which are usually associated with mental health.

The types of regulation are *licensure,* which means that the board must authorize a person to practice the profession according to the ASWB (American Association of State Social Work Boards, 1996); and *certification,* which is a term some states use but that generally has the same meaning as licensure. In Michigan the term *registration* is used and the regulation is somewhat different than is found in most other states.

Two types of laws also govern legal regulation. One is a *practice act* that establishes the criteria for authorizing people to practice a profession. The other is a *title protection* law that forbids those who are not licensed or certified by the board to use the title of social worker. Some groups, such as hospital workers and some who work for specific employers, are exempt from legal regulation in some states.

In most states there is an examination for licensing or certification. Most states also have several levels of licensing. Some license baccalaureate social work degree workers and provide them with various titles. All states certify MSWs. Others provide a higher level of licensing to those who hold master's or doctoral degrees and a required number of years of professional practice and supervision by a qualified, licensed social worker. A few states license people with associate degrees in social work as social work associates. As the ASWB describes it, states license social workers at four levels—BSWs upon graduation, MSWs upon graduation, MSWs with two years of practice that is professionally supervised, and MSWs with supervised clinical experience. Several states include doctoral level social workers in the last two categories. Although the ASWB describes four levels of state licensing, states range from providing one level of licensing to five. The top license is usually for those authorized to provide independent practice. Some specify a license for private practice. However, the names of the licenses and certifications vary among the states.

Many states require a degree in social work accredited by the Council on Social Work Education for both MSW and BSW licenses. However, some states provide opportunities for licensing to graduates of both accredited and unaccredited programs as well as to graduates who have studied in fields other than social work. The table in Appendix 6 explains the state-by-state licensing regulations.

States also usually provide a provisional license for social workers to practice while they complete the requirements for licensure. Some states also provide temporary licenses so social workers can be employed until the state board can make a decision on their status. The National Association of Social Workers, and individual, professional social workers worked for many years to achieve licensing and legal regulation in every state.

Licensing Examinations

There are four examinations developed by the ASWB: Basic, Intermediate, Advanced, and Clinical. Each state board chooses the examination or examinations it wants to use. The examinations are developed in consultation with professional social workers and testing experts. The ASWB publishes and sells study guides for each of its examinations. They include practice questions and score sheets, so potential licensees are able to assess their ability to pass the tests.

In addition, several organizations provide licensing preparation courses and materials. Local seminars, taped instructions and suggestions, and other approaches to preparing candidates for all types of credentials are regularly advertised in professional publications such as *NASW News*. It is always important, when looking at a job in a state in which you are not licensed, to find out about the licensing and regulation program and to determine the necessary steps to obtain the license to practice social work. Examinations are generally only part of the requirements. States may also require character and professional references and documentation of education. Some states also want candidates for licensing to complete examinations before their other credentials are evaluated. For detailed information on specific states, territories, or the Commonwealth of Puerto Rico, the listing in Appendix 6 is a good resource. Also, the toll free number for the Association of Social Work Boards is a good source of information—(800) 225-6880. The ASWB e-mail address is info@aswb.org and its World Wide Web homepage is www.aswb.org.

The ASWB is the primary national licensing organization. It develops the licensing examinations, based upon job analyses that it conducts periodically (American Association of State Social Work Boards, 1996) and also publishes information for social work boards and others who are interested in licensing (American Association of State Social Work Boards, 1997). Their "Blue Book" carefully describes the ways in which the exams are developed, constructed, and validated. The effort is to match the examination questions as closely as possible to the actual work of social workers.

The following are some sample questions from the ASWB basic examination.[1]

1. Following the birth of a son who has Down's syndrome and serious cardiac problems, a refugee couple asks that the child be allowed to die. What should the social worker do **FIRST** when working with these parents?

   A. Report the case to child protective services because of the at-risk nature of the situation.
   B. Offer the parents the option of relinquishing the child for adoption.
   C. Encourage the parents to meet with other parents of Down's syndrome children.
   D. Explore how this situation would have been addressed in their own country of origin.

2. The youngest child of a single mother with four children has been hospitalized four times for lead poisoning. The doctor has refused to release the child back into an unsafe environment. During an interview with the hospital social worker, the woman says that the landlord refuses to have the apartment where she lives repainted and make other necessary repairs. She would like to move, but she is unable to find affordable housing that will also allow four children. The **BEST** course of action for the social worker is to:

   A. advise the woman to withhold her rent until the repairs are made.
   B. inform the woman that the case must be reported to child welfare authorities.
   C. assist the woman with locating resources for suitable housing.
   D. report the landlord to the housing authority.

3. An adolescent has been referred to a social worker because of school-related difficulties. During the intake session with the family, the parents become angry and begin verbally attacking the teen. The social worker's **MOST** appropriate action is to:

   A. allow the parents to continue to vent their anger.
   B. stop the session and see the teen alone.
   C. focus on the parents' expression of anger.
   D. ask the teen to leave the room.

---

[1]*Source: Study Guide: A Guide for Candidates Preparing for the AASSWB Social Work Examination, Basic Level,* by the American Association of State Social Work Boards, 1999, Culpeper, VA. Copyright © 1999 by the American Association of State Social Work Boards. Reprinted with permission.

These are some questions from the clinical level examination administered by ASWB.[2]

1. A breach of ethical conduct may exist when a social worker:

   A. discusses sports scores with a client during a session.
   B. uses the client's first name.
   C. exchanges books to be read for pleasure with a client.
   D. exchanges social work sessions for babysitting services by the client.

2. A seven-year-old child frequently expresses worry about his parents' whereabouts, is afraid of the dark, cries easily, and complains of frequent stomachaches. The child is **MOST** likely exhibiting:

   A. symptoms of abuse and neglect.
   B. separation anxiety disorder.
   C. conduct disorder.
   D. panic disorder.

3. Using behavior therapy for treatment of depression reflects the view that depression is the result of:

   A. role confusion.
   B. negative cognition.
   C. poor interpersonal skills.
   D. absence of positive reinforcement.

4. A client, referred by his wife, walked into the social worker's office, talking in a loud and threatening manner. He stated that there is no problem except his wife and it is she who should be in therapy. The social worker should **FIRST:**

   A. assure the client that he will have the opportunity to discuss his situation.
   B. suggest to the client that his behavior indicates that he has a problem.
   C. instruct the client to leave the office until he is better composed.
   D. ask the client why he believes his wife needs treatment.

5. Which of the following characteristics is usually **NOT** found in families in which incestuous relationships have occurred?

   A. Enmeshment of family members
   B. Distorted patterns of communication
   C. Symbiotic mother-child relationships
   D. Moralistic attitude toward extramarital affairs

---

[2]*Source: Study Guide: A Guide for Candidates Preparing for the AASSWB Social Work Examination, Clinical Level,* by the American Association of State Social Work Boards, 1999, Culpeper, VA. Copyright © 1999 by the American Association of State Social Work Boards. Reprinted with permission.

Independent Social Work Credentials

For a more specific example, advanced levels of licensing are used for those who want to practice independently, or who want to obtain the highest level of credentials which, as suggested in this chapter, can be a wise career choice.

The credential, Licensed Independent Social Worker (LISW), is the highest-level social work license in South Carolina and is a typical type of requirement found in other states with similar approaches to licensing. According to the South Carolina Board of Social Work Examiners (1996) LISWs must have an MSW or doctorate in social work from a program accredited by the Council on Social Work Education. They must also have passed the Clinical or Advanced Level of the ASWB examination. In addition, they must have two years of supervised practice experience. The supervisor must have passed the same examination, and if a resident of the state, also must have been an LISW for three years prior to providing the supervision.

A contract for supervision has to be provided to the Board of Social Work Examiners that promises the supervision will be a minimum of fifty face-to-face hours over a twenty-four-month period. It has to be clinical supervision—about the clinical work the candidate for LISW does, not administrative—and it cannot be group or peer supervision. At the end of the supervision, the supervisor provides a report to the Board, an evaluation of the supervisee's work, and a recommendation about the license.

Complete details on social work licensing regulations, exams, and study guides are available from the Association of Social Work Boards, 400 South Ridge Parkway, Suite B, Culpeper, VA 22701, at the telephone number and web site mentioned earlier. In most cases, the ASWB sets up exams for individuals in their home communities on the basis of requests. The same information may also be obtained at college or university libraries or from the state licensing board offices.

To Be or Not to Be Licensed

Because the licensing and regulation laws and procedures are so different among the states, it is sometimes not clear whether social workers should be licensed in the state where they work. As mentioned earlier, certain jobs are exempt from the licensing requirements. A social worker may be able to work in some agencies, often large public agencies, without holding a social work credential from the state.

It is a good practice, no matter what the requirements are, to obtain the highest license or other credentials obtainable in the state. Even if no license is required, it is always advisable to have a license to document your job qualifications and to know that these qualifications are sufficient for another job that may be sought.

For example, George Planer is a social worker with a large department in his state that has been exempted from the licensing laws. He has worked satisfactorily for the agency for five years and has a solid reputation in his community. A local children's home is seeking a new executive director and the board contacts George, who it thinks is an excellent candidate. He interviews for the job and is well-regarded by the board, which offers him, beginning immediately, the job of executive director at a substantially higher salary. However, he does not hold a social work license and under his state laws cannot direct the home without a license in a field of human services. The next licensing examination is not to be given for three months. Therefore, he has to convince the board to wait for him to take the position, which they may be unwilling to do, or turn down the job, which he does not want to do.

Having a license and keeping it up-to-date is a good way to be prepared for career opportunities and to be able to make career advancements with less difficulty than those who do not bother to guarantee their credentials. Licensing usually requires an examination, as already mentioned, a fee that is paid for taking the examination, the cost of a study guide or participation in a preparation class, which may be offered in the community by the licensing board or another organization such as NASW, and an annual licensing fee.

Social workers who are licensed usually have some continuing education requirements, which are spelled out in the ASWB documents described earlier. For example, many states require licensed social workers to document that they have completed a specific numbers of hours of continuing education. In many states, the hours must be under the direction of a licensed social worker. In some states, publishing articles, leading workshops and similar activities, in addition to attending meetings and training sessions count toward the continuing education requirements. It is important for social workers to plan to continue their educations after graduation from a college or university.

In addition to maintaining the current license, social workers should also work toward achieving the next highest level of licensing, whenever possible. In South Carolina, graduates of the Master of Social Work program are able to take the examination for Licensed Master of Social Work (LMSW) credential when they graduate. After two years of professional work as a social worker under the supervision of a more highly credentialed social worker, an MSW can apply for and take an examination for the Licensed Independent Social Worker (LISW), which grants some additional privileges and is a higher credential. For that reason, many social workers want to ensure themselves that the job they take will provide the means to qualify them for the next higher license, and that appropriate supervision is available.

Voluntary Credentials

In addition to legal credentials required of social workers in most states, there are also various voluntary credentials for which social workers may apply. The three primary credentials are membership in the Academy of Certified Social Workers (ACSW), the clinical credentials offered by the National Association of Social Workers, and the credential in clinical social work offered by the American Board of Examiners in Clinical Social Work. In addition, social workers may be certified members of the American Association of Marriage and Family Therapy (AAMFT), a voluntary group discussed in more detail later, whose members must all have legally required licenses or other credentials. None of these voluntary credentials have any bearing on licensure.

Another voluntary credential is for sex educators, counselors, and therapists. Information can be obtained from the American Association of Sex Educators, Counselors and Therapists, 435 N. Michigan Ave., Suite 1717, Chicago, IL 60611. Professionals in sexual health work, including social workers, are eligible for membership. They provide professional education in addition to certification. Like the other credentialing groups, they have a code of ethics and standards for membership and practice.

It is generally a good plan for social workers to obtain as many voluntary credentials as possible. The voluntary credentials require specific educational and supervision experiences. They all require examinations.

Although the voluntary credentials are not required by all agencies, some agencies expect their staff to have them or to work toward them. Members of these voluntary programs pay annual dues, in addition to fees required to take the examinations and to prepare for them.

The suggestion to hold as many credentials as possible is for both quality and practical reasons. In terms of quality, a social worker demonstrates that the highest requirements of various credentialing groups have been met. For practical purposes, many agencies are reluctant to employ anyone who does not hold a specific professional credential. Holding professional credentials of various kinds increases your flexibility in changing jobs, relocating, and moving up in the profession. In some states, the licensing requirements are close to or identical to those of the voluntary associations. In South Carolina, requirements for a Licensed Marital and Family Therapist are essentially the same as those required by AAMFT, except that the state also requires a written examination.

Certified Social Work Manager

In addition to practice and clinical credentials, social work also has a credential for managers, the Certified Social Work Manager. To obtain the certification, a person must (1) be a member of the National Network for Social Work Managers, which administers the credential, (2) hold a BSW or MSW and have five years of postdegree experience, and (3) show competence in ten of twelve areas of management. Details for applying are available from the National Network for Social Work Managers, CSWM Program, P.O. Box 11391, Columbia, SC 29211-1391.

The Academy of Certified Social Workers

The oldest of the voluntary credentials for social workers is membership in the Academy of Certified Social Workers (ACSW). It began in 1962 and includes social workers of all specializations, unlike many other credentials which are limited to clinical or direct services work.

To qualify for the ACSW credential, which must be renewed annually, a social worker must meet the following criteria and have these qualifications (Academy of Certified Social Workers, National Association of Social Workers, undated; National Association of Social Workers, undated b).

1. Be qualified to provide social services and be certified for independent and self-regulated practice.
2. Have passed a national ACSW examination that covers assessment and service planning, intervention, professional development and ethics, and administration.
3. Have completed an MSW or a doctorate in social work from an accredited social work education program and at least two years of social work employment after graduation under professional supervision.
4. Provide professional references (a written evaluation of the worker) from a supervisor and two social work colleagues.
5. Be a member of NASW and agree to adhere to the NASW Code of Ethics and be subject to the NASW adjudication process.

The ACSW credential allows those who receive it to append the title after their names, as in Josephine Jones, ACSW. Members receive a framed certificate for their offices attesting to their ACSW membership. When they renew their NASW memberships each year, an additional amount is added for ACSW dues. Members receive a seal indicating that their ACSW credential is current.

Many agencies may use the ACSW as a screening device when hiring new employees or as an expectation for new graduates. In some cases, employers expect new employees who have not yet qualified for ACSW to do so within a reasonable period of time, as a demonstration of their knowledge and skills. The ACSW can also be used as the basis for applying for a clinical social work credential.

An application form and information bulletin can be obtained from NASW in Washington for the two tests given each year, once in the fall and once in the spring. Test sites are located all over the United States. The application kit also provides evaluation forms for supervisors. Because the application process is complicated, it is wise to begin it early. Early application is required for the tests. The deadline for applying for a June test can be mid-April.

The following are some sample questions from the application booklet and are not, of course, actual questions an applicant would be asked (National Association of Social Workers, undated b).

1. A four-year-old child who is extremely loving and oversolicitous of his new infant sibling is displaying which of the following defense mechanisms?

    A. Reaction formation
    B. Fantasy formation
    C. Introjection
    D. Regression

2. In an individual session with a social worker, a fifteen-year-old girl reveals her fears that she is lesbian. She has recurring fantasies about, and an ongoing intense attachment to, a female teacher who has taken a strong interest in her. The girl reports that her mother reinforces her fears by constantly commenting that the girl is not yet dating. Frightened by her intense feelings, the girl is experiencing acute anxiety attacks. The worker's most helpful initial response would be to:

   A. indicate that same-sex attachments are a normal part of growing up.
   B. explore why the girl is so fearful of homosexuality.
   C. deal with some of her mother's feelings about having an adolescent daughter.
   D. use a family session to explore openly the girl's fears about her sexuality.

3. A small oil and industrial community (population 3,000) has five multimillionaire families who own oil wells. The average annual family income in this community exceeds the state and national average. This fact suggests which of the following?

   A. There is little poverty in the community because of the presence of wealth-producing oil wells.
   B. The wealthy members of the community were concerned and shared their money with poor members.
   C. Annual income is not a good indicator of wealth.
   D. The mean is not a good statistical indicator of the distribution of wealth.

A full guide for preparing for the ACSW test is available from NASW at its toll free number (800) 838-8799 or at NASW, 750 First St. N.E., Washington, DC 20002. Its study questions and suggestions for analyzing examinations for other kinds of credentials should be helpful.

Clinical Social Work Credentials

In addition to the ACSW, which applies to all forms of social work, NASW and the American Board of Examiners in Clinical Social Work also offer special credentials for those who are clinical or direct service practitioners. NASW defines clinical social work services as consisting of assessment, diagnosis, treatment such as psychotherapy and counseling, advocacy, consultation, and evaluation. One or more of these credentials are often required by agencies that provide mental health services, and they are also often important for those who engage in private practice as a means of attesting to their experience and knowledge.

NASW Qualified Clinical Social Worker

NASW's two-leveled clinical credentials are available to both members and non-members of NASW. However, all who apply for the credentials must meet the same basic criteria. To be eligible for the NASW Qualified Clinical Social Worker (QCSW) credential, social workers must, according to the NASW Register of Clinical Social Workers Credentialing Office (1999), meet the following criteria.

1. Agree to abide by the NASW Code of Ethics.

2. Adhere to NASW's Standards for Practice of Clinical Social Work (available from NASW and summarized in the application materials for clinical credentials).

3. Complete 90 hours of continuing education every three years.

4. Have a master's or doctoral degree from an accredited social work education program.

5. Show completion of two years (defined as 3,000 hours) of postgraduate clinical experience in an agency or organized setting, supervised by an experienced clinical social worker.

6. Have a current state license based on an examination that requires an MSW or doctorate in social work or membership in ACSW.

The NASW Diplomate in Clinical Social Work

To be eligible for the higher level NASW clinical credential, social workers must

1. Meet all the requirements for the QCSW.

2. Complete three years, beyond the two required for the QCSW, of advanced clinical practice. At least two years of that practice has to have been during the past ten years.

3. Hold the state's highest level social work license.

4. Pass an advanced or clinical examination over a body of knowledge that applies to qualifications for independent practice and that requires the MSW or the social work doctorate.

5. Pass the NASW Diplomate examination.

NASW Register

Both levels of NASW clinical credentials are recognized in the *NASW Register of Clinical Social Workers* (1999), which is updated periodically in book form and CD-ROM. A fee is charged for each name published in the register. Some federal agencies and insurance companies consult the listing of names in the register to determine whether a social worker's services qualify for payment or reimbursement. Certificates are also provided to those who meet the requirements for the two credentials. Complete details on applying for clinical credentials are available from NASW Register of Clinical Social Workers, Credentialing Office, 750 First St., N.E., Washington, DC 20002-4241.

There are fees for taking the examination, for membership, and for listing in the Register. The Diplomate is a permanent title, while the QCSW must be renewed every two years. However, diplomates pay a fee for being listed in the Register.

The examination of clinical skills for diplomates is conducted at various sites around the United States on dates that change each year. The test was developed by examining the tasks that clinical social workers reported; the test items were written by clinical social workers, trained to prepare them, from throughout the United States. The examination questions are reviewed by clinical social workers, statistically analyzed, and tested with practitioners.

The Diplomate Examination
In 1996 the test consisted of twelve case scenarios with questions requiring short-essay responses. Applicants were allowed four hours to complete the examination. There were audiotape presentations of two scenarios. Some questions required some familiarity with the *Diagnostic and Statistical Manual of Mental Disorders.* Applicants receive a booklet that outlines the areas covered by the exam. In 1996 there were the following components:

1. Two questions on the initial stages of clinical work, such as defining the roles, examining legal issues, and developing rapport.
2. Three questions on diagnostic assessment.
3. Four questions on treatment.
4. One question each on using other systems and social action; risk management and legal liability; and documentation.

Two clinical social workers, trained to grade the examinations, graded the papers anonymously and independently. A third rater graded the papers on which the two initial raters did not agree.

Board Certified Diplomate in Clinical Social Work
The Board Certified Diplomate in Clinical Social Work is conferred by the American Board of Examiners in Clinical Social Work. It requires a master's degree from an accredited social work program with a clinical concentration; a minimum of 7,500 hours of direct clinical practice, 3,000 of which were under supervision in not less than five years; successful completion of a rigorous clinical examination; and registration or certification at the state's highest level.

Information about the American Board of Examiners Diplomate can be obtained from their headquarters, (800) 694-5285 or by e-mail, abe@abecsw.org. Their headquarters are at 27 Congress Street, Suite 211, Salem, MA 01970.

American Association of Marriage and Family Therapy
A valuable credential for clinical workers is clinical membership in the American Association of Marital and Family Therapy. Clinical membership is open only to those who have completed master's or doctoral degrees. Those who are working to-

ward clinical membership can become associate members for up to five years while they work to satisfy the clinical requirements. There is also a student membership category. The AAMFT educational standards are specific and the requirements for professionally supervised practica are also carefully defined. Social work includes marital and family therapy, but AAMFT requirements are more extensive. Therefore, the two-year MSW program may not include all the requirements of the AAMFT, so social workers who want to enter that field and pursue the credential may have to add to their educations after graduation. Graduates of some MSW programs will have completed all or most of the educational requirements as part of their graduate work. The organization has a Commission on Accreditation for Marriage and Family Therapy that accredits some graduate and post-degree training institutes, including graduate social work education programs.

AAMFT, like NASW, has insurance plans, its own code of ethics, and other attributes of a professional association. The AAMFT address is 1133 15th Street, N.W., Suite 300, Washington, DC 20005-2710. Telephone (202) 452-0109.

State Licensing for Marriage and Family Therapy
Several states also have specific licenses for marital and family therapists and licensed counselors in addition to the social work and other professional licenses such as psychology. Many social workers in those states seek the family therapy and counselor licenses, in addition to their social work credentials. As mentioned, in some states requirements for the license for marital and family therapy are the same as or similar to the AAMFT requirements. However, an examination is often a part of the licensing requirement.

The School Social Work Specialist Credential
NASW also administers a special credential for social workers who work in schools, the School Social Work Specialist Credential. Those eligible to apply for the credential must have completed the MSW from an accredited program. Also, they must have at least two years of supervised school social work experience after completing the MSW. The supervision must be provided by an MSW, who must provide an evaluation of the applicant's work. In addition, applicants must provide another reference from an MSW or doctoral level social worker familiar with the applicant's work. Finally, the applicant must pass the National Teachers Examination School Social Worker Specialty Area Test with a score NASW defines as passing.

Both members and nonmembers of NASW are eligible for the credential. Once awarded, the credential must be renewed every three years. Those who apply for renewal have to complete a minimum of thirty hours of continuing professional education for the three years.

According to one writer (Gill, 2000) some licensing and other standardized screening and credentialing examinations are compromised by those who are able to obtain the questions in advance and sell them to test-takers. Although the author does not mention social work or other human services examinations, any examination is susceptible to the theft processes he describes. Modern micro photography and recording make it possible to steal almost any written examination. The public emphasis placed on such examinations makes their theft and sale profitable.

Ethics and Personal Conduct

Those who hold professional credentials, either licenses or voluntary certifications from professional organizations, are bound by ethical mandates associated with those credentials. Violations of the ethical standards built into the licensing laws or the regulations governing the professional credentials can lead to their withdrawal. Failure to live up to the ethics required for a license in most states can lead to the termination of the license and the denial of the right to practice social work. In some circumstances, as mentioned in Chapter 1, criminal prosecutions may result. In the case of violations of professional credentials, inquiries into the conduct, and sanctions against the credentials holder, can follow. Possible consequences include denial of professional memberships and publication of information about the prohibited conduct.

Conclusion

Among the major concerns of all professionals are the rules covering their practice. This chapter covered some of the details of both public laws governing licenses and limits on practice and the major forms of public regulation. In addition, the chapter covered voluntary credentials provided by a number of groups, especially the National Association of Social Workers.

In developing a career, social workers need to begin planning for full licensing and credentials. The licensing and credentialing of professionals provide a valuable service to the public by certifying that they have completed the appropriate education and experience and that the professionals are committed to a code of ethics and conduct that will protect the public from the misapplication of professional services.

Part 2

Social Work Employment Settings

Part 2 consists of chapters that describe large areas of social work practice to help readers understand what social workers do in their everyday work. The focus is on the description of that work to help readers assess their interest in it, rather than providing a guide on how to do the work itself.

Chapter 7 addresses work in the broad field of government, which includes many of the most important social work functions such as public welfare, mental health, school social work, policy-level employment, and federal work with agencies such as the Veterans Administration, the Department of Defense, and the Peace Corps. Chapter 8 discusses health and mental health more broadly because these are two areas with large complements of social work employees. Work with the two population groups who are most commonly served by social workers—children and older adults—is the subject of Chapter 9. Services in the corrections field are covered in Chapter 10. In addition, international social work, rural or small community social work, industrial social work, social planning and larger systems services, and a variety of other areas where social workers are employed are covered in Chapter 11.

Information on job opportunities in these fields, including some of the applications processes, and information on the characteristics of social workers in these fields is also provided.

The material covered in Part 1 on the overriding professional and employment concerns of the professional social worker apply, of course, to the materials in these chapters about the places and the services that engage the time and attention of members of the profession.

There are several more detailed books on the social work field that cover information on various kinds of agency settings. *Social Work: A Profession of Many Faces* by Sheafor and Morales (1995) is a rich source of such information as are the National Association of Social Workers reference books, including the *Encyclopedia of Social Work* (Edwards et al., 1995) and the *Social Work Almanac* (Ginsberg, 1995).

7

Working in Government
Agencies and Services

*Local, State, and Federal Programs
and Public Welfare*

Many of the jobs for social workers are in government at all levels as Chapter 1 shows. For example, there is excellent employment in many federal settings and many social workers build their careers around federal employment. However, the numbers of federal jobs are not large and only a small percentage of social workers are federal employees. According to Gibelman and Schervish (1996) 3.5 percent of social workers who are members of NASW work for the federal government or serve as social workers in the military, or technically for the Department of Defense. Approximately 13 percent of NASW members work for state governments and more than 17 percent are employed by local governments.

Government service is not totally different than nongovernment service. Some voluntary organizations provide services that are also provided by government, especially in areas that are discussed in detail later such as health, mental health, and services for older adults.

Characteristics of Government Employment

The Bureau of Labor Statistics says that four of every ten social work jobs were in government in 1996. The work was usually in health and human resources, mental health, social services, child welfare, housing, education, or corrections for state, county, or municipal governments (Bureau of Labor Statistics, 1999a).

Government employment has characteristics that are different than working for private or profit-making organizations. Many social workers have long and enjoyable careers in government because government work, despite the frustrations that some government employees report, also has certain advantages that working for other organizations does not have.

Advantages of Government Work

The following are some of the advantages of social work in governmental or, as it is also called, public employment.

Steadiness
For the most part, government jobs are stable and steady. Once social workers are hired by a government agency and complete the probationary period, which is usually six months or a year, they are considered permanent employees and find that the jobs can be theirs for the foreseeable future. This relative certainty of employment for a whole career is attractive to many social workers who do not want to be concerned about the continuity of their employment. Of course, recent efforts to reduce the size of the government and to contract with private organizations for services traditionally provided by the government have reduced the permanence of government employment.

Generally, government jobs operate under merit or civil service systems and once social workers have achieved permanent status, they cannot be arbitrarily fired or laid off. There are specific rules governing reductions in employees that must be followed, including in the kinds of reductions described above.

Generally, government employment is permanent unless:

1. There is a major reduction in funds or a major cutback of some other kind in the organization. In that case, employees often have to be let go or moved to other positions to accommodate the reductions.

   Employees of government agencies have rights to their jobs and if they have seniority over others, they are usually not the first to go. In some situations, if their job classification is not one that is going to be reduced, they stay on the job, even if there is a general cutback. When they have seniority, if their job classification is reduced or eliminated, they have the opportunity to be considered for another job in a different classification for which they qualify.

   Despite some recent trends to cut government budgets and reductions in staff, the protection of government workers is still strong.

2. Public employees can be laid off or fired from their jobs for *cause*. If it is clear that they do not perform their jobs properly or if they are proven to have committed improper acts such as stealing, failing to come to work, violating confidentiality, or mistreating clients they can also be dismissed. However, government employees usually cannot be dismissed without an opportunity for a hearing or a kind of trial within the organization, if they ask for one. In many cases, it is less likely that a person will be removed from a government job than from any other kind.

3. A major agency reorganization may result in social workers losing their employment. For example, a state may eliminate or drastically reduce its public mental hospitals, which several have done, and rely on private nursing homes and client care in their own residences. Some of the social workers employed in the mental hospitals might find their jobs eliminated. However, depending on their qualifications and length of service, they may be eligible for vacancies in related programs and services such as helping provide the nonhospital care to discharged patients.

4. Some government agencies are shifting their operations from directly operating programs to contracting with private firms to provide the same services. For example, a state may enter into a contract with a private firm to manage one or more of its prisons or hospitals. In such cases, many of the public employees are no longer needed. Again, they are able to be considered for other vacancies that may exist. Former public employees may be hired by private firms, too.

Salaries and Benefits

Chapter 5 provides specific information on the salaries earned by NASW members who are employees of government bodies. It is noteworthy that government jobs usually pay approximately as much or more than jobs in nongovernment employment. Although, on average, federal employment is the best-paid, local and state government work is not always terribly far behind in terms of social work salaries. Of course, some state or local jobs pay more than some federal jobs.

Government salaries are somewhat cyclical. They may seem relatively high at some times but low at others when private employment increases its compensation. It is not unusual for government salaries to lag behind private industry for periods of time but, generally, they catch up. That reflects the necessity of all employers to pay competitive wages in order to hire enough people with the talents and skills they need to fill their jobs.

Historically, employee benefits in government work have been generally better than in other kinds of employment. That is partly because government wanted to attract people, despite sometimes lower than private industry wages, and because the total complement of government employees is so large that insurance and retirement plans can be financed at relatively low cost. The more participants in a health insurance or retirement plan, the lower the overall costs. Many governments are self-insured. Instead of purchasing health and other insurance from private companies, they, in effect, set up their own insurance companies, collect premiums from employees, and pay benefits to employees.

It was my experience—and it may be more or less universal—that government benefits are generous, in part, because legislators also participate in some of the same programs as do the government employees such as social workers. When the benefits of legislators are packaged with those of employees, employees are likely to benefit.

Sound benefits such as guaranteed retirement payments after a specified number of years of work and after the employee has reached retirement age have been an attractive feature of government employment for many. Such benefits provide an incentive to workers to stay with their government jobs even when the work becomes more difficult, or when the salaries are not competitive with work they might be offered in private agencies.

Significant Work

Perhaps most important to professional social workers is that government jobs provide significant and often challenging work opportunities. Social workers in public employment provide services with and for people that can make a large difference. For example, government workers provide financial assistance to people who are in need, mental health care to people who are emotionally disturbed, and training as well as other assistance to people who have disabilities. They also help provide vocational rehabilitation to people who are disabled, work with incarcerated and released youth and adult offenders, and help people prevent and deal with public health problems through work in departments of public health. Government workers also serve children and their families through the public schools. They assist with adoptions and foster care for children who cannot live with their biological families. Social workers who want to do important, helpful work often find that government employment provides an excellent vehicle for meeting their objectives.

Many social workers take their first jobs in government agencies such as departments of social services, mental health, or public health. Many devote the balance of their working careers to those same agencies. Other social workers spend relatively short periods of time, perhaps one to five years, as government employees; they often learn a great deal and then move on to voluntary organizations or administrative positions in other kinds of programs.

Disadvantages of Government Employment

Not everyone finds equal satisfaction with government work. Some of the frustrations that people experience in government employment are part of the reality of working in large organizations, or, as they are called by social scientists, bureaucracies, which is the technical name for large, complex organizations.

Bureaucracies

Bureaucracies have many layers of authority and supervision. Individuals in bureaucracies often find that they cannot act on their own. They often have to clear their decisions, their treatment efforts, and their statements to others with their supervisors. Although that is true in almost all organizations, it is especially an issue in bureaucracies because there is a hierarchy of supervisors.

People who work for large, government organizations find that they are often close to anonymous. They are not well-known to the top people in the organization, much less their peers, the clients, or the broader community. Government workers are paid to perform specific tasks and most do them well. However, they often are not fully recognized for their efforts or given any special acknowledgement in the community for what they do. People who want to be recognized for their accomplishments and to have well-known public personalities often find government jobs frustrating, except at the very highest levels. However, many social workers seek low-profile careers and for them work in large public organizations is ideal.

Public Criticism

From time to time, there is great public criticism of public employees, often without justification. At times, because the media or a vocal individual generalizes from one bad example to a whole set of public employees, government workers are ridiculed and chastised. People who are engaged in noble work on behalf of others may find themselves stereotyped as incompetent or as malingerers. In addition, some government programs in which social workers are employed such as financial assistance and child protective services are unpopular with segments of the population. Television news programs such as *60 Minutes, Dateline,* and *20–20* also frequently highlight social programs that may not, on the surface, seem rational, though they are usually just carrying out government policies. Although the criticism may be unfair, it is difficult for government organizations or employees to fight back. Government groups can point out the facts and explain but it is not appropriate for them to respond emotionally or with anger. People who cannot accept criticism when it is unfair may not prefer government social work jobs.

Both the larger public and the media also believe that government employees ought to be subject to greater scrutiny and criticism than nonpublic employees, because public employees are paid by everyone's taxes rather than by private employers. There are special laws that govern only public officials and employees covering conduct that would not be criminal if, for example, committed by a private employee of a corporation. The enforcement of those laws may make it appear that public employees and officials are corrupt when, in fact, the same behavior would not be improper in another circumstance.

Colleague Problems

Some people find it frustrating working with some of their colleagues in government jobs. Because of the strong emphasis on tenured job protections and the avoidance of removing people except under dire circumstances and for serious cause, a small number who have lost interest in their work are still employed by government agencies for years. Some of those workers lack motivation and some do not do their jobs as enthusiastically or as effectively as they should. Some employees who find it frustrating to work with such people may want to avoid working for government organizations. Similarly, if they tend to be hangers-on, they should also think about whether they should enter government jobs.

The reality is that "deadwood" and some burned-out workers exist in public agencies. Those agencies attempt to find ways to place such staff in work in which they can be effective or to find ways to terminate their employment. Their numbers are not great and the problem is not nearly as serious as some suggest. However, it is a source of discontent for managers and workers in public agencies. A realistic approach is to prepare to encounter it. Parenthetically, it is not true that such problems are only in government. Private organizations and corporations in and out of social work often encounter the same difficulties.

Structure

Government jobs are often carefully structured. People know to whom they report and they are not permitted to deal with anyone else or to go over the head of their supervisor. Decisions also go up the chain of command slowly and come back down slowly so that it may take months or years to have a decision on a policy or a case. People who have trouble being patient or accepting slow movement in an organization have to be careful about choosing careers in government organizations. This is also a bureaucratic pattern, similar to those described earlier.

Safety

Although it is quite uncommon, there are occasionally physical attacks on public employees of social agencies, especially those agencies that deal with controversial matters such as child protection services, adoptions, and foster care as well as people who work in programs such as economic assistance and food stamps. Over the years a few people with emotional problems have come to government social welfare offices and murdered workers who have taken actions that the attackers disputed.

There are ample procedures for unhappy public social work clients to address grievances. However, a small number of emotionally disturbed and violent people have taken more direct action against the workers they perceive to be the source of their anger.

Social workers in the mental health field may also encounter some dangers from clients. Although those with mental illness are no more dangerous, on the whole, than any other group of people, some have become violent and have directed their violence against social workers and other government employees.

Workers in public corrections, probation, and parole may encounter violence from those they serve or those known to their clients.

Locations of Government Jobs

As noted at the beginning of this chapter, government jobs are found at three different levels—the federal, the state, and the local. The procedures followed in applying for these and other jobs are discussed in Chapter 2.

The Federal Government

Although they are fewer than those at the state and local levels, federal government jobs are attractive. Only one percent of social workers are federal employees. However, their jobs are varied and often offer the best salaries (as mentioned earlier), benefits, and employee satisfaction. The following are examples of federal jobs.

U.S. Department of Veterans Affairs

The Veterans Administration (VA), the most commonly used name for the U.S. Department of Veterans Affairs, is one of the largest employers of social workers in the federal government. The VA was organized by the federal government to carry out many special programs for the first military veterans and these programs continue today. The United States, like other nations, believes that it owes a special debt to veterans because of the risks they took and because of their special contributions. During times of involuntary conscription or drafts, a large number of veterans served as a requirement of their government and VA benefits are seen by many as a form of additional compensation. The VA provides various kinds of benefits, including inpatient and outpatient health and mental health care to qualified veterans.

Social workers are located in the several VA medical and psychiatric hospitals, as well as long-term care facilities owned and operated by the agency. They are also located in a variety of regional offices, including Veterans Centers, which are found throughout the United States. Many who use VA health and mental health care are veterans with lower incomes because the VA focuses, in some circumstances, on helping veterans and their dependents who cannot afford to pay for their own health care.

Veterans who have service-connected conditions—veterans who were injured or became ill in combat or during their terms of service in the Army, Navy, Air Force, Marines, or Coast Guard—have preference over those whose conditions are not connected with their military service. VA services provide both outpatient and inpatient mental health service and medical service from periodic physician checkups to complicated surgery.

The social workers in the Veterans Administration provide counseling for individuals, families, and groups; help patients to arrange to leave hospitals and return to their communities just as social workers do in other kinds of hospitals; arrange for long-term care such as foster and nursing home care for people who cannot return to their homes; and otherwise perform a variety of duties, most of them connected with health and mental health care. Some social workers also serve in the VA central administrative offices in Washington. The social work services provided by the VA are often the same as similar services provided by states and by private organizations to nonveterans. The difference is that the VA serves a specific population.

In addition to its health and welfare services, the VA also provides a variety of help to qualified veterans that are authorized by federal legislation. They include low-cost, insured loans so veterans may more readily purchase real estate, grants for education and training, and cash benefits for those who have been injured or otherwise become ill during their military service. VA programs have also worked to improve community services and have helped to organize health, mental health, and social services that benefit the larger community. In many ways, VA social workers have responsibilities that are similar to social workers in social work jobs with similar services.

Federal Prisons

Most inmates of prisons in the United States are in state penitentiaries or local jails. In 1998, the federal government estimated that there were 1.8 million inmates in local jails and state prisons (Bonczar & Glaze, 1999). In 1997, there were an estimated 100,000 federal prisoners (Sabol & McGready, 1999). The network of federal prisons is operated for those who are convicted of violating federal laws. There are social workers employed in federal prisons throughout the United States who provide group and individual counseling to the prisoners and work with the prisoners' families.

The services that social workers provide to federal prisoners are similar to the work social workers do with corrections clients in state prisons. A more detailed discussion of services to corrections clients is provided in Chapter 10.

The federal government also provides probation and parole services and uses social workers as officers in those fields. The roles of probation and parole workers are discussed also in Chapter 10.

Services to Native Americans

Social workers are also employed to serve Native American clients through two basic organizations, the Bureau of Indian Affairs and the Indian Health Service.

Social workers perform a variety of tasks with and on behalf of these people such as helping arrange for health care, providing part of the care offered in the health care system, providing some counseling and mental health services, occasionally working with tribal governments on their social services programs and, in some situations, providing services directly to clients (Lewis, 1995; Lally & Haynes, 1995).

In an earlier time, most services to these groups were provided directly by the federal agencies responsible for them. Others were provided by the tribal governments, often with government financial assistance. Some tribal governments continue to provide social services and employ social workers to do so.

Under current U.S. policy most Native Americans and Alaskan Natives receive social services from the same agencies that serve other citizens in the states where they reside. Consequently, many social workers in areas with large Native American populations have large complements of American Indian and Alaskan Native clients, serve predominantly their Indian communities, and otherwise work extensively with those populations, though they are state or local rather than federal employees.

Federal Health Facilities

The federal government also operates health facilities for special populations or to serve people in federal territories and possessions. The District of Columbia is not in a state and is controlled by the federal government in ways different than any other city. An example of a special facility for those with mental illness is the Saint Elizabeth's Hospital in Washington, DC. Other programs include the National Institutes of Health, located in the Washington area, which conduct research and provide treatment for several health problems. Social workers serve in the federal health facilities, carrying out some of the same responsibilities as social workers in other health programs as well as being involved in research efforts conducted by the federal government.

Administrative Agencies

Large numbers of social workers are also employed by the several federal agencies that administer the government social welfare and social services programs. Those organizations include, among others:

1. The Department of Health and Human Services and all its units such as the Administration on Aging, the Children's Bureau, the Social Security Administration, Administration for Children and Families, and the Public Health Service (in which many social workers serve as commissioned, uniformed officers).
2. The Department of Labor.
3. The Department of Housing and Urban Development.
4. The Department of Justice (of which federal corrections is a part).
5. The Department of Agriculture, which manages the Food and Consumer Service, which is in charge of the food stamp program. It also provides food and financial help for food purchases to organizations such as day care centers and schools. The Department also studies social issues in rural areas and it is responsible for the state Cooperative Extension Service programs, which provide agents to help with a variety of rural concerns including social and personal concerns.
6. The Peace Corps recruits and places social workers in communities around the world to carry out a number of functions such as helping set up and manage social services programs, teach social work, and advise on social welfare.
7. The Executive Office of the President, which has included several social workers as consultants and advisors on social welfare matters.
8. The Department of Defense is responsible for civilian and military social workers in the various uniformed services.

In these agencies social workers are involved in a variety of activities, most of them administrative and consultative. For example, some social workers administer the large number of Health and Human Services federal grant programs designed to help state and local governments and certain voluntary organizations. Others monitor the large number of programs that are financed jointly by the state and federal governments and operated by state departments of social services, mental health, and health. They also collect and disseminate statistics, publish documents, respond to requests for information from Congress, and otherwise collect and provide data on social issues and social programs.

Social workers in these administrative agencies may be located in the central headquarters, which are almost all in the Washington, DC vicinity, as well as in the federal regional offices, located throughout the nation. An interest in and talent for social work administration and macro or larger system practice are key attributes for those who want to consider employment in these agencies.

The U.S. Congress

Some social workers also work in the U.S. Congress for the House of Representatives, the Senate, for various committees that deal with social issues and social legislation, and for individual members of the House and Senate. Those who work in legislative jobs devote their time to helping write legislation, organizing and conducting hearings, and carrying out research on social welfare issues; and, those who work in members' offices investigate constituent concerns (which are often about social welfare programs and Social Security).

Congressional jobs are an exception to the tenure and long-term employment described for the executive agencies. Changes in political party control of the Congress, which occurred in 1994, lead to many staff members' being replaced by others who are better related to and more ideologically in tune with the party that wins. Similarly, many staff who work for individual members of Congress are replaced when those members leave office voluntarily or lose reelection.

The Armed Forces

Many social workers work in the Armed Forces—the Army, Navy, and Air Force, under the Department of Defense. The U.S. Army has the most extensive social work program of all the military organizations. Social workers serve as both military officers and as civilians employed by the services.

Army, Navy, and Air Force social work officers and some noncommissioned officers or enlisted personnel with social work backgrounds, and other employees work in mental health clinics, in military hospitals, serving military personnel and their families. They also work in family advocacy programs and other services. There is special emphasis on employing social workers in programs dealing with child abuse and neglect and domestic violence, which can pose serious problems for armed forces personnel and their families.

The social work jobs are located at military bases throughout the world including the United States, Asia, Europe, and the Middle East. Some social workers are employed at the Walter Reed Army Hospital, located in the Washington area, which serves not only military personnel and their dependents but also government officials and members of Congress.

For uniformed officers, compensation and benefits are different than for other government employees. Salaries are based upon length of service and rank. Also, members of the military are able to retire with significant benefits—usually with half their salary—after as few as twenty years of service. While on active duty, service personnel have access to a variety of health care programs, low cost foods and other products at commissaries, social clubs memberships, and housing or housing allowances.

An Air Force recruiting document for clinical social workers in the Biomedical Sciences Corps says that those interested in such service should have a master's degree from an accredited school and a state license. They also prefer people with ACSW certification, who can also earn more by having Board Certified Diplomate Status. Most enter the service as first lieutenants but those with doctorates or higher degrees may enter at higher ranks. Clinical social workers may rise as high as the rank of colonel.

The recruiting material for the Air Force, which is comparable for similar appointments in the Army or Navy, says that social workers serve people of all ages as well as families in mental health, correctional, medical, and family advocacy programs. Some participate in research and training as well. Some serve as field instructors for social work education programs.

For information on armed forces social work careers, the recruiting services of the major branches have information and will consult with potential recruits regarding clinical social work opportunities.

Federal employment is attractive in terms of both working conditions and earnings and the satisfaction employees feel about the pleasure and significance of their work. Many social workers have had satisfying careers working exclusively in federal positions. Some social workers find that they must relocate or work in places they do not prefer, especially those in the military. Federal employment, like all other kinds, has its strengths and its limitations. It is highly attractive to some but has negative characteristics for others. Depending upon the kind of work and its location, federal employment opportunities may be highly competitive.

State Government

Jobs in state government are among the largest areas of employment for social workers because many of the programs that involve social workers are functions of state governments. The basic laws governing public social welfare are designed so that the states carry out the major programs such as assistance for families with children, the federal and state financed program for low-income people; mental health; public health; vocational rehabilitation; services to people with disabilities; and corrections. All of the social welfare functions are state functions under the U.S. Constitution. Only a few federal government services relate directly to individual citizens such as Social Security. In most cases, when the federal government provides most of the finances, as for food stamps, and Medicaid, state governments administer the programs to clients.

There are many agencies in state government that employ social workers such as human rights organizations, state legislatures, departments of education, and state colleges and universities. However, the largest numbers work in public welfare, public mental health programs, including hospitals and community mental health, public health, alcohol and drug programs, services for people with disabilities, and corrections. Social workers are also employed in state government employment development and placement programs such as JOBS, which is also a source for finding government jobs. State governments employ both MSW and baccalaureate level social workers in their various agencies.

Social services in state government are organized differently in different states. In some, the public welfare or social services agencies are separate. In others, several human services programs are combined into one comprehensive department that may include social services, programs for the aging, health and mental health services, and other functions that may be part of separate agencies in other states.

Public Welfare

A large number of state jobs for social workers are in public welfare. The state government organizations that provide public welfare go by various names. In some states they are the department of public welfare, in others the department of social services, and in others the department of human services (Ginsberg, 1983). The state public welfare agency provides financial assistance to families with children, which had been called Aid to Families with Dependent Children and which is now called Temporary Assistance for Needy Families under the new assistance legislation; food stamps; and Medicaid; as well as a variety of social services. Legislation in 1996 substantially changed the cash assistance program. Public welfare social work includes the following:

Eligibility Determination

The job of eligibility determiner does not always require a social work degree, but many states prefer hiring people with social work baccalaureate or master's degrees to carry out eligibility determination work. Many of those who supervise eligibility determination are social workers. The job of the eligibility determination specialist is to interview people who apply for benefits, help them complete a written application, and verify the information they have provided. Once the application is completed and verified, the person may begin receiving a monthly check, food stamps, and a Medicaid card, which makes them eligible for free health care in the state. In several states, the application process is conducted in whole or in part by computer, an example of the importance of computer literacy for social workers.

Mrs. Clarice Green recently lost her husband of ten years. She has two children, George, eight, and Susan, three. Mrs. Green has stayed at home caring for the children since the birth of the oldest and has not worked at a full-time job for the ten years she was married. Her husband had a job that was covered by covered by Social Security but his payments were very low and her benefits from Social Security are very small—smaller than the state's financial assistance grants for a family of three such as hers. The social worker, Ms. Evelyn Smith, takes the application and checks documents such as bank account statements, earning statements, rent receipts, and health care costs, and determines that Mrs. Green appears to be eligible. She presents the case to her supervisor for the family to begin receiving assistance.

As mentioned, eligibility determination supervisors are often social workers. They supervise a unit of eligibility determination workers. The focus of the eligibility determination supervisor is to ascertain that people who are eligible for assistance receive it and that people who are not eligible for assistance do not receive it. They do so by checking the work of the eligibility workers.

Eligibility workers and units also help people with personal problems by referring them to agencies and other social workers when they need noneconomic assistance. Extra help might mean counseling about problems they are having at home, helping them to find work, or helping them to live adequately on limited incomes.

Social workers with an interest in getting things done and moving applications and services promptly often enjoy the eligibility determination job. Although it often does not have a close connection with directly helping people by applying professional social work counseling skills, there is nothing quite so helpful to people who are in financial need as helping them obtain money for food, clothing, and shelter. Some people think that eligibility workers are the most important people-helpers in the human services.

At one time some states aspired to fill their jobs in eligibility determination and supervision with professionally educated social workers. The job included not only the mechanics of certifying eligibility but also helping clients become self-sufficient. However, through federal and state government action (much of the money for assistance programs comes from federal funds) the eligibility functions and the social services were divided so that most states now have separate units for determining eligibility and for providing services to clients who need them. Some of those who need social services are also recipients of financial assistance and some are not. The need for professionally educated social workers is often seen as more important in the services units than in the eligibility units.

Policy Interpretation

Understanding and dealing with public welfare policy is a complex process when public assistance laws are revised in major ways. The Personal Responsibility and Work Opportunity Reconciliation Act of 1996, which was popularly called welfare reform legislation, made some of the largest changes in assistance since the Social Security Act of 1935. It placed five-year lifetime limits on the receipt of assistance which is paid, in part, by federal funds (states may set shorter limits). It requires recipients to work or train for work. Teenage parents are required to live with adults and teen pregnancy prevention programs are required. The legislation, which concentrates on increasing contact with and supervision of assistance recipients by governments, may also require the employment of more human services workers to carry out its provisions, enforce its rules, and interpret its policies, Some social workers in public social services agencies work full-time to clarify, interpret, and explain policies. The following explains that function:

> John Basham works in the policy response unit of the state department of social services. He spends part of every day reading and updating the state policy directives based on decisions of courts, directives from the federal government, changes in state legislation, and administrative decisions made in the department that are sent to local offices.
>
> He also responds to county social services offices, which call him with questions about specific cases—is client A eligible for Medicaid, if the family has the following assets? Can client B receive assistance, without considering the scholarship income the youngest child receives from his private school? These kinds of interpretations are part of John's everyday job.
>
> He also looks at issues and notices patterns of questions. When he thinks he has discovered some basic concerns, he brings those to the attention of his unit director with suggestions for a change in overall policy or instructions to solve what appear to be common problems.

Child Support Enforcement

One of the major efforts in public assistance programs is the location of absent parents and the requirement that those parents pay for the care of their children through court-ordered or voluntary child support plans. A complex program of locating absent parents, establishing paternity, and collecting payments to offset the state assistance or directly help the custodial parent who is caring for the child, involves interconnected national computerized efforts and many human services professionals. That effort has consistently been strengthened by federal law, including in the Personal Responsibility and Work Opportunity Reconciliation Act of 1996, which, as has been discussed, made many changes in welfare assistance.

The Social Services

Since all the states began operating social services in the 1930s, many states have worked to fill as many social service jobs as possible with people who hold social work degrees because such work requires the knowledge and skills that social workers have.

The main social services provided by state departments are protective services for children and adults, especially older adults, and child welfare, which includes the protective services for children, foster care and group care for children who cannot stay with their families, adoption, and a broad range of other programs designed to help children and their families. Some state social services programs also provide help to young people who are in trouble with the law, either through community services programs or in institutions.

Protective services involve investigating reports of abuse or neglect of people who cannot care for themselves such as disabled or ill older adults and children. Protective services workers, who are often social workers, carry out the investigations and either take or recommend action. The action can range from determining that there was no abuse or neglect to calling upon law enforcement officers to make an emergency removal of the abused or neglected person from the residence.

Social workers in public agencies help families change their behavioral patterns, whenever possible, to stop the abuse or neglect and to preserve the family. When that is not possible, the social worker may help arrange for alternative care for the abused or neglected child or adult such as foster care with a relative or a nonrelative who is able to provide housing or care in a group facility such as a children's home or an adult residential care facility or nursing home. In extreme cases of child abuse and neglect, which can include psychological, physical, and sexual abuse, the worker's agency may call upon a court to permanently remove the child and allow the child's placement in an adoptive home.

Social services workers also help arrange adoptions and often also investigate and report on adoptions that are privately arranged.

Contracted Services

In some states, these social services are carried out not by government employees but by employees of other organizations such as private or voluntary social welfare programs. In those cases, the government agency monitors and establishes the contracts with the private agency that carries out the work. However, social workers are likely to be employed by the private organization that delivers the services.

Mental Health, Public Health, and Corrections

Many state government social work jobs are in the fields of mental health, public health, and corrections. Careers in those fields are discussed in greater detail in separate chapters later in this book.

Local Government Employment

Most of the large social welfare programs are state-run, often with federal help. Eventually, all programs are operated locally. In some way, clients must be reached by locally placed social services and by local workers. Many social workers, though they are employed by state governments, work in local offices. In most cases, the offices are part of county government or are state offices located in the county. Some social workers rotate among counties a few days each week or month. In a few cases, there are city offices. For example, some large cities have local social services offices which administer the programs that are cooperatively financed by the federal, state, and local governments.

There are also local health departments which are identified by counties, though some are designated as both city and county programs. In some states, public health programs are operated as multi-county organizations. A few areas of the United States have multi-county governments which are usually cities that cross over several counties.

Beyond the large programs such as family financial assistance, Medicaid, and food stamps, many services are organized and financed locally. Family service agencies, United Way organizations, programs serving people with AIDS, and a variety of other examples are typically local and are funded with voluntary contributions from the United Way and other fund-raising efforts as well as by city and county governments.

Cities may establish programs to deal with local needs such as children's services. A few cities have local councils on children and youth to deal with the problems and issues facing young people. Others sponsor shelters for homeless people, often with help from state and federal financing.

School Social Work

School social work is a large and influential part of social work employment at the local level. Social workers are employed by school systems, county school boards, or specific schools. Most school social workers are public employees, though some private schools employ them on their staffs.

The job dimensions of school social workers, according to a survey of them conducted by NASW in 1989 (National Association of Social Workers, undated c) are:

1. Helping relationships and providing services to children and their families.
2. Helping relationships and providing services to teachers.
3. Providing services for other school staff.
4. Performing administrative and professional tasks.
5. Working on interagency collaboration, prevention, and advocacy efforts.

NASW offers a special credential for school social workers, which is described in Chapter 6 on Licensing and Credentials.

Head Start

Social workers are also part of the Head Start program that provides preschool services for low-income children, shortly before they enter elementary school. In many cases, the children also need health screening and treatment and their families also need a variety of social services assistance, which social workers in the program help to provide.

Job Corps

Another important educational program is the Job Corps, which prepares people who have dropped out of school or who are unable to find satisfactory work with vocational preparation in many fields. The programs are operated in local Job Corps Centers throughout the United States and funded by the federal government, often through private contractors.

Other programs financed by federal and state funds such as vocational rehabilitation may be organized at the county or local level or by regions, which are usually groups of counties set up for administrative purposes. As discussed, many states organize their public health and some their social services programs by regions of several counties. Community mental health programs, programs for people with developmental disabilities, and probation and parole services are also usually organized by counties or by groups of counties, again in the form of regions.

Although the major funding for human services in governmental programs comes from the federal and state governments, most social workers work for local organizations or are placed in local offices of federal or state organizations. Usually a social worker is an employee of a regional or local office, with a salary that comes from the state, and with funds provided by the local, state, and federal governments.

Managers and supervisors of local offices may be responsible to state directors or regional directors who are, in turn, responsible to state directors. Many community mental health center directors are responsible to local boards of directors that are appointed by local governments.

Conclusion

The patterns of organization of government-sponsored social services are quite varied throughout the United States. However, it is always important for social workers to know how the specific job for which they are applying is organized, the sources of the financing, and who has the major administrative and policy control over the organization.

The personnel rules and policies vary among the states and within localities within states. Therefore, a sound and detailed awareness of the structure of programs and the operation of programs is one of the essential factors that social workers always want to understand when looking at career opportunities.

Social work education provides students with understandings of agency structures and government in order to help them become well-informed social work employees and to help them develop skills in influencing government policy for the well-being of clients.

8

Social Work in Mental
Health and Health

Nearly half of all social workers who are members of the National Association of Social Workers are employed in health and mental health. These two areas have been large employers of social workers for many years and they continue to engage members of the profession in large numbers. Hospitals, public health departments, community mental health centers, alcohol and drug abuse treatment programs, employee assistance programs, and many other locations directly or indirectly related to the health and mental health fields are examples. The employment opportunities in these fields of social work practice are described below. The large numbers of social workers who are engaged in full- or part-time private practice are mostly engaged in health or mental health services.

Social Work in the Mental Health Field

The mental health field is one of the largest employers of social workers. According to Gibelman and Schervish (1993a) over one-third of NASW members identify mental health as their primary employment. In fact, in many mental health systems social workers are the largest single group of professional employees—more than psychiatrists or psychologists. In some mental health settings, social workers are second in number only to nurses, especially in residential facilities. Whatever the situation, mental health is a major source of employment for social workers, and social workers have a high degree of involvement in and influence over mental health services.

Of all the human services, mental health has probably changed the most during the past forty years. From the beginning of mental health care centuries ago until the 1950s and 1960s, care for those who were emotionally disturbed was provided primarily in mental asylums or hospitals and most hospitals were part of state government. In the 1950s tranquilizing and other psychoactive drugs began to be developed and made widely available for the first time. These drugs made it much easier to control and work with mental patients. Much less emphasis was placed upon custodial security and control of patients and much more emphasis was placed on working with patients and their families. Court decisions also placed limits on the rights of government to deny freedom to people who were mentally disabled, which drastically reduced the incidence of involuntary commitments of people with mental illness to public hospitals. Ultimately, the mental health strategy in most of the United States was to release patients from hospitals and place them, instead, in community settings such as group homes, foster families, and in their own homes with help from service agencies and professionals in various fields.

The Magnitude of Mental Illness in the United States

In 1999, the Surgeon General of the United States, Dr. David Satcher, presented a 500 page report called the Surgeon General's Report on Mental Health and Mental Illness, which is available on the National Institute of Mental Health Internet site, *http://www.nimh.nih.gov* (U.S. Department of Health and Human Services, 1999). The report was released on December 13, 1999.

Dr. Satcher reported that 20 percent of the U.S. population is affected by mental illness in a given year. Among adults, 22–23 percent have diagnosable mental illnesses. Six percent of the population has an addictive condition such as alcoholism or drug dependence and 3 percent have both a mental and addictive condition. Of those who consider themselves to be—or are considered by others to be—in need of treatment, 15 percent of adults use mental health services of some kind. Eleven percent of them receive those services from the general medical care sector or a specialized mental health service in approximately equal proportions. Five percent of adults use human services programs such as social agencies and 3 percent become involved in voluntary support services. Some, of course, use more than one service.

Among children and adolescents, some 20 percent have the signs and symptoms of diagnosable mental illnesses in any year. However, only 5 percent of children are sufficiently affected to have extreme functional impairments.

Given these large numbers and the government's desire to prevent and treat mental illness, it is not surprising that the mental health field is a major source of social work employment and the site of many social work services.

Community Mental Health

The community mental health movement arose from the changes in care of the mentally ill. Instead of employing a large number of professionals to watch over and provide services to people in mental hospitals, governments began developing community mental health centers and services to provide assistance to people in their own communities. Federal legislation was passed providing state and local governments with money to help pay for community mental health and, by the end of the twentieth century, the United States was dotted with community mental health programs that provided access to services for mental patients virtually anywhere.

The transition from hospital to community services changed the ways in which mental health professionals, including social workers, carried out their responsibilities. Both mental hospitals and community mental health centers, along with a network of private services and hospitals, were developed to deal with mental health issues.

Current Mental Health Services Programs and Social Work Employment

Although their populations were much smaller in the 1990s than they were in the 1950s, public mental hospitals are still a significant part of mental health services. The patients stay in them for shorter periods of time and the focus of the work in hospitals is on assessing patients and working to determine the best long-range plans for them.

For social workers, a major part of the work in mental hospitals, in addition to providing treatment, is discharge planning—helping patients return to their communities by assisting them with housing, supervision and companionship from their families or friends, and making connections with community mental health centers that can monitor the patients once they are discharged and that can help them with a variety of treatment.

Patients continue to be housed in hospitals and provided services throughout the day and night, though the average stay has been reduced from as long as a lifetime, which was the pattern until the early 1960s for many patients, to a period of only weeks or a few months.

Many critiques of long-term hospitalization in the past demonstrated that many patients, while provided with custodial care, were not treated for their illnesses. In many cases, patients were involuntarily committed to receive treatment. Several court cases ordered that patients be released to their communities if they were not receiving treatment or if there was no evidence that the hospital services were helping overcome the patient's problems. The rights of people to stay in the community combined with the problems of providing adequate service in hospitals and the development of psychoactive medicines changed the basic ways social workers and other professionals cared for those with mental disabilities.

Forensic Units

Some functions continue to be performed in public mental hospitals. Extensive attention is provided in most state inpatient mental health facilities to forensic work, evaluating persons accused of crime for their suitability to stand trial, to determine the extent of their understanding of the crimes with which they are charged, and helping to determine where those convicted of crimes will be held or how they will be treated if they are given probation. Courts refer those accused of crimes who may also be mentally ill to such units so they can make recommendations about handling their legal cases.

Social workers are among those who assist in assessing the accused and in developing recommendations about their trials and their sentences if found guilty and convicted.

Private Inpatient Hospitals

Although mental hospitalization in public facilities has declined with the development of psychiatric medicines and the widespread use of those medicines for patient treatment and as a result of court decisions, other inpatient hospitalization has increased. Community hospitals and private psychiatric hospitals that use large numbers of social workers on their staffs continue to treat people with mental illnesses. Again, the periods of hospitalization are much shorter than they were in the past. Now hospitalization is a few days, a few weeks, or, usually at most, a few months.

Hospital care in psychiatric facilities is paid for under health insurance policies, Medicare, and Medicaid. The emphasis in the private psychiatric hospitals is similar to that in many public institutions. It is to treat as well as assess or diagnose the patient, to develop treatment plans for the patient, to determine the medicines that are most effective in helping the patient function, and to assist the patient in making community connections with family, friends, and community mental health centers outside the hospital.

Private psychiatric hospitalization is relatively expensive—the daily costs are in the hundreds of dollars at least, and, therefore, most people cannot afford long-term private psychiatric hospitalization with their own funds. However, the third-party payments discussed above make such care possible.

Long-Term Care Facilities

Many of the people who might otherwise be residents of inpatient mental hospitals are unable to live in their own homes or apartments. Therefore, they are placed in extended care or long-term care facilities such as nursing homes, personal care homes, or foster care homes. Social workers in hospitals, both public and private, usually maintain close connections with community residential facilities so they are better able to help their clients find places to live and to be cared for once they are discharged from inpatient mental health facilities.

Nursing home care has grown significantly with the decline of mental hospitalization. It is the most expensive form of community care because it provides intense health and mental health services with the assistance of physicians, nurses, and social workers, and other professionals. Adult residential care, which is provided for people who cannot live in their own homes but who do not need extensive medical services, or adult foster care, in family homes, are less expensive alternatives than nursing home care. Social workers assist in developing, supervising, and licensing long-term care facilities as well as working in them as social work service providers.

Children's Mental Health Facilities

Each year, a large number of children and adolescents display behavior resulting from mental illness that makes it impossible for them to live with their families, attend their community schools, and live satisfactorily in their communities—even with the help of child and adolescent units of community mental health centers. For such situations, a variety of short-term and long-term residential facilities are operated for young people. These include portions of the same public and private psychiatric hospitals that were described for adults. In addition, there are private residential treatment centers throughout the United States that provide care exclusively for children with mental illnesses. Among other available services are residential schools that focus on children with mental health problems and a growing number of wilderness programs that provide residential care for young people in outdoors settings.

The hospital settings are usually populated by children with severe mental disorders such as schizophrenia and others that require the treatment of a mental health expert. Residential schools and wilderness camps are more likely to be geared to children and adolescents whose behavior is problematic—children who use illegal drugs, truants, and children with other problems that place them in conflict with the law. These camps are a relatively recent development. In such programs, children live with full-time counselors in tents or other rustic arrangements. They prepare their own meals, often build their own housing and educational facilities, and function totally in groups with the guidance of their counselors, who help peers in the groups help one another. Usually, placement in a wilderness camp is for no more than six months or a year.

A variation on the wilderness camps is the marine academy, a similar facility located in coastal areas that focuses on helping children but always has a major boating and aquatic component. In addition to their regular studies, decision making, and counseling, students learn to sail and maintain boats as part of their overall therapeutic and educational program. Marine academies are used by many juvenile delinquency programs, which also use boot camps, which are described in Chapter 10 of this book.

Community Mental Health Centers

Community mental health centers are, in effect, multipurpose organizations that deal with several aspects of mental health and mental illness. Their function is not only to treat people with emotional problems but also to educate the public about mental illness and to prevent mental illnesses from developing in the population. Social workers participate in the following mental health center functions.

Case Management

The term *case management* is widely used in social work. Some organizations prefer the term *service coordination* but both mean approximately the same thing. A professional is given responsibility for the management of the care of an individual or family that is facing mental illness. The case manager or service coordinator meets periodically with patients, refers them to various services, and monitors the services that patients receive. The case manager stays in touch with the service providers who are assisting the patient or family. Services may include education, housing, nutritional services, recreational programs, counseling sessions with social workers, psychologists, or psychiatrists, and many other kinds of assistance. Community mental health centers and other human services organizations make extensive use of case management and case managers.

Child and Adolescent Services

Many community mental health programs have special programs for children and adolescents with mental illness. They counsel with them and their family, refer patients and the family for services such as a prescription of psychiatric medicine, work with the schools, make referrals for summer camps and similar kinds of programs. Also, the programs assist in connecting the young person with recreation and leisure time programs, and generally work to improve the well-being of the young client.

Hospitalization Services

Although the main function and feature of community mental health centers is outpatient care for people with mental illness, community mental health centers also provide hospitalization services, usually for short-term care. The community mental health centers typically have arrangements with community hospitals for inpatient care and their psychiatric units for people who become mentally ill in emergency circumstances and need immediate hospitalization. Community mental health centers often make use of hospital emergency rooms for care of people with sudden and serious mental illnesses as well as of the needed inpatient hospital care. Also, community mental health centers maintain close contacts with public mental hospitals and, when necessary, place patients in such hospitals for the stabilization, assessment, and treatment, including prescription medicines, that they need.

In addition to traditional hospitalization, many community mental health centers also provide partial hospitalization. Some mental patients can function adequately with hospital care only during the day. The hospital places them in day hospital programs that provide supervised care, medicine, and some leisure time activities. This arrangement enables their families, if they are living with families, to work and otherwise carry on their activities, and to know that their family member with mental illness is being cared for while they go about their regular duties. Similarly, some partial hospitalization programs provide night hospital care for patients whose problems are more severe at night or who have arrangements for care such as recreation and leisure time activities during the day. Community mental health centers have major roles to play in the hospitalization of people with mental illness.

Information and Education Programs

Another responsibility of community mental health centers is to inform and educate the public about mental illness. Community mental health workers who are specialists in information and education, many of whom are social workers, work with civic groups, churches, private physicians, teachers, and others who have frequent contact with people to help them understand the problems of mental illness and the ways in which mental illness can be treated and overcome. They similarly educate other professionals, appear before civic and professional groups, and work with the larger public to reduce the incidence of untreated mental illness.

Long-Term Community Care

Many community mental health centers operate programs of long-term community care. They provide services to people who need long-term supervision but who can function within their communities if they receive supervision. The workers in these programs visit with the patients often, monitor their medicine and ensure that they are taking it, and provide some of the case management services described earlier. Social workers have been extensively involved in these programs, as they have in other elements of community mental health.

Programs of Intensive and Assertive Care

A relatively new trend in community mental health, a variation on long-term community care, and one that has involved many social workers, is the treatment of mentally ill people through intensive, assertive care. Such programs, which have been called assertive community treatment, assign social workers or other professionals to provide regular supervision and guidance to clients with severe mental illnesses. The workers take the clients shopping, visit them several times a week in their own apartments or other residences, in which they live independently or with others, including family, help arrange for them to have meals, monitor their budgets, which may come from Supplemental Security Income for the disabled, and otherwise provide much of the care found in a hospital situation but that is community-based.

Intensive, assertive care is expensive because it requires a high ratio of workers to clients. Some have suggested that it may be as expensive as hospitalization. However, most current thinkers and policy makers in mental health agree that it is better for patients to have aggressive treatment and care in the community than it is for them to be hospitalized.

Day Treatment Centers

A number of community mental health centers operate day treatment centers for mentally ill people. These are sometimes called club houses. They provide a place for people with mental illness to go during the day and function as leisure time or recreation programs. Patients can play games, participate in arts and crafts activities, receive health services, follow current events, involve themselves in educational programs, and otherwise pass their days in useful and meaningful ways. These programs help patients give meaning to their lives and provide them with productive ways to pass their days.

Alcohol and Drug Treatment

Social workers are heavily involved as workers in the alcohol and drug fields. Alcohol and other substance abuse problems constitute one of the most costly and dangerous of all American social issues and are critical issues within the mental health field and law enforcement. Many community mental health centers have alcohol and drug treatment units as part of their service components. In some states and cities, the alcohol and drug program is separate from the community mental health program. Some states also have residential facilities for alcohol and drug abuse treatment.

In addition to public programs for alcohol and drug treatment, there are also a variety of private services to deal with alcohol and other substance abuse. Some of the best known are self-help groups such as Alcoholics Anonymous, which is mentioned earlier in this book. However, there are also private treatment facilities and hospitals in which patients who abuse alcohol and drugs may be hospitalized for periods of intense treatment for their abuse.

Social workers who work in alcohol and drug abuse use a variety of individual and group counseling methods to help people control their abuse. Many of the private clinics and hospitals that deal with drug and alcohol abuse have specific programs for specific periods of time through which substance abusing patients is processed to help them deal with addiction. Many rehabilitation programs for children and many of the wilderness and treatment center programs discussed earlier in this chapter deal with children who have been or who are drug or alcohol abusers.

Developmental and Other Disability Services

Among the services provided by governments, often through contracts with nongovernmental organizations, are programs for people with developmental disabilities such as mental retardation, cerebral palsy, autism, and other long-term or lifelong conditions. Services include: training and education programs, special help for people with physical disabilities, and special residential services. Many social workers are employed in programs for people with such disabilities. The services often also include family support services to assist families in working with those members who face disabilities.

Family Service Associations

Although their work goes well beyond mental health, family service associations or societies are among the most important providers of counseling and other services designed to help people overcome their personal and family problems. The family service societies, which have traditionally been heavily staffed and directed by social workers, preceded the community mental health movement in the United States. In some ways, these associations, which are voluntary and directed by boards of community leaders, are descendants of the charity organization societies discussed in Chapter 1.

In addition to family counseling, which is a core function of these organizations, family service agencies also provide credit counseling, often provide employee assistance services under contract with corporations, involve themselves in community planning and problem solving, and are also often engaged in some of the child welfare services, especially adoption and foster care, also carried out by public welfare agencies.

Most large and many smaller communities have family service society agencies that are affiliated with a national organization called Family Service America. Typically, they are financed by the local United Way, voluntary contributions, fees, and contracts. They often advertise for professional employees and most are also interested in applications from social workers who are seeking careers in their field.

Private Practitioners

A substantial portion of mental illness and mental health problems is treated by private practitioners such as psychologists, psychiatrists, and social workers. Many social workers maintain solo private practices or work in partnership with other social workers. Some social workers practice with psychologists and psychiatrists.

In many ways private practice mental health services are similar to those provided by community mental health centers, depending upon the mix of the professionals. In many states, medication for mental health patients can only be prescribed by physicians. Private practices that include psychiatrists or other physicians, at least part-time or on consultative bases, are more likely to be able to use psychiatric medication with their patients.

Many of the social workers who work in mental health are called or call themselves clinical social workers. Being a clinical social worker means providing treatment to individuals with problems, especially emotional problems. Certification for clinical social workers is available through a variety of organizations and procedures discussed in Chapter 6 on legal regulation and licensing.

Social Work in the Health Field

As several other chapters explain, social workers are heavily involved in various health services. For much of its recent history, the social work profession has been involved in what is sometimes called medical social work. Social workers work in hospitals and with hospital staffs to assist the hospital with the social elements of illness and diseases. Physical health conditions often also have social components. For example, patients who have had colostomies face social concerns in addition to their share of technical and physical problems associated with the condition. Patients with terminal illnesses need help in dealing with the end of their lives. They may also need help in making the transition into a hospice program or to some other long-term care services after they leave the hospital. People with less severe but chronic health problems need help in coping with elements of those problems such as continuing to use medicine, making behavioral changes in their lives that help them accommodate to the health condition, and dealing with physical changes. Others have to cope with problems such as amputations or blindness. Loss of mobility requires some social help and adjustment that the social worker may be able to help the client achieve.

Over the years, physicians and other health specialists have discovered not only that much of modern health care requires the services of the physicians and nurses who deal with the physical and treatment sides of the problem, but that there are also social components which may be equally important. Helping people maintain the proper diet, helping them learn to participate in exercise, and assisting in making other life adjustments are important elements of promoting patient well-being.

Parents who have children with disabling conditions may use the help of a social worker in providing the kind of care that will make it possible for the child with the condition or conditions to survive.

Prevention is also an important element in the health care system and many social workers assist in educating the public and individual patients about the prevention of illness or the spread of illness. Preventive work is especially important with terminal conditions such as AIDS, diabetes prevention, highway safety, avoiding tobacco and illegal drugs, and other kinds of issues that can make a difference between long-term physical illness and good health.

Social workers are employed in various elements of the overall health care system including:

Hospitals

Many hospitals of medium and large-size have social service or social work departments that are staffed by professionally educated social workers, including the Veterans Administration hospitals in most large community and voluntary hospitals. The social workers help patients arrange for financing their health care, help them arrange for their discharge from the hospital into satisfactory long-term care or family relationships and housing, and assist them in budgeting their resources so that they can survive adequately outside the hospital.

Some social services workers also work with patients to assist them in dealing with organ transplants. The issues of waiting for and dealing with the surgery associated with transplants are often major social problems. Helping patients follow the rigorous health routines after surgery poses some serious social—as well as medical—problems for patients and their families. Social workers are essential in helping people deal with those elements of their lives.

Some health conditions also require major behavioral adaptations and changes that go far beyond the medical dimensions. Conditions such as asthma, heart disease, and cancer require social guidance and personal behavioral adaptations that social workers help patients and their families make.

The tasks of working with hospital patients are massive and intense. In 1997, some thirty-one million people, other than newborns, were discharged from U.S.

hospitals. However, the average stay was only about 5 days (5.5 for men and 4.8 for women) and 39 percent of patients were age sixty-five and over (Lawrence & Hall, 1999). That meant that hospital social workers found it necessary to arrange effective discharges for large numbers of people, many of them elderly, with only a few days of lead time. Of course, many patients simply return to their homes, but even they may need special help and adjustments in order to become satisfactorily cured or rehabilitated. Thus the task of hospital social workers often requires concentrated and complicated efforts.

> William Barrett is a social worker in the Children's Hospital of Metropolitan Community Hospital. He works with a thirteen-year-old boy who has been diagnosed with childhood diabetes that requires regular injections of insulin, careful attention to diet, and regular exercise. William meets with the teenager and his family daily while the child's diabetes is being stabilized in the hospital. He also works with the boy and his family to help them make plans for using insulin in school, to prepare lunches, to avoid foods that worsen the problem of diabetes, and to participate in regular exercise to control the illness. The child has difficulty understanding the reasons for the special behavior but comes to terms with it with William's help. The family also finds it difficult to monitor the boy closely, while still caring for their other three children. Planning with them for the care of their diabetic child requires frequent meetings and conversations with Barrett, who visits them in their homes and in his office. Occasionally he brings them together with their physician to help them deal with the child's serious health conditions.

Social workers in hospitals also work to assist the hospital administration in policy making for the hospital. There are so many social dimensions to many elements of hospital care that the guidance of a social worker is of significant importance.

Social workers also frequently work with neonatal units of hospitals. Their work is particularly important with children of low birth weight, many of whom must remain hospitalized for periods of time until their health stabilizes and they can return home. Frequently, their mothers need assistance in caring for their low birth weight children.

Many children are also born with specific health problems that are associated with behavioral issues such as mothers who use alcohol or narcotics and mothers with AIDS. Children who are born with drug dependencies and AIDS need special treatment and care, much of it social in addition to medical.

In some hospitals, the social work programs have been especially designated departments of discharge planning. That is because the major function of the social workers in those hospitals is helping with the post-hospital care of patients, particularly elderly patients and low-income patients. As Chapter 9 on older adults and children clarifies, many ill older adults need long-term care in nursing homes or other residential facilities. The social worker's discharge planning job is to help find and make arrangements for locating patients in such facilities.

The patients may also have difficulty in paying their hospital bills and, in some hospitals, a major social work function is helping the patients obtain assistance from public and private programs to pay for the care they have received and that they will need. Social workers are often experts in helping people complete the application process for Medicaid or, in the case of children, for handicapped or crippled children's services. Nursing home care often requires the person to be eligible for Medicaid, which pays for nursing home services for a large number of low-income older people. Again, the social worker helps the patient or the patient's family qualify the patient for Medicaid so they can be placed in a long-term care facility.

The following may be considered a typical, complicated case for a hospital social worker:

Marjorie Dawson is a social worker in Summers Memorial Hospital, a large community hospital in a city of approximately half million people. She is assigned to make an appropriate discharge plan for William James, a forty-five-year-old man who has entered the hospital after being found unconscious in the street by police. After James is revived, Marjorie learns that the client is homeless and that he has been living in shelters and on the streets for ten years. The hospital staff diagnoses an operable brain tumor. Marjorie, who arranged for the patient's surgery, physician costs, and hospital care for him by obtaining Medicaid coverage, has now been told that he has recovered sufficiently to be discharged from the hospital and that he no longer needs hospital care.

She finds a nursing home that will accept his Medicaid coverage and arranges for him to be transferred there by ambulance within a few days after he has recovered sufficiently for discharge. The nursing home will follow his case, too, and if he becomes sufficiently healthy, the nursing home social worker may arrange for him to be placed in a foster care home or adult residential care facility and to begin work training that may make him self-sufficient.

Public Health Social Workers

Some of the most important contributions to the health and well-being of people come from public health, rather than the treatment of illnesses or health problems. Public health focuses on several kinds of activities such as health education, which is sometimes provided by specialists in public health known as health educators; preventive measures such as services to mothers and infants; screening for health problems among young children to assure that they receive early and adequate treatment; and immunization to prevent children from contracting severe illnesses such as diphtheria, measles, and polio. Public health social workers also serve in the community to educate the public about preventive medicine practices and sound health practices about diet, regular health checkups, and immunizations.

Public health services are available in most counties in the United States. Although the major functions are in areas other than direct work with people to prevent illnesses, that is also an important part of their function and social workers are heavily involved in that series of functions. Other activities deal with issues such as regulating restaurants to make sure that their food preparation is safe and sanitary, monitoring water supplies for safety and purity, visiting public facilities such as day care centers, schools, and hospitals to ensure their compliance with health regulations through licensing. They also have major programs of keeping records of communicable diseases such as sexually transmitted diseases and viruses to determine whether epidemics are developing and to prevent the spread of serious health problems. Social workers are major participants in the provision of health services to their communities and in preventing health problems through their public health services.

Managed Care

A growing role for social workers in health care is called managed care, which is also discussed from the perspective of employees in Chapter 5 on salaries and benefits. Social workers in managed care play a leadership role in or assist in evaluating patient conditions to determine the kind of medical care that should be authorized for them. According to Poole (1996) almost all Americans are under a managed care plan of some sort. A special issue of the journal *Health and Social Work* (Poole et al., 1996) describes the managed care field and some of the ways in which social work is involved in it.

Both health and mental health services are delivered through managed care companies. Several managed care firms operate in the United States to organize and control health services so that only the proper quantity of services is provided to those who need them. These are measures designed to hold down the costs of medical care through preapprovals and monitoring of procedures and other steps designed to rationally handle the rising costs of health care. They are closely connected with health insurance companies and hospitals, including hospital corporations. Managed care is usually delivered through a health maintenance organization (HMO) or a variation of the HMO approach.

Working with Physicians

Social workers also serve closely with physicians in many different specializations including pediatrics, gerontology, oncology, and others. Social workers assist physicians in working with the social problems families face about their family members' illness or condition. Sometimes, the social worker's role is to help family members to find ways to pay for the care that the patient receives. Because social workers are typically experts at knowing about and helping people secure resources such as Medicaid, crippled children's funding, and other assistance, they are often especially helpful to physicians in keeping patients in the hospital and paying for the care.

Conclusion

This chapter has covered the roles social workers play in two of the areas that employ them in large numbers.

Mental health is one of the major employers of social work. It is also one of the major areas of social services and social problems in the United States.

Almost every social worker, in some way and at some time, becomes engaged in the mental health field, either as a clinical social worker, as a direct service provider to people with mental illness, or by referring clients from other agencies and other settings to mental health services. It is possible that mental illness is the most pervasive of all social problems, other than economic need, and, therefore, social workers are heavily involved in and heavily employed by mental health and its related agencies. Although the emphasis has shifted from inpatient hospitalization to community mental health services, both still exist and both are part of the practice of professional social workers.

As discussed, the health services employ a large number of social workers. The employment of social workers in hospitals, public health departments, clinics, and physicians' offices is a significant portion of the responsibility social workers assume in their field.

Social workers not only engage in direct services to clients and in preventive services, they also are involved in the administration of health and mental health programs. Many social workers work in health maintenance organizations and for health insurance companies in evaluating patient claims, consulting on the approval of payments for care that is recommended by physicians, or sought by patients, that is part of the managed care process.

Employment in health and mental health is arranged through a variety of means. Many jobs are listed with the JOBS Service and are advertised in professional as well as general circulation publications such as newspapers. In some public programs, applicants follow the merit system procedures discussed in Chapter 7 on government. In private mental health and health programs, applicants go directly to the personnel offices of the employing organizations to complete formal applications. For several reasons, these fields have high turnover so there are frequently vacant positions either available or about to become available. Personally visiting programs that interest the applicant will often provide specific information on opportunities that may not otherwise become known immediately.

Health and mental health are not only large users of social work services, they are also popular fields for social workers, who are often quite positive about their experiences in both areas of employment.

9

Working with Older
Adults and Children

Older people and children are the two largest population groups of social work clients. Social services and social welfare programs are, to a large extent, established to benefit older people and children because those two age groups are the most vulnerable in American society. Many of the programs financed by government as well as many of the services operated by voluntary organizations are, in large part, devoted to serving older adults and young people. Medicare and Social Security, the largest of all social welfare services, are designed for older people, families with children whose economic supporters have died, and people with disabilities, many of whom are also elderly. Public adult and child protective services, which are also dedicated to meeting the needs of those two groups, are extensive social services programs in every state. Day care, nutrition assistance, and hospital social services, are also often likely to be geared to older adults and children.

This chapter describes some of the key services provided for older adults and children in addition to those already covered in the chapters on government programs, and health and mental health.

Networks of Services for the Aging

The U.S. population is becoming older. By 2000 there were some thirty-five million Americans sixty-five and older. By 2010 that number is expected to grow to almost forty million. By 2050, a quarter of the U.S. population will be over sixty (Begun, 2000). Better health care, better public health, large birth rates in the 1940s, Social Security (by providing older people with the resources to stay alive) and other factors are increasing the proportion of the population that is older.

Those interested in comprehensive and detailed information on the elderly and the services provided for them have access to many resources on the subjects. A number of textbooks detail the issues facing older adults and the services available for them. For example, see Harbert and Ginsberg (1990) and Tirrito (1996). Several entries in the *Encyclopedia of Social Work* (Edwards et al., 1995) discuss the details of various aging issues and services.

Aging programs are operated and financed at the local, state, and federal levels. Most of the direct social services programs provided for older adults are organized and delivered at the local level through senior centers that are financed through state governments. The states receive large portions of their money from the U.S. government agency, the Administration on Aging that is part of the Department of Health and Human Services.

States have planning and organizing groups that administer funds for local aging programs. The states give their organizing and planning groups different names. Local programs have the direct service contact with older people through city and county senior centers, which provide a variety of services. Those services include educational and recreational activities, some health screening, often in cooperation with public health programs, dining programs to provide daily meals to older adults at low cost, and a number of other activities designed to assist older people in living well and enhancing their lives.

Some local programs for seniors operate transportation for older adults to travel to the centers as well as to doctors and clinics, reach other social services offices, and otherwise meet their transportation needs.

Social Work Roles in the Aging Network

Social workers are involved in many different ways in organizing and delivering services for older adults (Bureau of Labor Statistics, 1999a). Many social workers are involved at every level of aging services planning including the federal Administration on Aging, the state aging offices, which are part of the executive branch of government, and in coordinating and directing senior centers. Some state legislatures have committees on aging, which often have social work staff experts. There are also local councils on aging in some communities that coordinate senior services, including senior centers. Many social workers direct or are professionally affiliated with those councils.

The social work emphasis in programs offered for older people is not ordinarily on direct services or counseling. The emphasis is on working in programs that help older people meet a variety of economic, health, and social needs, rather than counseling with them about individual problems, though there are exceptions.

Of course, that does not mean older adults have no personal problems with which social workers might deal. Many older people have serious, pervasive emotional problems such as depression. Instead of providing counseling through the senior centers or other senior programs, it is the usual procedure to refer people with personal problems to other services such as community mental health and family service agencies for help by social workers and other professionals.

Health Care Programs for Older People

The largest portion of the money spent on health care in the United States is spent by and on behalf of older adults because older people, as a group, have more health problems and more severe health problems than any other population. The Medicare program, a federally financed insurance program to provide health care for Social Security recipients, is almost totally devoted to providing health coverage for older adults. Medicaid covers low-income people with disabilities, including, particularly, those who receive Supplemental Security Income through the Social Security program. It also serves a large number of older adults, among the millions of Americans that it helps with medical care payments. Medicare is administered directly through the Social Security Administration. People who have reached age sixty-five receive Medicare credentials that enable them to access coverage that includes hospital care and some physician services.

Low-income older people are certified for Medicaid through state departments of social services, human services, or public welfare (the name varies with the state) so many social workers are involved in certifying older people for eligibility for Medicaid.

Hospital Social Work

Social workers who work in hospitals are also frequently involved with older people through the normal course of their hospital social work duties. Social workers in hospitals often work to help them come to terms with and plan for dealing with their health conditions, as discussed in Chapter 8 on health and mental health services.

Nursing Homes and Other Residential Facilities

Social workers also often help older people and their families arrange for care of the older person upon discharge from the hospital, perhaps in a nursing home or other extended care facility, some of which are described below.

Some of the most important health services provided to older people are nursing home services. Nursing homes provide long-term health care for people who are not so ill that they must be hospitalized but who are too ill to stay at home. Social workers are employed at every level of the nursing home field. Some function as social work consultants or advisors. Many are owners or part owners of such facilities.

Although many nursing home residents are elderly, the homes also care for adults with long-term disabling physical or mental conditions, including AIDS. Private health insurance funds, private funds, pensions, and Medicaid are used to pay for most nursing home care. A small but growing portion of Americans carry long-term care insurance, as discussed in Chapter 5 on salaries and benefits. Medicare pays for some nursing home care for people who are covered by the program when they are discharged from hospitals.

There are lower-cost, long-term residential arrangements for people whose medical problems do not require nursing home care but who require housing, meals, and some supervision. Adult residential care homes and foster homes provide alternatives for many older adults and people with disabilities. Residents are able to pay for their care with their private funds, pensions, Social Security, or Supplemental Security Income benefits. Medicare and Medicaid do not normally cover this kind of nonmedical care but, in some cases, that rule is waived and adult residential care and foster care are reimbursed by Medicaid. Some social workers have organized and owned such facilities. In some foster care arrangements, families care for older people and people with disabilities in their private residences.

Social workers in agencies such as aging programs, social services departments, hospitals, and the Veterans Administration make many of the arrangements for nursing home and adult residential care.

Other Services

Home services, including home health care, are among the services provided to older adults. Many older people are able to remain in their own homes, rather than moving to adult group residences or nursing homes, if they have help. Therefore, many agencies provide assistance of various kinds to older people.

Home health care is one of the primary forms of assistance to older people. Nurses and other health care personnel come to the residences of older people and provide them with medical treatments, monitor their prescriptions and medicine use, discuss their general health and eating habits, and generally provide them some of the services they would receive in a hospital. Social workers also often direct home health services.

Other nonmedical help is provided to older people in their homes. The two main forms of help are chore services and homemaker services. Chore services are often provided by someone known to the older adult. For example, money paid to a grandchild might enable that person to remain with a grandparent and provide help in the home, rather than seeking a job away from the residence. The provider cleans, cooks, and otherwise helps with the basic living situation of the older person. Some recipients of chore services are people with disabilities and many are both aged and have disabilities. Social workers often screen people for their eligibility for chore services and also supervise chore services providers. Homemaker services are provided by trained homemakers, who assist in the home but who also arrange for cleaning and food preparation assistance and other kinds of help for the older person. Homemakers also provide some education and training in household maintenance to older adults.

Both chore services and homemaker services that enable older people to stay at home make it much less expensive to care for older people than to provide them with nursing home or other residential care. These in-home services are financed through a number of mechanisms such as the federal Social Services Block Grant, aging program funds, payments by the recipients of services, and other resources.

Home-delivered meals are another important service for older people who live at home. Sometimes called Meals on Wheels, this service brings prepared meals several times each week, often with the help of volunteers. The availability of delivered, prepared meals makes it possible for some older people to remain in their own residences. Social workers often coordinate home-delivered meals programs as well as training and supervising those who deliver the meals.

Hospice

One of the programs in which social workers are heavily involved with older people is the hospice movement. Hospices are programs that provide social services and some care for people who are terminally ill, including people with AIDS. Although hospices serve people of all ages who are facing terminal illness—usually with visits in their own homes but sometimes in residential facilities, apartments, or group care facilities—many of those served are older adults. Hospices provide a more natural and, in some ways, humane and dignified living situation for people who are nearing the end of their lives. It is less expensive than hospital care and those who use its services are frequently not likely to be helped by the intense services of a hospital. However, they need some support and some assistance. They also need reassurance and some companionship, which are also functions of hospices.

Adult Protective Services

One of the ways in which social workers serve older people is through investigating and working to overcome problems of abuse or neglect. Reports are made to abuse and neglect services, which usually are part of the state social services agencies that also certify for Medicaid. Tatara (1993) estimated that there were 735,000 incidents of domestic elder abuse in 1991, only a fraction of which were reported to authorities.

These agencies send social workers to investigate the cases and to work with the individual older person and the family to address them. The abuse of older people is a much greater and less well understood problem than many others. The abuse may be physical, emotional, or economic. Many cases are found in which an older person's resources, including monthly Social Security checks and other pension funds, are taken by family members and used for their own purposes rather than for the older person's benefit. Older people are also, at times, forced into sexual activity with younger people, locked in their rooms and not allowed to leave; or denied adequate food or medical care. Older people are abused in ways that run the entire gamut. Some older people are also neglected by those who are supposed to care for them. Many other older adults neglect themselves—fail to maintain their hygiene, limit their diets, or do not make use of health care services when they need them.

Social workers who deal with abuse and neglect of older people try to assist the older individual, the family, or their caretakers, in ending the abuse or neglect. Sometimes the services described previously such as home health services, chore and homemaker services, and home delivered meals are used to address the problems. When the situations are so severe that they cannot be addressed through negotiation, services, and counseling, older people may be removed from their living situations and relocated to group care facilities, group residences, or other preferable environments.

Organizing Older Adults

Of course, not all old people face the kinds of problems discussed already. Many function quite satisfactorily on their own. Many work, maintain families, lead active leisure lives, and participate as leaders in civic and political activities.

I personally well remember beginning a community program for older adults when I was a social worker for a community agency in Oklahoma. In many cases, both the adults I wanted to serve and the board that had to be convinced of the needs of older people were the same ages. The board members, though they eventually provided the funds for the aging services program, wondered why being elderly was a social problem. Of course, it isn't. There is probably a greater range in the capacities and socioeconomic characteristics of older adults than of any other population group, though the problems faced by older people are often severe. The reality for large numbers of older adults is that they have few resources for overcoming problems such as poverty, compared to the opportunities of younger people.

Many social workers are employed helping organize groups of older people who want to deal with matters of interest to themselves and the larger community. One of the largest organizations of any kind in the United States is the American Association of Retired Persons, which employs social workers in its national and state offices. One of the most active and aggressive organizations for older people, the Gray Panthers, was organized by a social worker, the late Maggie Kuhn. Social workers with an interest in administrative and organizational activities often enjoy working for groups such as these. They lobby in Congress and the state legislatures for senior programs and benefits. They advise the executive agencies of government about the development of aging services. Because older adults are more likely to vote in elections than any other age group, they have great influence in politics.

Securing Positions in the Field of Aging

In services to the aging, applications for local and private employment should be made directly to the agency. For state government positions applications should be made to the state employment or civil service system. In both children's and older adult or aging employment, there is an active network of people who are engaged in those efforts. Local senior center staff will often know about jobs in other senior centers. Local councils on aging will have information about programs in the state government aging office, and, perhaps, the local Council on Aging. Children's home workers will often know about the Child Protective Service employees in the state agency department that deals with child welfare.

Older Adults Summary

Because services for older people are so pervasive in the U.S. social welfare system, most social workers, no matter what their position, become involved in working with older people and in delivering services to the elderly. Whether their job is in a department of social services, mental health, health care, or corrections, in which long sentences are yielding a growing population of elderly prisoners, the need to know about older people and the services available for them is critical.

Services for Children

Children have long been one of the main preoccupations of social work, as Chapter 1 and the chapters on government, health and mental health, and corrections show. The protection of children, promotion of the well-being of children, treatment of children with health and mental health problems, and work with children who are in difficulty with the law are among the functions performed by social workers with young people. They are also high priorities for social services in the United States. In addition, however, many social workers help young people who are not, in particular, experiencing problems, but who need and want leadership skills and other kinds of help to enhance their lives.

Child Protective Services

Protective services for children is a major field in the public social services, as is mentioned in Chapter 7 on government services and employment. All states now require that professionals and others who suspect a child is abused or neglected report that suspicion to the state child protective services agency, which is ordinarily a part of the state public welfare, human services, or social services program— names used by states for their various economic and social assistance agencies.

Many social workers operate and respond to calls on twenty-four hour toll free telephone lines that provide statewide access for those reporting child abuse or neglect. The reports are investigated, usually within twenty-four hours, under the laws governing child protective services. Reports of child abuse and neglect are frequently anonymous and, in any case, state laws protect the anonymity of those making such reports. Social workers are also involved in making child abuse and neglect investigations, which follow the initial reports. They visit reported neglected and abused children in their homes to determine the extent, if any, of the maltreatment.

There are three levels of solutions used by social workers who investigate child abuse and neglect. The first is to find that there is, actually, no such problem. In some cases, reports are made that cannot be verified because there is no evidence there is either abuse or neglect. Families may have different housekeeping standards than the persons who reported them and that does not constitute a problem that requires public action. Some reports are made by noncustodial parents—a mother or father who does not have custody of the children who complains about the care of the children by the parent who has custody.

If there is evidence of abuse or neglect, the worker in the agency may decide that there is a need for counseling by a social worker from the agency, who visits the home periodically, monitors the situation, and attempts to ensure that the child's health and well-being are not endangered by remaining in the home. By far, that is the solution most commonly used in dealing with abuse or neglect.

The third approach requires the removal of the child from the home. When the situation seems very difficult and problematic for the well-being of the child, the worker may take steps to have the child immediately or eventually removed from the family. A child can be taken into custody and placed temporarily in a short-term children's shelter. Most large communities have children's shelters that operate around the clock and are directed by people who are trained by and trusted by the agency. In a less onerous solution, the child may be placed temporarily with a relative such as a grandparent, an older sibling, or an aunt or uncle.

The courts may become involved in the case and, if the abuse or neglect seems sufficiently severe, the courts may order that the child be temporarily—and eventually, if the problems are not resolved, permanently—removed from the family and that all the parents' rights to the child be severed. But more commonly, services are provided to the family in their own homes to make it possible for the child and the parents to stay together. For example, homemaker and chore services may be provided. Or the agency may arrange for respite services so that the children are cared for and the parents are provided with free time to deal with some of their tasks and for recreational purposes.

For those families that are separated, there are usually efforts to reunite the family. After a period of counseling with the family by the child protective services worker or by a community mental health, family service, or other agency and the provision of services, the child is returned to the family and the family is monitored for a period of time to ensure that there is no more danger of abuse or neglect.

For long-term care of children who cannot safely be returned to their houses, agencies may place a child in substitute care, usually in a foster home with substitute parents, who may be relatives, or, if situations warrant it, in a group care facility such as a children's home.

Children's homes are often former orphanages that provide care for children who cannot live with their biological families or, for various reasons, with foster families. Those reasons usually are age—older children and teenagers may have difficulty in foster homes—large sibling groups that do not want to be separated, and behavioral problems that make it difficult for foster parents to house the child. Many group homes use the consultation and other services of social workers and social workers frequently are also members of the staffs of group homes, sometimes as directors.

The protective services social worker consults with the children's teachers, counselors, and school social workers (see the case below) to try to help them succeed in school and to try to ensure that they attend school regularly, no matter where they reside.

Social workers are engaged in every part of the child protective services continuum from the investigations, previously described, to working in children's homes, training and supervising foster parents, operating and working with emergency child shelters, and otherwise being engaged with those programs and services that help children.

A recently growing role for social workers has been in the field of specialized or treatment foster care (Meadowcroft & Trout, 1990). In traditional foster care, people who have other employment provide care for children for a fee. That fee is considered to be enough to pay for the extra cost of the child being in the home but is not sufficient to serve as a sole salary for the foster parents. In specialized or treatment foster care, children with special problems, especially emotional problems, are placed with professional foster parents. At least one of the foster parents devotes a large portion of his or her time caring for the child or, in some cases, children in the home. The social worker may help select, train, monitor, and evaluate the home and the foster care arrangements.

As in children's mental health, there is a strong emphasis in child protective services on keeping children out of institutional care such as is provided in group care facilities or children's homes, and an increased emphasis on keeping children in their own families and on placing children in their own communities with foster parents, including treatment foster parents.

Melissa Brown, who works for a public child protective services agency, has been given the case of a mother who has physically punished her nine-month-old daughter so severely that the child has died from trauma. She investigates the case with care, interviews the mother, and works with the authorities on prosecution of the case. She studies the way that the case had been followed and learns that her social services department had investigated complaints about the mother earlier but that there was insufficient evidence to take action. Melissa wants to know how the agency may need to bolster its training of protective services investigators and its policies about when action should be taken. She thinks that early intervention with the mother and the child might have saved the child's life and she wants to find ways to avoid further tragedies in the future.

The week before, Melissa was assigned to investigate a case reported by neighbors of an infant child who had failed to thrive. The child was very small and had not achieved the developmental milestones one expects of a child at its age. She investigated the case and found that the child was not sufficiently cared for. Although there was no beating of the child, the child was left to lie in a urine-soaked bed most of the day. Food was provided by bottle on occasion but the bottles were not sterilized. The mother rarely held the child.

Melissa recommends to her supervisor and to the court that the child be at least temporarily removed to a shelter for emergency care and that the case be examined periodically for the quality of the mother's understanding of the care she has provided the child. If the mother leads a disorganized life and if that continues, Melissa will recommend after six months that the child be permanently removed from the mother and placed in an adoptive home.

School Social Work

As discussed in Chapter 7 on government work, a large area of employment for social workers is school social work. Many school districts and schools have programs of school social work, that provide social workers to help meet the needs of children, especially those who are having difficulties. They counsel with children, work on abuse and neglect complaints, consult with teachers who are having special problems with children, and otherwise involve themselves in the range of services that some school age children need.

School social work is a large subspecialty of the field, and has its own professional journals and also several books (Constable, Flynn, & McDonald, 1991; Winters & Easton, 1983) are excellent sources for preparation for work as school social workers.

Maternal and Child Health

Health services for children is another area of social work practice and many social workers are engaged in programs such as maternal and child health, children's hospitals, and other programs designed to help children facing health difficulties. Hospital social workers who serve children's health function in many ways like social workers in other hospital situations.

Social workers also work with public health departments on issues such as helping mothers more adequately care for their children, encouraging and ensuring that children have the correct immunizations to prevent serious illnesses, and assisting families in obtaining adequate nutrition through programs such as the Women's, Infants, and Children's Program (WIC).

Child Mental Health

As discussed in Chapter 8 on health and mental health services, there are hospital, residential treatment, and community mental health programs that specialize in services for children. Many social workers are involved in those efforts. Some social workers are full-time employees in offices of pediatricians and child psychologists and psychiatrists. They work with their counterpart professionals to understand and deal with the problems faced by the children.

In addition to outpatient services for children, there are also extensive networks of residential treatment centers and specialized schools for children who are in difficulty. Many work with children who have drug and alcohol addiction problems. Others deal exclusively with children who have behavior problems. Many treat children who have specific mental illness, diagnoses such as schizophrenia, borderline personality disorder, and others. Some state mental health programs also maintain children's residential treatment. Many social workers are employed in residential treatment of various kinds for children.

Young People in Difficulty with the Law

As described in Chapter 10 on corrections services, many social workers are involved in serving young people who are in difficulty with the law. The ways in which they work with children are described in that chapter. However, it is noteworthy that social workers tend to think of children who are in trouble with the law as children with special needs, rather than criminals. The approach that social work takes with these children is significantly different than the position that is taken with adults in the field of corrections.

Social work in the youth corrections field is a large area of employment for many in the profession.

Leisure Time, Leadership, and Recreation Programs

Some services for children, many with long histories, are not designed especially for those who have personal or family difficulties, but are designed to enhance the well-being of children whose family situations are satisfactory. These children are maturing normally and succeeding in their various roles. Social workers, for much of the history of the profession, have been involved in programs such as the YMCA and YWCA, the Jewish Community Centers, the Catholic Youth Organization, Boy Scouts and Girl Scouts, and camping. These are programs designed to help children better enjoy their lives and enhance various skills. Leadership, arts and crafts, outdoor and wilderness activities, and a variety of other life-enhancing lessons are learned informally and outside the school setting. Social workers developed and maintained many of these programs under a variety of agency auspices. They remain a major part of the social services system and social workers continue to be active in them. United Way funds are often allocated to support these programs.

Advocacy, Planning, and Organizing Activities with Children

Another major tradition in work with children is developing and organizing programs for them, particularly advocacy programs but also programs of policy analysis and development. Several national and state organizations carry on major programs of child advocacy and administer programs that include the work of volunteer and professional lobbyists who work on behalf of young people. Organizations such as the Children's Defense Fund and the Child Welfare League of America make a major impact on legislation involving children in the United States. The Kids Count program makes a statistical report on the well-being of children in every state and in the nation every year with funds from a national foundation. Social workers also help serve the needs of children as members of legislative staff in state legislatures and in the U.S. Congress.

Finding Children's Services Jobs

Those interested in finding jobs in services for children should usually visit and apply directly to the children's programs they want to explore. It is sometimes possible to start working part-time in an agency as a student, and to secure a social work job by the time of graduation. That seems particularly true of children's homes, in which many house parents or cottage parents are employed to deal with the daily living of the children in residence. People with experience as house parents or cottage parents have the potential for moving into professional responsibilities as social workers or counselors. However, applications are made directly to the children's home.

Some positions in child mental health and especially in children's protective services are a part of the state civil service system described in Chapter 7 on government jobs. For those positions, interviews in advance with the agency that employs the workers are a good idea but the formal application process has to be handled through the state application, testing, and appointment system, as is discussed earlier. Making application and becoming part of the registers for appropriate jobs is the critical step. Many of the job titles in public children's services are similar to to those for other kinds of work, in many state government systems.

Conclusion

Services to the aging and children are among the largest, oldest, and most important in social work. Large numbers of social workers find themselves employed in working with these two groups. After mental health clients, children are the largest focus of social work practice. Those who work with the aging are less than half the size of the social work complement of those who report they are social workers with children. However, the aging population is relatively small and is only beginning to grow. Also, many social workers work with older people in mental health and health clinics. Therefore, those who report that they primarily work with the aging are a relatively smaller group than those who actually work in a large number of ways with older adults.

10

Crime and Delinquency Services

Among the growing social problems in the United States is crime and delinquency. Although crime and delinquency statistics show some reduction in the incidence of crime, the number of people arrested and imprisoned for committing crimes appears to be increasing.

Allen (1995) points out that society uses three ways for punishing convicted offenders against the law. These are probation, in which a person is punished by being required to perform certain kinds of activities and complying with certain restrictions, while remaining in the community. The second form of punishment is incarceration, which involves removal from the community and being placed in an institution. Parole is provided for persons released from prison for good behavior but who continue to be supervised in the community after their release.

Services to Incarcerated Offenders

The proportions of the U.S. population who are in prison continue to increase. That is increasingly true of members of minorities, who comprise more than one-half of the U.S. correctional population, despite their much smaller representation in the general population.

As mentioned in Chapter 7, there were close to two million people in prisons in 1998. The population of correctional facilities grew significantly in the 1990s. In 1990, there were 4.3 million people in jails, prisons, or on probation or parole. By 1998, that figure had grown to 5.9 million. According to the federal government estimates, in 1998 there were 1.2 million people in prisons such as penitentiaries, 584,372 in jails, 3.4 million on probation, and 704,964 on parole. About one in every thirty-four American adults or about 2.9 percent of the U.S. adult population was incarcerated or on probation or parole in 1998 (Bonczar & Glaze, 1999). The fact that some four million people are serving under probation or parole is especially important for social work and related fields since so many probation and parole officers are counselors, human service workers, or professional social workers.

The increased corrections population reflects the increase in court convictions for felonies. In 1996, for the first time, state and federal courts convicted a combined total of over one million adults. When those convicted were added to the existing corrections population, the growth was dramatic. The average sentence in 1996 was about 5 years in state courts and 6½ years in federal courts (Brown & Langan, 1999). Of those felony convictions, 35 percent were for drug offenses, 30 percent were for property offenses such as theft, violent offenders were 17 percent, and convictions for weapons offenses and other nonviolent crimes were the other 18 percent.

Nearly half of those convicted of felonies were members of minority groups. Although women are a small portion of those convicted of felonies, their percentage is growing. In 1988, women were 13 percent of convicted felons but in 1996, 16 percent were women. Of all felons, some 90 percent pled guilty and only 9 percent were convicted during trials (Brown, Langan, & Levin, 1999).

The time served in connection with sentences is also growing longer, especially in federal prisons. In 1986, the average time served in federal prisons was fifteen months. In 1997, it was twenty-nine months (Sabol & McGready, 1999).

It is not a coincidence that among the growing job placements for professional social workers are services for offenders against the law in penitentiaries and related organizations and services.

Social Services for People in Correctional Institutions

Social workers in prisons and penitentiaries provide a number of services to inmates. Some of the same functions discussed for social workers who serve people with mental illness and patients in hospitals also apply to correctional facilities.

Scott Edinboro is a clinical social worker in his state's maximum security prison. All of the prisoners are men who have been convicted of a number of different felonies including murder, sexual assault, armed robbery, and, in disproportionately large numbers, drug offenses. Scott's work involves a variety of counseling services for inmates—individual meetings with those who ask to see him; counseling with those who are about to be released, both individually and in groups; contact with families about their concerns for inmates; and group therapy sessions with inmates who have abused or been addicted to illegal substances such as cocaine or heroin. He assists the prison administration in making work assignments for inmates and he helps ensure that the work is performed. A wide variety of work is one of the two most important activities for prison inmates—the second is education—and most prisoners want jobs so they are able to pass their time more quickly and productively. Scott has been employed by the institution for five years. Although his original objective was to work in mental health, he was persuaded by some of his course work as a social work student and a field placement in a probation and parole agency that he should explore and perhaps try a career in corrections.

Scott finds that, contrary to public opinion, prisoners are people with social and emotional needs not different from those of other clients he encountered or learned about in his studies. He finds the corrections clients appreciate the help he provides them and also believes that many want to behave within the law once they are released. His reactions to his prison work are similar to those of other social workers who serve in correctional institutions. The work is interesting, those he serves want the help he provides, the working conditions are good—better than some of his fellow graduates have experienced—and the salary and benefits are satisfactory.

Some social workers resist working in the corrections field. Its inherently authoritarian and involuntary nature seems to conflict with traditional social work values. However, many social welfare programs and social workers are involved in involuntary situations. And it is often the involuntary client who is most in need of help from a social worker.

The kinds of services described for Scott are typical of the work many social workers perform in adult correctional institutions. Another major task involves working with the classification process, which is an assessment procedure for determining the ways in which individual prisoners are handled. Social workers also help organize prison activities, consult with the prison administration on inmate issues and individual inmate behavior, and assist in planning modifications in prison procedures.

One of the public's misunderstandings about prisons is that they are designed to punish prisoners and it is agreed that it is wrong for social workers to be involved in punishment. Some potential social workers in prisons assume they may be called upon to participate in punishment. However, it is not the fundamental purpose of prison programs to punish inmates. The punishment is the separation from society—the isolation. Prisons are designed and operated to be secure and to protect the public from criminals. They are not designed to be or expected to be punitive.

Central Office Planning

In some states social workers direct central social work planning offices for entire state corrections systems. They outline programs, train and supervise workers, and help develop human services policies for the system. Such jobs constitute the large systems approaches to corrections that involve social workers. As in all other fields, social workers serve at differing organizational and program levels. In the central office work, they take responsibility for a number of indirect services such as those described.

Probation and Parole Services

Social workers are also heavily involved in state and federal probation and parole services. According to Allen (1995) social work is among a few professions that fit into the probation and parole fields. The others are criminal justice, law, psychology, and sociology. Probation is a kind of sentence—a nonprison sentence by a court for a person who has been found guilty of a crime. The probation officer meets periodically with probationers and assists them with the problems they are facing. If the probationer is sentenced to perform community service, the probation officer may monitor the performance of the service. Sometimes, convicted persons who are ill are placed on probation to preserve their health and to provide them with opportunities to obtain treatment. Some probationers are placed under "house arrest." They are not removed from their communities to prisons but are required to stay in their residences.

During the sentencing process, the probation officer may conduct an assessment of the convicted person and report to the court. Probation officers may also assist the court in determining the most appropriate sentence for them. Investigating offenders is one of the functions of probation officers.

Conditions are typically imposed on probation to ensure that the convicted person does not commit additional crimes or deal with others convicted or suspected of crimes. The probation officer may also monitor the conduct of the probationer and report concerns to the court. Monitoring may be conducted by the convicted person's wearing an electronic bracelet or anklet that allows the probation officer and the probation department to know that the parolees are where they are supposed to be—often at home under a form of house arrest.

Parole is considered an early release from prison for those whose conduct has been good and for those who are not deemed a threat to the community by a parole board. The released prisoner reports to a parole officer periodically. The officer counsels the released prisoner and helps with reintegration into free society. The other role of the parole officer is to ensure that the parolee is complying with the terms of the release.

Juvenile Delinquency Services and Corrections

Youth offenders and young people who are deemed to be juvenile delinquents are also groups social workers serve. Historically, social workers have believed that juveniles are not criminals in the same sense that adults are. Instead, social workers, and the rest of society, have treated young people who violate the rules differently—with an emphasis on assessment and services rather than punishment.

Although there have been recent changes in many states allowing for youths, in certain cases, to be treated as adults and to be tried and punished as if they were adults, in most cases young people continue to be treated as a special category with emphases on service rather than punishment.

The Juvenile Court

Historically, young people in difficulty with the law have appeared before juvenile courts that operate quite differently than adult courts. The courts' procedures are not considered adversarial. The court's purpose is to help the child, rather than prove that delinquency occurred and to impose punitive action, such as incarceration, on the youth.

Because of specific federal and state laws the courts also determine whether the improper behavior constitutes juvenile delinquency or a status offense. An act of juvenile delinquency is behavior that would be criminal if it were committed by an adult such as sexual assault, murder, robbery, and similar acts. A status offense is one that would not be considered a problem if it were committed by an adult. Status offenses include truancy, drinking alcohol, violating curfews, or refusing to obey parents. In most states the laws require status offenders and juvenile delinquents to be treated separately.

Social workers are heavily involved in juvenile courts as probation officers and in other kinds of social work roles. They investigate the child's life, discuss the offenses with the child and the parents, as well as with the child's teachers, and develop an assessment of the child. They also recommend services to help the juveniles overcome the problems that brought them to the unacceptable behavior.

The Range of Services for Juveniles

The range of options for juveniles who have committed offenses is broad. Part of the skill of those who work with juveniles is to select a service that will help overcome the problem behavior and not exacerbate it.

Help within the Family

When possible, efforts are made to help the child and the family stay together so as to avoid disrupting the children's lives. They may be required to make restitution to victims or perform community service, in addition to carrying out normal home and school responsibilities. Or the requirement may be for the young person to attend school regularly, perhaps take a part-time job, and remain out of trouble for a specified period of time.

Community care programs may provide youthful offenders with group activities such as camping and recreation or services programs. Children stay in the community but are expected to participate in mental health services, youth organizations such as Scouting or Boys or Girls Clubs, attend tutoring classes, and otherwise enhance their lives.

In some cases, youthful offenders are placed in foster or group care homes for children similar to the way that young people receiving protective services may be placed, as described in Chapter 9 on older adults and children.

In extreme cases, youth may be placed in correctional institutions, which are sometimes called reformatories or schools. In the past, institutional care was the primary form of treatment of juvenile delinquents. However, such facilities have been deemphasized to the point that some states have done away with them completely.

A few juvenile services programs have experimented with shock incarceration and boot camps, which are exceptionally unpleasant institutional experiences that last for only a short time. The theory behind them is that the young person will behave properly in the future in order to avoid such treatment in juvenile or adult institutions later. Students may be involved in such programs for a few hours or a few days. They are designed to persuade young people to avoid the kinds of behavior that lead to their incarceration.

An important preventive service for young people in danger of becoming offenders are shelters for runaway children. These facilities, located in many larger cities, assist young people with housing and food as well as assistance in relocating or returning home. Social workers have been heavily involved in organizing and operating runaway youth shelters.

Victim Assistance Programs

One of the emerging areas of work in the justice and corrections fields are programs for crime victims including financial compensation and social services. Concern for victims is a major issue for public officials and most states have laws providing services to those who have been harmed and whose families have been harmed by criminals. Many social workers are involved in programs of victim assistance as service providers, researchers, and case managers.

Domestic Violence Services

Social workers were among those who helped found some of the early programs dealing with domestic violence, one of the programs of victim assistance. Virtually all large cities and many smaller communities have programs of domestic violence services. Domestic violence programs deal primarily with victims of violence or abuse in the family, especially women who have been physically assaulted by their husbands or male partners. The victims are provided with temporary housing in shelters, often at unpublicized locations, with some social services for themselves and their children as well as counseling and referral for legal help, employment, job training, and education. Social workers often direct domestic violence programs. Some of the social services provided are also delivered by professional social workers who are employed by domestic violence shelters or by volunteers.

Social Work Jobs

Social workers are among those employed at every level of the juvenile justice system, as the entire juvenile, delinquency and juvenile court system is called. They may be directors of state programs or work as planners and supervisors in central offices of such programs, just as they are in adult corrections. As mentioned, some social workers work with the judges of juvenile courts. Some work as community workers with juvenile programs and as juvenile probation and parole officers. They also are employed as managers and social workers in juvenile institutions. A few social workers who also have law degrees have served as juvenile judges.

Some states have contracted their juvenile services programs to private corporations. Many social workers are employees of those private contractors. Social workers are also involved with demonstration and experimental programs in the juvenile justice field, along with others who conduct research on juvenile delinquency and status offenses. Social workers also work in the field of research about juvenile justice programs, collecting data and planning programs and services. Others work with legislative bodies in developing data about and preparing legislation on juvenile issues.

Many social workers are also involved in crime and delinquency prevention activities by organizing programs of education, community involvement, and working with schools and teachers. They also assist youth organizations in developing crime and delinquency prevention services. The prevention services, though not as well-funded as treatment and incarceration programs, can be an inexpensive way to reduce the problems. Social work, in general, has a variety of strengths in the development and operation of prevention programs because prevention has been linked historically with social work. Social work's focus on client strengths blends readily with prevention efforts.

Conclusion

For the immediate future, one of the likely growth areas for social work employment is corrections and justice, including programs for victims of crimes. An increased emphasis on reducing the use of drugs and eliminating drug sales and trafficking, growing rates of unemployment, the growth of gangs and gang violence, and broken families, all tend to increase the rates and levels of crime and encourage governments to take steps to reduce crime. Social work is among the disciplines that increases while such conditions prevail. Social work, with its emphasis on rehabilitation, future planning, and family services, has a great deal to contribute to the prevention and treatment of crime and delinquency. These areas of work also provide challenging opportunities for many social workers.

11

Social Work Jobs in
Smaller Communities,
Employee Assistance,
and International
Settings

The Special Nature of Rural Social Work

Social work began as an urban profession. Most social agencies and most social workers carry out their duties in metropolitan areas. However, there is a significant amount of social work activity in smaller communities and many social workers work in small towns and rural areas.

Part of the reason for social work growing in the smaller and rural communities is the increasing understanding by policy makers and public officials that small communities often have more social problems than metropolitan communities. In many cases, when they have opportunities, the most healthy, best educated, and youngest citizens of small communities leave to work in cities. The people who remain in smaller communities often have fewer options and opportunities than their large community or city counterparts. There are disproportionately large numbers of older adults, people who are poor, disadvantaged minority group members, and children with problems in smaller communities.

There is a constant interest in social agencies to better equalize services between smaller and larger communities (Ginsberg, 1999a). However, it is sometimes difficult to attract and retain professionally educated social workers in small towns. Professionally educated social workers are somewhat less likely to accept professional positions in smaller communities. They are likely to relocate to cities when they have more opportunities, for some of the same reasons that the citizens of small towns have moved to the cities in the United States and elsewhere. Approximately 75 percent of the U.S. population lives in metropolitan areas or cities with populations of more than 50,000 while the nonmetropolitan population is only 25 percent of the nation's total.

Social Work Opportunities in Smaller Communities

Because smaller communities are not popular with some social workers, those who are willing to live and work there often find attractive opportunities available to them. There are often jobs for social workers in the rural areas of states when there are no jobs for social workers available in cities or metropolitan areas.

The range of services in smaller communities is likely to be narrower than that in larger cities. Most social work jobs in small towns and rural areas are in basic fields such as public welfare, public health, and community mental health (Ginsberg, 1999a). In some cases, social workers in rural communities are required to serve several areas, perhaps working a day each week or a few days each month in different places, rather than concentrating all of their work week in one community or location. Some find the geographical diversity encouraging and stimulating and for those who like to deal with a different clientele every few days, small community work is often attractive. At the same time, many workers in smaller communities serve only a limited number of people in a limited geographic area. In those circumstances social workers who like to know their community and their clients well and to be both well-known and community leaders tend to flourish.

Generalist and Independent Social Work

Social workers in smaller communities are likely to be able to use their generalist skills that they learn in BSW and MSW programs. Because they are the only social workers in the community or one of only a few, many small community workers have opportunities to deal with large and small system efforts. They may be administrators, organizers, planners, and consultants, as well as direct practitioners. Social workers in smaller communities are likely to have special status in their community as experts on social problems and social programs.

In addition to having a broad range of responsibilities, in a rural or small community social workers usually find that they have extensive opportunities for independent work. That is because they are distant from agency headquarters and from supervisory social workers and many workers in small communities have greater discretion in their jobs and less need to report to a higher-level social work professional. The independent-minded social worker who wants to exercise authority and responsibility in a wide range of professional areas is often ideally suited for rural and smaller community work.

> Jennifer Reynolds is a child protective services social worker in her county's department of social services office. She investigates and works to resolve the occasional child abuse complaints that are brought to her attention.
>
> In addition to her normal duties of interviewing families and children in which there may be abuse or neglect and finding ways to overcome them and protect the children, she also plays a number of major community roles. She becomes a board member and consultant to the local children's advocacy group that works to improve social services in the area. She is called upon to present programs for civic groups such as the Rotary and Lions. At the invitation of the superintendent of schools, she conducts a workshop on child protective services for local teachers and counselors.

As the foregoing example indicates, social workers in smaller communities become multifaceted and are expected to perform functions that are not the usual, specialized activities of social workers in metropolitan communities.

After a period of time on the job, this worker has the opportunity and skills to transfer to a state office leadership position or as an administrator, rather than a line worker in this or another nonmetropolitan county.

Rural Social Work Summary

Social work in smaller, nonmetropolitan communities, offers employment opportunities that are often unavailable in larger cities or metropolitan areas. Frequently, a younger, talented, and ambitious social worker can move quickly into a job with major responsibilities in a small town that would require years of experience and slow movement up the employment ladder in a large city. Some newly educated social workers have found that small community work is ideal for entering the profession and, for some, the basis for an excellent and responsible career.

Employee Assistance Programs

Among the responsibilities of many social workers are employee assistance programs. These are organized in several different ways. Some basic concepts of EAPs, as they are known, and the principles underlying them developed in other nations. The fundamental purpose of an EAP is to assist employees of organizations with personal and social problems. In the United States one of the primary purposes is to help employees who have drug and alcohol problems overcome those problems so they can be more effective employees. However, EAPs also provide casework and counseling services to assist families in overcoming family conflicts, in arranging appropriate child care and parent-child relations, and in dealing with older adults such as parents of employees.

Although EAP work is effective in helping people solve some of the same kinds of social problems other social agencies address, the EAP function is to improve the workplace, the employing organization, and the performance of the workers.

Contract EAPs

A typical pattern in the United States is for EAPs to be established to operate under contract with existing agencies. Many family service agencies, described in Chapter 8 on health and mental health, provide EAP services under contract with employers.

Many EAPs provide a screening and referral service. Some of the work under contract EAPs is provided directly to employees by employees of a contracting organization. However, in other cases, those who receive help are referred to other agencies or to private practitioners, many of whom are social workers. Employees are also referred to hospitals and other inpatient or residential settings to assist with their problems.

Employer-Located EAPs

In this field of providing services to the workplace, which is sometimes called industrial social work, some programs are operated by the employing organization itself, and the professional workers in the EAP are corporation employees. They provide services directly through their own efforts to employees who come to them or who are referred to them for help.

International Social Work Careers

Many social workers have long careers in international work because social problems and social welfare programs are a significant part of the agenda of world organizations and social welfare services.

The United Nations

Social workers from various parts of the world, including the United States, have long been part of the activities of the United Nations. Although the United Nations is primarily known for its international peace efforts and its intervention and disputes and conflicts, the social welfare role of the organization is an important one and one in which social workers have long been heavily involved. Most social workers in the

United Nations are employed by units of the Economic and Social Council, one of the main arms of the international organization.

The United Nations identifies social problems and makes recommendations and projections about social programs and the social development issues associated with them. They study various kinds of social problems around the world, make reports and recommendations about those problems, and consult with nations about the solutions. In addition, social workers are often part of the U.N.'s health programs such as the World Health Organization.

There are jobs in the headquarters of the United Nations which are located in New York City. However, there are also regional organizations of the United Nations in many parts of the world. Social workers have been employed in most of those regions, especially the Vienna offices of the U.N.

Peace Corps

Among the major opportunities for social workers in international programs is the Peace Corps, a program originally founded in 1961 under President John F. Kennedy, to send American experts to various parts of the world that request them to help deal with social, health, educational, and other problems. Since its founding in 1961, the Peace Corps has placed more than 145,000 volunteers in 130 countries. In 1996 ninety-four countries were being served by Peace Corps volunteers, many of them in Eastern Europe. Social workers served in the following regions: Africa, Latin America, Europe, Central Asia, the Mediterranean, and Asia and the Pacific (Cunningham, 1996).

By sector of activity, 37 percent of volunteers were involved in education projects; the second largest group were in environmental programs; and the third largest in health; others were in business, agriculture, and other activities.

Social work has long been part of the Peace Corps groups that have assisted other nations. Several types of positions are appropriate for those with social work backgrounds, including community services, urban youth development, urban planning, or public health. Social work positions cross over several of the sectors described above. Many positions require a bachelor's degree plus a demonstrated interest and experience in the field for which one is being considered. Professionally educated social workers who join the Peace Corps may, after completing their training, expect to work in various parts of the world. They are required to learn the language of the country in which they are locating.

In recent years, some social workers in the Peace Corps have been social work teachers in Eastern European nations, which had ceased educating social workers when they were part of the Soviet Union sector of influence. Others have helped with community development projects in every part of the world. Still others assist with health programs, child welfare services, programs for the aging, and many other kinds of social work that have been described in this book.

Persons interested in joining the Peace Corps may obtain advice and information as well as applications forms by calling a toll free number, 1-800-424-8580, or by calling the toll free number directory assistance line. Information is also available on the World Wide Web.

There are eleven regional Peace Corps offices and each can provide information and advice on applying. Although there are regular recruiting efforts, the standards for selection are high because the work is often exceptionally challenging emotionally and physically. Application packets provide details on some of the difficulties that volunteers experience as well as some of the health concerns that volunteers face. Detailed physicals are required and people with several kinds of health problems are excluded or delayed from entering the Peace Corps.

For someone who is adventurous and who meets the standards, Peace Corps can be a valuable opportunity to learn and a significant career enhancement. Many social work employers are attracted to candidates with prior Peace Corps service. At least one MSW program has provided special stipends and educational opportunities for returning Peace Corps volunteers.

In 1996 the average age of the nearly 7,000 volunteers was twenty-nine. Eight percent were over fifty. Fifty-five percent were women and 45 percent men. Only 8 percent were married. Thirteen percent were members of minority groups. Almost all had bachelor's degrees and many had graduate degrees. About one-third had a year or more of work experience (Cunningham, 1996).

Other International Organizations

Some social workers also work with other international organizations such as the World Health Organization, a part of the U.N. mentioned earlier, which has major projects for dealing with AIDS. Others have been involved in the United States Agency for International Development, which sends experts to other countries to assist them with various projects, including social welfare projects. Some embassies have social welfare consultants attached to them to help the countries in which they are located deal with social welfare programs and services.

International Industrial Social Work

Many countries have employee assistance programs of various kinds and many are more comprehensive than those of the United States.

I recall that when I taught in Colombia, South America, in the 1970s most of the social services were delivered by corporations to their employees. That is, in addition to providing wages and American-style fringe benefits to their employees, many organizations had their own extensive social services programs. It was quite common to find a social work section in the textile and petroleum plants of Colombia. Even the government agencies had employee assistance programs. It was a government requirement that services be provided to employees by corporations as a condition of doing business. Sometimes the organization's expenditures for services exceeded the amount spent for the employee payroll.

These services were, as mentioned earlier, more comprehensive than the direct practice efforts described in EAPs in the United States. In Colombia the programs included literacy training, music lessons, and sports for the children, some educational programs, often for wives who had not completed school, and, occasionally, housing for workers. All these services were designed to make it possible for workers to discharge their responsibilities effectively. They also included activities to enhance the well-being of families, much as the overall social services system in the United States does.

Sometimes the agency's employee assistance program is tied to its other benefits such as health insurance and retirement, especially retirement planning. In other cases they are separate functions.

Conclusion

This chapter has covered three special areas in which social workers work, outside the more typical settings of American urban or metropolitan area social agencies. Opportunities for social workers are interesting and often promising for those who are willing to work independently, often in areas removed from their original residences. That is especially true of work in smaller communities and international work. In many ways it is also true of industrial social work in corporate settings, separated from the more typical settings of social agencies, institutions, and hospitals. These areas are worth exploration and consideration for those who pursue professional social work careers.

12

Macro-Social Work Careers

Some writers call the social planning and social administration functions of social workers macro-social work. That is social work within larger systems such as communities, organizations, and institutions.

Social Administration

In every agency that has been discussed in this text so far, and, in every social agency, there is an administrative component. These are the efforts to rationally and efficiently direct the organization. Social work students are exposed to social administration or social agency management and supervision, as some refer to them, in every educational program.

The role of a social agency manager or administrator is to ensure that the organization runs smoothly while reaching its objectives. That means hiring and dealing with personnel; supervising some staff and making sure other supervisors oversee their staffs; working with and managing the agency budget; ensuring that there is an adequate flow of clients from referrals, self-referrals, and outreach to the community; and making certain that the agency missions are pursued. Management is a complex and extensive subject on which there is extensive literature in the form of books, journal articles, videotapes, audiotapes, and films. According to Weinbach (1994) there are five functions of managers including planning, organizing, staffing, directing, and monitoring. Social workers learn the skills associated with these five functions in courses they take in undergraduate and graduate social work programs, by reading the extensive literature of management, and by attending workshops and seminars on effective management of programs.

160

Many people think that social administration which, as Chapter 1 shows, is one of the oldest methods and approaches to social work, is the most important of all social work jobs. Without adequate administration, programs are not organized and delivered. Without effective management, it is hard to build an effective and high-quality program. Therefore, social administration pervades all of social work and is probably the most basic of the larger system or macro skills in the field.

Styles of Management

There are various styles of management that one encounters in social work. The more traditional management follows the same kinds of patterns as traditional organizations or bureaucracies. However, some "alternative social agencies" as they are defined by Perlmutter (1995) are less centrally managed. Workers are able to help in the decision-making process and many administrative actions are defined by peer discussion and group decision making.

Boards of Directors

Almost all social agencies, and, in particular, private and nonprofit social agencies, are governed by boards of directors. These boards, which are composed of citizens who usually have no financial connection to the agency, meet regularly and make decisions about the organization's program and mission. Generally, their most important function is to employ the executive director, who makes the administrative decisions for the organization, within the guidelines of the organization's constitution and bylaws, as determined by the board of directors or, in some cases, by the total membership of the organization.

In general, the agency, under the executive director, employs supervisors to lead, educate, and otherwise control the functions of line workers in the organization. The special skills of supervision are critical for workers in agencies.

Social Planning

Another of the functions of social workers in larger system work is that of helping plan and finance human services programs. Workers in such programs are called social planners or community organizers. The classic description of their function is to balance community needs and community resources. If the community calls for more mental health services, additional services to protect children, or special services for older adults, the social planning function is to discover and document the extent of the need. The other major function is to help plan solutions such as social services, for dealing with the problem. Of course, another function is to develop the resources to pay for the resolution of the difficulty.

The United Way

One of the most important of the social planning organizations is the United Way, which studies community needs, makes recommendations about meeting those needs, develops budget for financing programs to overcome community needs, and organizes and operates campaigns to raise funds to address community needs. The United Way is the principal fund-raising organization for many volunteer services in U.S. communities. Organizations that participate in United Way campaigns forgo their right to mount independent fund campaigns without special permission from the United Way. An umbrella organization called the United Way of America, with offices in Alexandria, Virginia, helps the local units carry out their responsibilities through public relations activities, training, and the preparation of materials (Brilliant, 1990).

Corporations tend to approve and support the United Way because it screens agencies for their needs and quality, and represents effective and less expensive means for organizing and raising money through campaigns among employees and managers of businesses. Rather than a corporation being confronted with fifteen or twenty fund-raising campaigns each year for various organizations, the United Way operates one campaign for many organizations and distributes the money from the campaign on a basis that is carefully studied and planned.

United Way workers, many of whom have social work backgrounds, are often involved in specific studies or specific social problems or issues. They may also assist various planning and allocation committees in determining how the campaign's money will be spent. They also become heavily involved in operating campaigns for raising money, based on a specific goal. The goal is constructed from compiling all the needs of the organizations funded by the United Way that can be identified by the community's boards of directors and that the United Way believes can realistically be achieved in the fund-raising program of the community.

Other Planning Functions

Many other organizations are involved in social planning and community organization, in addition to the United Way. There are many state government planning bodies, some of which are affiliated with public social services programs, that are designed to study needs such as health care, crime reduction, delinquency deduction, services to people with developmental disabilities, and many others. These planning groups conduct research—or commission others to do research—to help them identify the extent of various problems and identify the means for reducing those problems in the future.

Social Research

One of the supportive services in social welfare macro-services with a long history is social research. Many large organizations have their own research programs, often with financing from federal agencies that are part of the Department of Health and Human Services or one of the other departments that sponsor social programs. Social researchers examine social problems to determine their origins and their extent. They evaluate alternative treatment programs in mental health and engage in the study of social issues.

Administrators and planners make extensive use of research findings in determining how to proceed to deal with social problems. The results of research projects are also disseminated to larger audiences through professional journals and government publications so that others will be able to use the results to deal with the issues covered in the research.

Many social workers become social researchers within agencies, as members of think tanks that study social issues, or as members of university faculties or staffs. Although well-known social work researchers often hold doctoral degrees, there are also large numbers with BSW or MSW degrees.

As discussed earlier, the major approaches to research in social work are evaluation of one's own practice and program evaluation. However, the contributions of social work research to understanding and planning solutions to social issues and problems are also great.

Volunteer Supervision and Training

In many agencies, volunteers provide substantial portions of the services to clients. However, in order to be effective, volunteers have to be carefully screened, trained about the agency and the volunteers' efforts, and supervised in their work. Effective volunteers can often do more for clients than professionals. Some are professionals such as physicians, social workers, and teachers. Others come from a range of other fields. People of exceptional talent who cannot or do not choose to pursue professional social work or similar careers are often willing to volunteer their services for a few hours. A large number of social agencies have staffs of volunteer coordinators and trainers, who locate, screen, train, assign, and supervise volunteers. Many volunteers in the social services are adults but volunteers can be young children who play a variety of roles in the operations of many programs as well as adults in their senior years.

Working with volunteers represents an important skill in the social services. One element of volunteer work is volunteer recognition, making certain that volunteers receive nonmonetary rewards for the services they provide to others. This work is another of the indirect services or macro skills of which social workers should be capable and which are of major importance to the effective operations of social programs.

Information and Referral

Among the classic functions of social workers is the provision of information to clients and the public at large on the availability of services and the means for accessing them. Many communities maintain one or more information and referral programs that centrally maintain data on available services. In some cases, these services are the most important help provided to a client or a group of clients. Programs for individuals and families who are homeless sometimes serve by informing people of where and how to obtain various kinds of help such as employment, housing, health care, and food. In some cases, services are co-located, so that homeless people can reach a number of different programs in one office or one location. In other cases, the information is provided and the referrals made by telephone.

Among the programs provided to homeless people are emergency shelters in which people can live for a short period of time while they await assistance that might help them with more permanent arrangements. Many social workers as well as religious organizations are involved in operating shelters.

Public housing, or community housing, is another available resource for people who lack adequate housing. Again, social workers have been involved in planning and operating housing programs; this is a macro-service.

Of course, homeless people are only some of the users of information and referral services. All kinds of clients of all ages are also users of such help when they find they need assistance from social welfare agencies.

Grassroots Organizing for Social Change

One important way in which social workers provide larger system services is through organizing people to solve their own problems at the grassroots or local level. Some social workers are involved in organizing and working with labor unions. Some of these are unions of social workers who organize and bargain with their employers to improve their working conditions and compensation. Social workers also work with workers in other industries to help them organize and negotiate for their own well-being. Social work and the labor movement have had partly shared histories. Many social workers are employees of labor unions and the AFL-CIO, in particular, has long operated programs of community and social services.

Social workers have also had a long history of organizing disadvantaged people to improve their circumstances. The grassroots, confrontational-organizing efforts are led by many but they were made most popular by the late Saul D. Alinsky (1969). Out of these efforts came the organization of people to confront landlords, government officials, and others to improve programs for people with low incomes and other disadvantages.

Community Action Programs

The National Welfare Rights Organization was one of the best examples of organizing the disadvantaged for their own well-being and involved many social workers during the heighth of its operations (Kotz & Kotz, 1977). The community action programs of the War on Poverty or Office of Economic Opportunity are another example of programs designed to help people help themselves, often with the help of a mobilizing social worker. There are detailed and elegant discussions of several of the origins of these projects in *Dilemmas of Social Reform* (Marris & Rein, 1967).

Many social workers are attracted to organizing for change and, in some ways, social work has made major contributions to the human services through such efforts.

Association Management

Association management is a social work career that attracts many professionals. One of the best examples, perhaps, is NASW which employs a large national staff and fifty state chapter staffs, most of whom are social workers. There are also many other national, regional, and state associations dealing with a range of subjects and causes that use a large number of professional social workers, mainly BSWs and MSWs, to manage their programs.

Fund-Raising

Many social workers have traditionally been involved in fund development for human services organizations in addition to working for the United Way. Many social workers are also employed by groups such as Jewish welfare federations, which play a similar role for the Jewish community in fund-raising, planning for services, and allocating funds for financing those services. There are similar efforts in other ethnic groups.

Fund-raisers always appear to be in short supply in the human services and the need for effective fund-raisers always seems to be greater than the pool of skilled people from which agencies can draw.

Conclusion

The macro-component of social work practice ranges from classic social work administration, which is similar in nature and skills to any other kind of management, to grassroots organizing. Planning, fund development, and many other skills are also part of the social work profession's range of roles and responsibilities. In some cases, agencies that employ macro-workers seek older and more experienced social workers than those who have only recently graduated from social work education programs. However, many such employers, looking for a fresh viewpoint and, perhaps, lower-salaried workers, consider and often employ younger and newer social work professionals.

Although there are many more job opportunities in direct social work practice than in macro-areas, larger systems work has a steady history throughout social work history and often provides attractive and exciting opportunities for social workers interested in that area of professional responsibility.

Part 3

Success and Satisfaction on the Job

All knowledge is not formal and not all work is based on professional concepts and skills. Being successful in a social work job and, for that matter, in any job, often requires knowledge that is not taught in professional schools. Some physicians with great skills, who might have been first in their medical school classes, never quite succeed in practice because they lack the skills necessary for running an office. Teachers who may know their subject matter better than anyone else may find their work frustrating because they do not know how to manage student classroom behavior.

Social workers, like other professionals, need some practical skills that are fundamental to all others but that are inappropriate subjects for social work schools. Chapter 13 is about some of the things social workers need to know but may not have been formally taught. In other cases, practitioners may find they immediately need knowledge of some subjects that are not required in social work education programs but are central to the agency where they work. All schools are obviously not able to teach each student what will be needed in the future. A quick catch-up on some specific subjects may be essential. Psychiatric assessment and diagnosis, which many agencies perform, are mentioned as examples.

In Chapter 14, the book sums up the keys to successful social work careers by discussing some ways for surviving on the job and for maintaining physical and mental health while employed. The chapter acknowledges that all work is difficult, often more difficult than expected. Preparation for the problems encountered on the job, along with the positives that have been covered already, is one of the primary objectives of the book and especially this last chapter.

13

Things Social Workers Need to Know That They May Not Have Been Taught in Social Work School

Although most of the knowledge, values, and skills that are important in social work jobs are taught in social work education programs, there is always some information that students may have missed, their school did not teach, or that does not quite fit with the social work curriculum but is important, nevertheless. These are some facts and skills that social workers need to know for successful job performance and that should be learned before employment.

Technology

There are a number of resources and services that effective social workers should use if they are to do their jobs properly. Many of these resources are not always discussed in education programs but are critical for effective work. It is an almost daily occurrence in most agencies for social workers to cry out in frustration when their dictating wasn't recorded on the tape or when it is inadvertently erased; or to find that a lengthy document prepared on a computer has not been saved and cannot be retrieved. Cyberspace carries a heavy load of case notes, Medicaid reports, and minutes of meetings, that were written or dictated but lost forever because a dictating machine or a computer was incorrectly used. Outstanding professional performance may be overrun by technological insensitivities or failures. Some of the following suggestions may help avert some of those problems.

The Telephone

One of the most pervasive problems in social work but one that is not often discussed, is the difficulty in reaching an agency and an individual social worker by telephone. Such difficulties may be encountered in trying to find out about jobs with a particular agency or when trying to make an appointment for an interview. Many social agencies, at least many that I try to reach, are practically unreachable. That is especially unfortunate because people try to contact agencies by telephone to help them with mental health problems, to report child and adult abuse and neglect, to learn about licensing regulations, or to obtain health and financial services that may make a vast difference in their lives.

An effective agency will have sufficient telephone lines and answering systems to accommodate all who call.

The ways social workers, themselves, use the telephone is often an important element in their careers. Returning telephone calls promptly may be viewed as a sign of efficiency and dedication to the agency's work. And answering the telephone crisply while at one's desk is often important. Answering with one's name, "Susan Jones," is always appropriate, as is, "Human Resources Department, Susan Jones." The reactions to telephone courtesy are often the basic reaction to the person on the telephone.

Cell Phones

Cell telephones are probably too new for a consensus on their etiquette to have evolved. They are increasingly pervasive and can play a positive—or negative—role in professional social work. They are flexible and make their owners available, wherever they happen to be.

In some of the emerging ideas about courteous and safe cell phone use, some driving safety experts say that drivers who simultaneously use cell phones are road hazards who are disproportionately involved in accidents. At a minimum, many suggest, headsets that allow drivers to keep both hands on the steering wheel are essential.

Some cell phone users also place and engage in calls in ways that interfere and endanger others. I once saw a cell phone user standing at the top of an escalator, obliviously talking and blocking the free exit from the moving stairs of those who followed.

Because they can ring anywhere, some cell phones interrupt conferences and meetings. Turning them off ought to be a common practice when a social worker is involved in a professional activity, lest the talker neglect both the face-to-face activity and the caller. Some things demand one's full attention, which should not be compromised.

Cell phones are a convenience but they also require conscious and thoughtful use lest they interfere with one's health and well-being as well as one's efficiency on the job.

Answering Machines

Agencies also have detractors who are furious over their telephone calls not being answered or being answered by incomprehensible answering systems. Extensive amounts of business are conducted by telephone in social work, just as is the case in other places of business. Many agencies use automated telephone systems and answering machines to accommodate the needs of their clients and constituents.

Increasingly, workers have personal answering machines or access to answering systems so that they can hear from their clients and return calls efficiently. It is important for social workers to understand their own answering systems or machines and to make good use of them. The first step in good social work practice is to be accessible to clients. If the client can't reach the social worker, the abilities of the worker to solve problems are irrelevant. Workers need to know how to access their machines from remote sites such as their homes, and should check their machines regularly. They need to return phone calls that are made to them promptly. They need to erase the messages that have been left so there is room on the tape or in the system to take new messages. Imagine how clients, who have very serious problems, feel when they place a call to a social worker only to find that the worker is unreachable or that the worker's answering machine or answering system is filled with messages. Few events could arouse more hopelessness in a client.

I occasionally encounter answering machines that have no message from the person called. Or the machine has a flippant message such as "You know what to do—so do it!" One person I called spoke painfully slowly, and played rock music in the background. Callers need to know that they reached the person or organization they were calling rather than an incorrect number. At work, the answering machine owners should, in most cases, identify themselves by name and affiliation and should also repeat the telephone number so callers are assured they reached the number they were attempting. Being entertaining may be pointless. That was not what the caller expected or wanted from the number that was called.

It's possible to be more circumspect with a personal answering machine at a residence. Some people are unwilling to identify themselves or want to obscure the fact that they live alone. In those cases, just stating the number and indicating that "we" are not immediately available may be sufficient.

When leaving a message, the caller should clearly leave the name and affiliation and also slowly and clearly state the number where the caller can be reached.

Menu-based answering systems also have drawbacks that can be easily overcome. Some businesses, including social work organizations, use recorded answers with a menu that has, in turn, five or six options. The problem is that none of the options may fit the objectives of the caller—who may not know the name of a person who can help, an extension number, or what division handles the problem.

In some cases, callers and recipients of calls fail to use the answering machine to its maximum, acting as if nothing significant should be left as a message. For example, Ms. Smith, who knows she will be away all day, calls another agency and says "I need directions to your agency for my client, Mr. Brown, who is scheduled to be with you on November 5 at 10:30 A.M. Please leave the directions on my answering machine." The agency called returns the call with, "I'm answering your message. Please call me back." There is no reason to tie up both callers' time talking to one another. Leaving simple directions would solve this simple, straightforward problem. Instead, both people will have to spend time the next day trying to make contact and obtaining such simple information as directions.

A good test for social workers and social work managers is to call their own offices, answering machines, and answering systems to understand how the agency appears to clients and to the larger public. People's impressions are often based almost totally on whether or how the telephone is answered.

Cellular telephones make it possible to stay in touch with callers when one is away from the office or home. Some social workers also use pagers or beepers to be alerted when telephone calls come. Agencies that are required to provide twenty-four-hour coverage such as protective services programs and some community mental health services often rotate pager assignments on nights and weekends, with social workers taking their turns at responding to after-hours calls.

Dictation Systems and Equipment

Many agencies are equipped with central dictating systems or provide their workers with dictating machines so they can prepare letters and reports. These documents are transcribed by support staff or a secretarial service within or under contract to the agency. Knowing how to dictate effectively is not regularly taught to social work students, though many find that they spend a large portion of their time each day dictating. Learning how to dictate is critical to avoid one of the more frustrating agency practice experiences—dictating for an hour and finding that none of what was said remained on the dictation tape. I have seen it happen—it has happened to me and almost everyone who dictates.

The dictation process is not complicated. It usually only requires being explicit about the instructions to the person who will type so it is clear where the document starts and when it ends. It also involves carefully including the punctuation and capitalization in the dictation so that the typist knows where paragraphs begin, and where there are commas and periods. There are many different kinds of dictating machines and each operates somewhat differently from others. Knowing how to operate the particular machine is the immediate task of those who need to prepare reports by dictation.

Dictating machines require the person who dictates to think and express ideas orally. Some social workers have greater oral expression skills than others. Dictation is an area of skill development that is critical. Agencies use dictating machines because they are a much more efficient way to get information and ideas on paper for records and reports than is dictating to a typist or writing reports in longhand and having them later transcribed. People who have experience in dictating can record their ideas much more rapidly than they can by typing or writing their notes, reports, and other documents in longhand. Dictating makes it possible for a social worker to do the necessary paperwork and still have time to meet with clients.

In some organizations, more than half the time of social workers is taken up with writing reports—a poor use of their expensive training and time. So learning how to dictate is an important skill that many social workers are called upon to use very early in and throughout their careers. Many workers learn it as part of their field instruction or field practicum. Those who do not should arrange to learn to dictate some other way such as asking a faculty member, field instructor, work supervisor, colleague, or support staff person for help.

Computer Use

Almost all social workers are required to use computers or must be able to understand and use computer-prepared reports and other documents. Many schools now teach computer use or provide computer labs for students to learn computing on their own. There are many different kinds of computers and many differences among the computer software programs that make them work. The Macintosh systems, used in many schools, operate differently than the IBM systems which are more common in social agency administration. Mastering a system and mastering a software program, especially a word processing program, are not difficult tasks. Most educated people should be able to operate any computer and use any software program effectively within a few hours of work. A particular job should not be avoided because the organization uses a computer system that is unfamiliar. Learning a new system is a minor task, especially if one already knows another, and should never be a deterrent to accepting a job, if everything else about the job is positive. Switching between computer systems is only slightly more complicated than shifting from one brand of automobile to another (moving from automatic to standard transmission is a bit more complicated). Long-term Macintosh users ought to be sufficiently competent on an IBM or IBM-compatible system to perform their job with a minimum of lost time.

The basic skill in computing is not particularly modern. It is simply typing or, in the more modern terminology, keyboarding. Effective computer users must have the skill of entering information quickly on a QWERTY keyboard, which is the standard configuration for typewriters and computers. Knowing how to use the keyboard and knowing how to use the other function keys on a computer are important attributes for people embarking upon social work careers. Taking a class in touch-typing or keyboarding, for those who do not have those skills, is a sound investment of time and money. Of course, many people have highly individual skills in typing their own ways. Some older-era newspaper reporters mastered two-finger typing and were both well-regarded and successful. But knowing some means of efficiently communicating with a computer is indispensable in social work practice.

Knowing what computers can do and being able to make them do it is also critical. Social workers who prepare a ten-page report that vanishes into the air because they did not know how to save it testify to the importance of mastering the fundamentals.

Social workers need familiarity with two basic kinds of software. As indicated earlier, software makes the computer work. When computers were first used in social work, it was necessary to construct individual programs in order to make the computer useful for social agency functions. Now, prepared software programs provide the skeleton on which computer uses are built by social workers.

The first software classification is *word processing*. Programs such as Microsoft Word, WordPerfect, and many others are available to make it possible to use computers to write letters, reports, articles, and any other kind of document.

All computers are capable of using one kind of word processing software or another and every social agency has its preferences for software.

If a person knows how to use a computer, it is not difficult to use any word processing software. Other employees will usually show newcomers how to use the agency's word processing system. Manuals are also available that provide complete information on each program. There are also training courses taught at community colleges and computer stores that will help workers learn what they need about word processing. The programs, themselves, usually have "help" menus, that outline the answers to the questions users may have. When in doubt or trouble, a computer user may tap into the help function of the program.

Word processing is important because, in many agencies, workers are expected to produce their own notes, documents, and letters. Those agencies that do not rely on dictation or handwritten notes will probably require computer software usage instead. Knowing how to use word processing is a basic skill required for most social workers and most jobs.

It is likely that many readers already have the required computer word processing skills. During the 1990s, social work faculty members saw students as a group change from rarely having word processing skills to almost universal computer competency. Most students know how to use computers for all kinds of functions and large numbers own and use their own computers.

A second kind of computer software that is necessary to understand is a *spreadsheet* or other forms of record-keeping software. Many agency records such as statistics, billing information, appointment schedules, and, in some cases, case or client notes are kept on spreadsheets. There are many different kinds of spreadsheet programs, all of which do the same things—they allow people to set up charts that show clients, workers, and other larger subheadings with data such as budget information connected to those headings and subheadings. Workers in social agencies are often required to enter data on a spreadsheet. They are almost always required to be able to read and interpret information from it.

There are other kinds of computer software programs that are more important in some agencies than others, but if they are important, the worker must be able to use them. One is the *database.* This is information about clients, programs, or other categories important to the agency. A mailing list or a record of all agency clients or information for referral for other services contained in one place and alphabetically or numerically arranged is an example of a database. For example, it is possible with a database to identify all the clients of the same age or diagnosis, all the people who live in a particular neighborhood or zip code, or all of any group that fits a specified variable. Many agencies constantly use their databases to work with their programs and their clients.

Another kind of software program that is becoming increasingly important is electronic mail or e-mail. Many agencies use e-mail for all or most internal communications. The sender of a message simply types the message on a computer and then sends it to the computers of one or more other people. In agencies that use e-mail extensively, if an employee wants to ask the supervisor a question, it is often done by e-mail. If workers want to get a message to all their fellow workers, it is done by e-mail. Increasingly, agencies are moving away from memos and other paper message systems and toward e-mail systems. E-mail can also be sent around the nation and the world at little or no cost and certainly at much lower cost than either fax or telephone.

Another important software application is the family of programs for searching the Internet or World Wide Web. Extensive information is available for workers about programs, medicines, services, legislation, and almost everything else, on the World Wide Web. Software and hardware (modems) are available for connecting any computer to the Internet and World Wide Web and to obtain information from it on virtually any subject. Many agencies have home pages that provide basic information on their work. The Web is an important resource in the human services. It is also a source of information about job vacancies in some agencies.

Many workers also find it convenient to maintain their records and carry out their responsibilities by using portable computers such as laptop or notebook computers. They set up their home visits or daily appointments on the laptop and enter their records on the computer. Increasingly, workers in some agencies find it unnecessary to go to their offices except for meetings and supervisory conferences or to pick up their mail. Many workers spend most of their time in other agencies, in the homes of clients, or in their own homes performing their duties. In such situations, a good knowledge of computer technology is required. The kinds of computer knowledge and skill suggested here go well beyond what is taught in most social work education programs. However, the knowledge and skill are relatively easy to acquire and use, with the help of colleagues and computer specialists, most of whom are always willing to help newcomers to the computer world learn how to improve their use of hardware and software.

Knowledge of English

In some cases, social workers lack skill in oral and written English. Effective communication requires knowledge of grammar and punctuation, and a good ability to spell. There are small spelling dictionaries available for very low cost that can help writers. A paperback dictionary, as well as guides to grammar and to writing can also be assets for many social workers. Almost all computer word processing programs have "spell check" capabilities, which will help the writer correct spelling errors. Many also have grammar checking functions, which help correct punctuation and other dimensions of proper English usage. However, some people may want to bolster their writing skills through community college courses, tutorials, or help from friends and relatives.

It is possible to lose a social work job because of a lack of writing skills. Social work students who plan to teach should know that professors have difficulty earning tenure if their writing skills are poor. Colleges and universities do not always guarantee that their graduates are adequate writers. Multiple choice exams, a reduction or elimination of term papers, and other new styles of teaching make it possible for some people to graduate from baccalaureate and master of social work programs without knowing the English language. Lack of writing skills is a common problem; however, it is a technical, not a moral or conceptual, shortcoming. Therefore, social workers ought to be enthusiastic about improving their writing and not overly defensive about any lack of skill. Poor writing can be corrected with a modest investment of time and dedication to improvement.

Skill in a Second Language

In the increasingly multicultural United States, knowledge of a secoond language is often helpful to social workers. For example, knowledge of Spanish facilitates interacting with Spanish-speaking only clients. French is also valuable in working with some immigrants from Carribean and African nations. In addition, a large number of other languages are spoken by clients in the United States. Native American, Asian, and many European languages are the first languages of many social work clients. Being able to communicate in another language increases the opportunities and abilities of social workers.

Basic Math

Many Americans lack familiarity with basic mathematics—the kind taught in elementary and middle schools such as long division, multiplication, and addition. Converting whole numbers to fractions or calculating percentages is not possible for some otherwise well-educated people. Many find it necessary to take refresher courses in basic math and to learn to use calculators to complete expense accounts, calculate statistics, and otherwise carry out basic computational functions that are required on the job.

Refreshing individual mathematics skills—sometimes just to the extent of what one knew in the sixth grade—often helps enormously in a social work career. Familiarity with a simple scientific calculator may also be a major boost for effective social work practice.

Map Reading

Map reading is another skill that social workers may lack but that is sometimes of inestimable importance. Workers often need to visit agencies, institutions, and individual clients or client families in unfamiliar neighborhoods. The ability to read and follow maps is, therefore, a necessary part of their skills.

Public Speaking

In the course of their work, almost all social workers are expected to make speeches to various groups—the staff, groups of clients, boards of directors, churches, community groups, professional associations, and civic clubs, among others. Whether the presentation is to a large or small audience, it is always important for social workers to present themselves and their materials well. In fact, public speaking may be the source of more phobias among most of us than many more commonly recognized fears. For some reason, we are anxious about appearing before a group to explain or inform. Many social workers should have developed public speaking skills during the course of their educations while making class presentations, but that is not the case for everyone. And those with some experience in presenting to others may remain uncomfortable with the process. I know one able, intelligent, and articulate person who is immobilized even by answering machines. She is more likely to call back than to leave a message, for fear of having her voice recorded and being heard by others. A large number of capable professionals limit their potential and their career options and opportunities because of their aversions to making public presentations.

Therefore, it is important for social workers to understand that they will make presentations and to work to overcome their concerns about doing so. Making presentations—public speaking—is a normal expectation of most social work jobs. Doing so effectively is a route to success and promotion for many in the field. Books and guides to speechmaking are plentiful. Reading one occasionally is a sound way to keep some ideas about presenting to others in mind.

Peterson (1996) developed a simple guide to giving speeches for those she called "petrified at the podium." The following are adaptations of her main points:

1. Arrive early and chat with some of the audience so they will seem like friends rather than strangers. Remember that they want you to succeed and think they can learn from you. Why else would they be there? So don't apologize for being nervous or any other problem. Why call attention to something the listeners may not have noticed?

2. When preparing the speech, know the fundamental points to get across—which should be stated in a sentence or two.

3. Know and target the audience. Every group is different and even if the speech is a repeat, it should be adapted to the special interests of the audience. For example, speaking to parents about child mental illness is quite different than speaking to social workers about the same subject.

4. Keep it short—fifteen to twenty minutes in most cases. When delivering a full paper at a professional meeting, the expectation may be for something longer, and it is not a good idea to cut short a workshop or other session that is supposed to last for a specified period. But when presenting with others at a formal meeting—a luncheon, for example—be brief and punchy. It is rare for the audience to be negative about a talk that is a bit shorter than they anticipated.

5. Use simple language, short sentences, and active verbs. Written language and spoken language are different. Speeches don't read as well in print as they sounded and written materials don't sound as good as they did when they were read.

6. Be cautious about humor—no sexist, racist, or other demeaning humor. A short one- or two-line funny statement is a good ice-breaker. Try it out with friends or family well in advance to make sure the audience will get the joke. A punch line that elicits bewilderment is much worse than no humor at all.

7. Write out the speech—the whole thing—a few days before the presentation and then lay it aside for a while. Then it can be revised or rewritten, depending on how it looks.

8. Don't read the speech. It is better to speak from note cards covering the key points. If speaking from a full manuscript, put it in big type, double-spaced with wide margins—and thank the inventor of the word processor for making it all possible.

9. Practice the speech in front of a mirror, before friends or family, read it into a tape recorder, or perform in front of a camcorder.

Many of the great careers in social work and other disciplines have been based on great speechmaking ability. It is an art worth mastering.

Psychiatric Assessment and Diagnosis

Social workers who want to pursue licenses and other credentials often find they need familiarity with the *Diagnostic and Statistical Manual* (DSM) published by the American Psychiatric Association. The edition in use in 1997 was number 4 (or IV, as the editions are designated by Roman numerals.) However, it is updated periodically and the most current edition should be used.

Many social work education programs, especially MSW degree programs, require course work on the DSM. However, it is not a requirement for accreditation, and some education programs that emphasize elements of social work other than mental health do not make it part of the required curriculum. Questions about psychiatric diagnosis and assessment are asked on many licensing and credentialing exams, even for those social workers who do not plan to work in mental health or provide direct services of any kind. Some of those social workers may not have studied the DSM in their social work education programs. Therefore, they should become familiar with it either by taking an elective course on the subject if it is not required, by studying the DSM as part of a test preparation course offered by the licensing board or a professional organization such as NASW, or by individually studying the manual. Clinical credentials, such as those listed in Chapter 6, all require familiarity with the DSM.

Conclusion

Professional education in social work is a great way to begin preparing for a career in the field. It provides the background needed for beginning practice and it provides the tools for knowing how to learn whatever else that needs to be known.

However, remember that professors prepare students for a profession that exists, that is known. Neither they nor their students can possibly know what the future will be for every social worker. The social worker of the 2000s will provide services and work in settings that were not dreamed about in the 1950s. So every social worker, like every other professional, needs to stay current and to be aware that things will change, sometimes drastically.

Also important to realize is that social work education programs have only limited amounts of time—a finite number of quarter or semester hours—to get it all across. Many would like to include full courses on language and composition, public speaking, math, and some of the other basic information that this chapter suggests is important. However, they cannot do everything and, therefore, it is up to the individual professionals to learn what they need in other ways. That is true of every profession, although few have changed or are as likely to change over the course of the coming years as much as social work. Learning what was not taught in school and continuing to learn are essential elements of the professional work and life of a modern social worker.

14

Surviving on the Job

Getting work in social work—finding a job and filling a professional position—is only the initial step in beginning a social work career. One fact of professional life in the United States and in social work is the difficulty and complexity of work itself. People are often frustrated, disillusioned, and may even become depressed after just a short time on the job, when they realize the work isn't what it might have seemed initially. The disillusionment of people taking jobs for the first time in the United States in many kinds of work becomes a barrier to happiness and sometimes to completing a professional career. Such reactions to the work in situations as diverse as teaching, medical practice, law, and social work, as well as working in any other kind of job, are severe impediments to effective work for many. I often find it surprising, when I talk to young people about their plans, especially when they choose not to pursue a higher education, that they have not carefully considered what working is like. They often tell me that they are going to "get a job." It sounds easy and straightforward but getting a job and finding satisfaction in a job are among the most difficult problems people face. They often sound as naive as those movies in which the romantic couple marry and are assumed to live happily ever after.

Possible Problems and Solutions

Although it is true that eventually most people find satisfactory work and perform their jobs in ways that make it possible for them to be self-supporting, the road to independence through work is rarely simple or easy. Most people change jobs and even careers several times before they settle into work that is more satisfying than unsatisfying. Many newly educated social workers hold at least one job for a short period of time, such as a year or two, before they find the kind of work that satisfies them and which they can perform satisfactorily for a longer period.

Ideally, professionals should not change jobs more often than every two to five years. Potential subsequent employers may question an applicant's persistence and stability if job changes are more frequent. However, sometimes the difficulties of a job are such that one cannot continue with it, or the opportunities for financial and professional advancement through changing jobs are so great that some people find it necessary to make changes in shorter periods of time.

If change is not for professional advancement but as a result of job difficulties, it is important to understand their dimensions. There are several bases for work difficulties and they occur in restaurant employment, retail sales, skilled labor, and almost any other kind of endeavor, in addition to social work jobs. These are some of the reasons for people finding it impossible to continue in their jobs:

Inability to Perform the Required Tasks

Whether it is serving fast food, making child abuse investigations, or writing reports for a mental health program, many people lack the skills for the jobs to which they are appointed. In many cases, those skills may simply be communication abilities such as the capacity to talk effectively to colleagues, superiors, and clients or the ability to use correct English in writing reports. It is often an ineffective communication skill, more than a lack of skill in understanding and working with clients, that causes the greatest difficulties for people new to a job.

Developing effective communication skills, especially writing skills, is an important component of being able to do a job effectively. Knowing how to touch-type, an old skill from the early part of the twentieth century, is more, rather than less important in the new millennium because of the pervasiveness of computers and the fact that using computers requires typing or keyboarding skills, as discussed in the last chapter.

Effective communication requires the ability to speak to others, the ability to write and use English correctly, and the ability to process words or keyboard thoughts into prepared materials.

Disillusionment

Many workers on their first job become disillusioned in the work environment. They begin their work with enthusiasm but discover that some of their fellow workers are less enthusiastic than they are. They find people who cut corners by reporting to work late, leaving early, taking extra long lunches, or simply not performing their jobs and covering up their failure to do their work. There is a surprising, and for new workers, disillusioning amount of careless job performance in the United States. Some observers of work in the United States suggest that just doing a job—only what is expected and only working full-time for the number of hours required by the employer—makes a worker appear to be exceptional because so many other people employed in the same organization do not perform their assigned duties and work less than is expected of them.

Other sources of disillusionment are many. New workers may hear or may observe that management has improper personal relationships with other employees and that may be troubling to them. They may find that the organizations in which they are employed, especially in social work, seem more concerned about financial success and survival than about their ability to serve clients. They may find special treatment for wealthy citizens or influential people such as members of the board or leaders in government or central fund-raising organizations such as the United Way.

Young and idealistic people often have great difficulty with their work environments. There are lawyers and physicians who stop practicing their professions soon after they begin their careers because they cannot tolerate elements of the job. Social workers may change careers because they do not like what they see in the agencies that initially employ them.

The unfortunate truth is that these kinds of disillusioning experiences may be found in any kind of organization. It is not particular to social work. In fact, it may be less common in social work than in other endeavors.

It is often difficult for a new worker, at the beginning of a career, to judge exactly how bad the situation is. Is it simply a manifestation of the kinds of problems encountered in any work setting or is it beyond the normal limits? Are circumstances likely to change? Is the situation one in which the new social worker should complain to higher authorities or is it not sufficiently serious for such drastic action? There is always a degree of complaining by employees in any work site about the boss, the fairness of the work schedule, and the quality of the work performed—whether it is the Army, a public welfare agency, or a university. Knowing whether the situation is simply normal or reflective of serious, unresolved problems should help the new worker decide on a course of action—waiting things out, moving on, working internally for improvement, or filing grievances with higher authorities.

Inability to Get Along with the Boss or the Management

One of the most common difficulties in work environments, especially for people who are employed for the first time, is the inability to tolerate their bosses and the way they perform management tasks in the organization. The boss may be abrupt, insulting, or vague in directions but concrete and specific in criticisms. The employer may be unreasonably neglectful of the job or the boss may make decisions that seem to be inimical to the interests and needs of clients or to the success of the organization. The boss may seem to stifle leadership and creativity and make it difficult for enthusiastic and talented employees to do their best work. Over the years, I have known and worked with many local newspaper and television journalists who have faced difficulties on the job and quit or been fired for doing what seemed to them to be right and proper for the organization's best interests. It is encouraging that later many of them appear on network television, with major assignments, or as reporters with top national newspapers or magazines. I have seen similar career progressions for social workers.

The fact is that management in most organizations is not as good as it ought to be. Many managers of all kinds and in all walks of life, including those in social welfare organizations, are not especially well-prepared for their work. Many have never studied management or supervision of employees and may have been selected for their jobs by default. Some are chosen by others who do not understand or respect sound management behavior. The reality of poor management is that business and government organizations in the United States spend billions of dollars every year training their managements to be more effective. Poor management is a common and expensive problem.

Social work education programs require all baccalaureate and master's students, as has been mentioned, to have some exposure to organization and management ideas because management is so important and because so many social workers spend at least part of their careers managing agencies and the work of others. But despite such efforts, management is still not of the quality that it ought to be and many people find that they clash directly and dramatically with those to whom they report, whether they work in the military, in public and private social services programs, or in hospitals.

Ideally, each employee has the right to make comments and participate in decisions and in managing the organization. However, that is not often the reality. Organizations that operate in those ways often have a lower proportion of disgruntled and disillusioned employees than those that do not. When that is not the style of the organization where workers are employed, it is usually best to do what they are told and to follow the directions of the supervisor. Answering questions, making suggestions, and generally showing an interest in the program may be rewarded with more formal involvement in organizational decision making. If the situation is untenable, it is sometimes necessary to relocate. However, that ought to be a later step, for some of the reasons discussed below.

Dealing with Adversity and Disillusionment on the Job

There are many ways, of course, to deal with problems on the job. The most important is to be prepared for them, and hopefully this chapter will help achieve that objective. Knowing that disappointment or disillusionment is possible is the first step toward dealing with those feelings and reactions to work.

There are many other ways to deal with adversity and job difficulty. It is usually much better to solve the problems at work rather than quitting the job and taking another because, unless the situation is so extreme that it requires immediate departure, a similar problem may be encountered on another job. All jobs have their drawbacks and all jobs are sources of disillusionment for many workers.

The following are some practical steps to take when job difficulties begin:

1. If inability to do the job for reasons of communication skills or others is the basic problem, these skills ought to be improved. That can mean taking a keyboarding course at a local community college. Most college educated people can learn all they need to know about keyboarding in a few weeks and with an investment of a few dollars. Being serious about solving the problem is the major solution. Keyboarding is a minimal skill, compared to psychiatric diagnosis or interviewing a client. But it requires time, effort, and dedication—all of which are worth devoting to it. The same can be true of any other skills. Writing well is a learnable skill that is taught in community colleges everywhere. Taking the time to learn how to spell, use a dictionary or spell checker, how to punctuate, and how to use the proper verb with the proper noun are all important skills that can hurt a career if they are not learned. While one is learning, getting help from others such as secretaries, or colleagues, friends, teachers, or family members with editing reports is a good thing to do, especially if confidentiality is not a concern. I know many very able social workers and a few college professors who call upon their sons and daughters for help with writing. Many of the problematic skills new social workers face are not with their social work skills. They are simple difficulties with basic knowledge and communication.

   2. When the problems are disappointment or displeasure with the behavior of others on the job, it is always a good idea to discuss those concerns with a supervisor. Of course, the supervisor may be the person who is behaving improperly and that may mean a frank discussion with that supervisor. It may also mean some discussion with the executive director or the person to whom the supervisor reports.

   3. It is usually not wise to make accusations or to tattle. For some reason most people resent those who are critical of others even if their behavior is wholly unacceptable. Although it is often useful to talk directly with a supervisor or perhaps the supervisor's supervisor about problems encountered on the job, it is usually not productive to personally criticize others without great amounts of evidence and good reason. However, questions can be asked and those questions do not necessarily need to be tied to someone else's name. If it is an ongoing problem, the supervisor or the higher level manager would probably know about it without your observations, and will or will not do something, depending on the situation. Many times, organizations are not able to deal with personal misbehavior or misconduct, even if they have fairly good evidence that it exists. That is often the reality of the supervisor's job.

   It is often disillusioning for people who have spent most of their lives in school, as I had until I took my first job in my twenties, to see people who drink too much, who fail to do their jobs, who stay out all night and are therefore unable to perform their duties the next day, and who otherwise behave in ways that interfere with effective work. My first jobs were in television news and in the U.S. Army, but social work and higher education are not, I learned, significantly different. There is a problem with inadequate job performance and with improper behavior no matter what the circumstance or the setting.

   Although it may seem right to bring out problems and pass along the information to others, there is virtue in observing before making charges and in watching carefully before talking or drawing conclusions. It is easy to be wrong in making judgments, particularly when a person is in a vulnerable position, that are unjustified or incorrect, or that the organization knows about and has decided not to address. But discretion and caution are always advisable, especially until someone knows what the organization's standards and history are. There is nothing quite so frustrating as giving up on a job or losing it and moving to another job where exactly the same kind of problems exist.

4. When the problem is getting along with the boss, especially an incapable boss, there are several solutions that are at least temporary in nature. Individuals may find it useful to ask for a meeting with the boss to determine if they are doing the job well and if the boss is satisfied with the work or has suggestions for improvement. Even poorly trained and incompetent managers enjoy meeting with people who want to improve their performance and who want guidance. Staying in touch and keeping the lines of communication open are always good resolutions to such problems. Bosses, managers, and supervisors that seem hopelessly unskilled probably want to do better work and need the cooperation and support of their subordinates to perform more adequately. Staying in touch and working to make the job satisfactory are useful on-the-job strategies.

Writers in a popular magazine cite a number of bosses' and supervisors' comments about annoying one's superiors (Wild, D'Agostino, Schulz, Dolan, & Batistick, 2000). Among their examples are employees who: seek constant reaffirmation that they are performing well; fail to do what they're told or who delay in carrying out instructions; fail to tell the truth about mistakes they have made; take credit for the work of others; interrupt conversations with others; fail to keep their offices neat; fail to report serious problems; and regularly come to work late—among several dozen others. Common sense, alone, won't help workers understand possible annoyances they create in their work.

Periodic evaluations can also be requested. In most jobs, as is discussed previously, employees are given regular and formal evaluations. However, that does not prohibit employees who think there may be difficulty on the job from asking for an evaluation of their work—either orally or in writing. If supervisors seem uninterested in the workers or less than enthusiastic about the workers' performance, it is often worthwhile to confront the problem and get an idea of how the supervisors would actually put their observations in writing for the employees. It is also often useful for workers to meet with and obtain an appraisal of their work from someone higher up in the organization, but that should be done only if it is impossible to reach some satisfactory resolution with the immediate supervisor or boss. In some situations, going over the head of a superior is grounds for dismissal and, in almost all situations, arouses the anger of the supervisor and perhaps others.

The purpose of these discussions is to help workers avoid quitting their jobs before they have gained what they can from them in both experience and credentials. As stated previously, employers are suspicious of people who have changed positions too often and too early in their careers. It is also part of the discussion's purpose to help people avoid being terminated involuntarily from jobs. Being fired from a job is a terribly unpleasant experience for most people. It also is a problem that stays on an individual's record. Almost every job application asks if the applicant has ever been terminated involuntarily or fired from a job. Answering honestly is essential but a positive answer may raise questions about the employee's abilities or character.

Client Conflicts and Liability

Workers often have conflicts or find themselves under attack from clients. Social workers deal with such a broad range of sensitive problems that it is not always possible to satisfy those served. At times, a social worker may be blamed for the problems the client or the client's family faces. At times, too, a social worker inadvertently or, because of poor judgment, commits an error in client relations.

For those reasons, it is crucial for every practicing social worker to have some form of liability or malpractice insurance, which will cover the worker in case of a lawsuit or an ethical complaint to the licensing board or the professional association. To be sure one has coverage, the social worker should do one or more of the following:

1. Purchase malpractice insurance from a commercial carrier or a professional association such as NASW, which has low-cost and reliable malpractice policies.
2. Check individual homeowner or other liability insurance to determine whether charges of professional liability or malpractice is covered. Be sure that information is in writing and that the provisions are specifically spelled out. Do not rely on a conversation with an insurance company representative.
3. Determine whether the agency has malpractice insurance for its staff. If it does, it may not be necessary to purchase individual coverage.

It is often wise to have several kinds of coverage, which is generally inexpensive. Most social workers never have a claim of malpractice against them. However, one claim, no matter how justified or unjustified it may be, can wipe out a social worker's savings and create a debt for many years. That is because engaging an attorney for representation in a malpractice or liability case is likely to be costly, whether the worker is found to be liable or not.

Anyone with whom a social worker has professional contacts, including clients, can make complaints in at least three different arenas—the courts, to the licensing board, or, if the worker is a member of NASW, to the state NASW chapter, which has a committee and set of procedures for hearing complaints. The negative consequences of a complaint can be severe—loss of a license, expulsion from NASW, requirements to pay damages to a client or plaintiff, or all three. The ability to provide a defense in such cases is critical and the best way to do so is with insurance coverage. It is especially important to have coverage if a social worker is involved in private social work practice.

Complaints of all kinds can be and are made against social workers—failure to provide services, a charge that can be made by an employer as well as by clients; violating client confidentiality; engaging in sexual relations with clients; financially exploiting a client; and many others based on the codes of ethics of licensing boards and professional associations.

Peer Relations

Sometimes, a worker's difficulties on the job are related to peer problems and difficulties with others because of competition for promotions, jealousies, or other kinds of reactions that may lead to conflict. For most workers, the best course of action is to maintain friendly and positive relationships with every other employee but to avoid close personal ties with fellow workers. Close personal ties, especially if they are romantic in nature, can sour and lead to difficulties at work. It is sometimes wise to choose friends away from work, while maintaining only friendly relationships at work.

A special peer-relations issue involves working with support staff or secretaries. Professional social workers are usually paid much more than secretaries in their organizations and also have higher status than the support staff. However, acting in authoritarian ways with support staff may cause others to consider the social worker arrogant or insensitive. It is also true that secretaries and other support staff members often possess and exercise enormous power in social welfare agencies. Many top organization managers have more faith in the opinions and suggestions of support staff members than they do of newly employed social workers. They can also help directly with office arrangements and supplies, completing work on a timely schedule, and many other practical necessities. Moreover, they have the power to render the social worker ineffective. A story about restaurants, which may not be true, is that servers who treat cooks poorly do not receive their food orders correctly or in a timely manner. The analogy of social workers with secretaries is applicable. Most support staff members view themselves as professionals who are as capable of carrying out their duties as other employees. Treating support staff members, maintenance staff, and others with respect and learning how to work effectively with them can be a major factor in job success. Working effectively in an organization is more difficult than it might seem, and staying on the job can be complex.

Unions and Employee Associations

Some social agencies have labor unions or employee associations to which their workers belong. The social work labor union movement, though not enormous, is relatively large, especially in states that are heavily unionized in other kinds of employment. The National Association of Social Workers staff is one example of a social work employment setting that is unionized. In unionized employment, unfair evaluations and negative relations with bosses as well as peer relations problems may be reduced because the work rules are carefully spelled out in union contracts. For some social workers, a job in a unionized setting is especially attractive. Grievance and appeals procedures as well as most other aspects of the work situation are likely to be spelled out in the union contract, which is periodically renegotiated.

Employee associations are more likely to be voluntary than are unions, although either may represent employees with the employing organization on issues such as compensation and working conditions. There are two kinds of employee organization arrangements, especially in terms of unions. One is the union shop in which all employees are required to either join the union or, if they prefer not being members, to pay the equivalent of dues to the union nevertheless. In the second arrangement, the open shop, union membership is voluntary.

However, in both situations, employees and employers may collectively bargain, or agree to employment conditions and arrangements that are mutually satisfactory and which become binding on all employees, members or not.

In most situations, if there is a union or an employee association, it is wise to affiliate with it and participate in its activities as a way of influencing individual work and having a voice in employment arrangements.

Employee Burnout

Burnout is one of the problems that social workers face, as do people in any other occupations and professions. This is characteristically a feeling that an individual is no longer useful, becoming cynical on the job and about work, and loss of enthusiasm. Many times the manifestations of burnout are much more severe than these suggestions would indicate. Employees who are burned out may become ineffective and alienated from their jobs. It is important to recognize the signs of burnout and to cope with them through taking leaves of absence, counseling with others, transferring and learning new skills, or even changing jobs. The phenomenon of burnout has been a sufficient problem for many social workers and many social agencies and some of the literature on the subject helps explain it (Arches, 1991; Bly, 2000).

One important step for avoiding burnout is to protect oneself from becoming a workaholic. There is nothing inherently wrong with working hard or long. Being dedicated to a program is admirable. However, if work becomes all-consuming, it is important to recognize it and develop some balance. Bernstein and Ma (1996) suggest some telltale signs of becoming a workaholic: using work life to avoid social commitments; letting work life interfere with family life; spending fifty hours or more per week on the job; letting work keep one from having other interests and hobbies. Being a workaholic is often a clear route to burnout, which helps neither the clients nor the organization.

Time Management

For most professionals, the primary asset they own is their time. In essence, professionals sell their expertise and provide that expertise to others in the time that they have available. Wasting professional time is a major error for social workers and other professionals. It is also often tempting for social workers to forget their priorities and use their efforts on other worthwhile but low-priority activities instead of those that are most important to their professional responsibilities.

For example, some workers become so involved in their professional associations that they limit the number of contacts they may have with clients though, in most cases, client work should have a higher priority during working hours than professional association business. Sometimes workers may become so involved in consulting work that they neglect the core responsibility of providing services to their agency's clients. Social work educators who neglect their students and their courses or do not spend their extra time writing articles and conducting research, which have high priority in colleges and universities, may damage their careers. Knowing what to do and doing it is a simple but central rule for effective social work practice.

A key to on-the-job success is effectively managing time, which entails appearing for and performing all responsibilities. A good attendance record is a requirement in most jobs and certainly a requirement for job success. Although social workers should not come to work when they have contagious health conditions or are too ill to perform their duties, staying at home is a serious decision, even if one has accrued sick leave. Workers do not want to develop a reputation for missing work or for being too ill to work regularly or for staying away and making excuses for doing so. Sick leave is a humane fringe benefit that allows people to continue earning if they are too ill to work. It should never be used as a substitute for vacation time. More important, performing a job well means being available to do so. Some have suggested that much of life consists of simply showing up—being around. That is partly true in social work, just as it is in other fields.

Perhaps a greater problem than problematic attendance is failing to keep appointments or to attend required meetings without an excuse. Most social workers avoid those problems by keeping carefully constructed calendars with all their appointments and meetings listed by date and time. Many others use more complex, formal time management systems that help them allocate their working hours to plan, provide services, to develop professional activities such as keeping current with the professional literature, consulting with colleagues, providing community service, supervising others, receiving supervision, and writing records. There are many systems sold in office supply stores and through management consulting organizations (Priority Management, Dayrunner, and Day-Timers are examples) that provide forms, charts, instructions, and, sometimes, classes to help with time management. A large range of electronic planners made by the major electronics firms such as Casio, Hewlett-Packard, and Sharp are effective devices for keeping schedules. Computer software programs are also available for entering appointments and keeping track of them. For some, a simple office calendar is as effective as the more expensive time management systems and equipment. Consulting the calendar each day and updating it every time a change is made will help the social worker avoid conflicts and ensure that everything necessary is accomplished.

Whatever procedures a worker follows, it is critical to have some arrangement to ensure that scheduled professional activities are not forgotten. More specifically, the ability to set priorities and to have some control over time is critical. An address book or address listing on an electronic organizer or computer is also essential. Keeping track of clients, colleagues, collateral service providers, and others is the basis for effective work. Others keep business cards in special business card organizers, which also are the basis for a good address book and directory.

Staying Healthy

Maintaining good health is a prerequisite for everything else accomplished on the job. There are rules for good health maintenance that have been documented by health researchers and that are part of the Bureau of the Census's periodic studies of samples of the population. Those who follow those practices are less likely to become ill. Older people who follow the following rules are as healthy as younger people:

- Keep your weight down
- Don't eat between meals
- Exercise regularly
- Eat breakfast
- Drink alcohol only moderately
- Don't smoke cigarettes

It is notable that none of these rules mention periodic visits to a physician, or regular checkups, or medicines, or even vitamin pills. Mostly, they are about not drinking heavily or smoking cigarettes (two major causes of preventable illness), exercising, and maintaining sound eating habits. Contrary to everything written about cholesterol and other nutritional issues, the rules suggest that simply avoiding eating too much is the key to adequate diet. These rules will not necessarily prevent cancer or heart disease or save someone from an accidental death in an automobile. However, they appear to be excellent guides to maintaining health for most people at most times.

Exercise is valuable not only for good health but also for mental health. Many people find that they are able to overcome anxiety, frustration, and other discomforting feelings through exercise. According to *Time* magazine (July 22, 1996) quoting a Surgeon General's report, a fourth of Americans do not exercise regularly. The same report suggests that people can burn 150 calories in a variety of ways, some of which take more time but less vigorous exercise than others. The report suggests exercising the equivalent of twenty minutes or more three times per week, depending on the intensity of the exercise. For example, jumping rope, running ten-minute miles or faster, and playing basketball are more likely to provide sufficient exercise in a few minutes than washing and waxing a car, fishing, or walking. However, the value of physical activity is clearly demonstrated as a factor in building and maintaining health—mental as well as physical.

Credit and Finances

How earnings are managed is a factor in how satisfied and successful an employee is able to be. Although social work salaries are not large, on average they are generally comfortable. And, as Chapter 5 on salaries and fringe benefits shows, most social workers are able to make economic progress throughout their careers.

Managing individual funds is a complex problem for many Americans and, for many, a social problem. In fact, one type of work social workers perform with clients is credit counseling—helping people unravel financial difficulties that often result from circumstances or from simply spending more money than they earn. For most wage earners, some kind of plan or budget for handling family income is critical. Knowing in advance how the available money will be spent is a major step in avoiding overspending.

A sound budget includes sufficient funds for basics such as food, clothing, shelter, and health care (the deductible portions not covered by insurance in particular). An employee must always consider deductions from take-home pay. Actual, disposable income is always significantly less than the overall earnings, after taxes, Social Security, retirement contributions, and health insurance deductions are made. Some experts on family economics suggest that one-fourth to one-third of the family income be allocated for rent or house payments, which is probably a reasonable estimate.

In addition, one needs to allocate funds for unexpected expenses such as illnesses, major auto repairs, and other contingencies. Planning for the unplanned is always a good idea. In fact, some recent analyses show that many bankruptcies are the result not of overspending but of expensive crises such as serious automobile accidents and major illnesses, both costing money for treatment and care but also often costing months or years of income from wage earners who are at least temporarily unable to work.

Several principles appear to apply to effective budgeting and finance and they are summarized here:

1. Be cautious with credit and interest. More people face financial crises because they overuse credit such as installment accounts and credit cards than for most other reasons. It is important to remember that credit debt is often easy to obtain but difficult to pay off. Stores, banks, finance companies, and credit card companies offer credit constantly, often in amounts greater than many wage earners should assume. That is their business—they sell money at a profit. They loan the debtor $1,000 and, in return, they are to be paid pack $1,100, more or less. They have allowed someone to use their money, which costs them something, too, for a fee that is greater than their costs. That is one of the primary means in which those who provide credit earn their profits.

However, excessive credit can be financially deadly. For one thing, interest is simply an expense and does not provide the payer with anything other than the convenience of paying for a purchase over a long period of time, instead of paying cash. It is likely that for many people, interest is their largest single expenditure each year—interest on a house, car, appliances, and credit card purchases. Often, the cost of interest is hidden or unapparent to the payer. A car payment of $300 per month may be almost all interest, at least in the early part of the purchase.

However, one thinks not of interest but of car payments. Interest rates for cars may be advertised as 10 or 12 percent but a four-year car loan carries 10 or 12 percent interest per year times four years so that the overall interest for the car may total close to 50 percent. On credit cards, if only the minimum requirement is paid, the combination of principal and interest may require many years to repay, even for a relatively small amount of debt. Some people are so accustomed to some forms of debt, such as monthly auto and house payments, that they do not think in terms of erasing their debt but only about the amounts of their payments. An acquaintance showed me his new car, on which he had traded another car, that was still not paid for. As he put it, "And my monthly payments only went up $20 for a much better car." Of course, he extended the number of years he had to make payments. And it never appeared to occur to him that he might be able to free himself of debt by not exchanging cars. Another acquaintance, when he learned home mortgage interest rates were declining, refinanced his house mortgage at lower rates and reduced his payments. But he had enough savings to pay off the existing mortgage and thereafter to pay no payments and no interest at all. Although he thought his money, which was invested in stocks, was better kept in savings, his interest costs were one of his largest annual expenditures. At the rate he was paying, with interest and principal combined, his house would cost twice or three times the purchase price—he would pay $200,000 to $300,000 for a $100,000 house over thirty years. Few investments would yield as much benefit, even with the tax deduction for home mortgage interest.

2. When possible, pay cash or charge the expenditure to a credit card and pay it off before the interest is added. Saving the money for a cash purchase and avoiding interest simply spreads money further. Pay for the item over two years at ten percent interest and it instantly costs 20 percent more.

Saving money for the same number of years as one would make payments and buying an automobile, for example, for cash, would require much smaller monthly payments—payments to themselves.

3. Buying a house with a home loan is a reasonable use of credit. Few people can purchase a house with cash and, therefore, they have to pay interest to borrow the money. But look at an amortization schedule. In the early years of the loan, a person is likely to be paying less than $50 toward principal in a $500 per month mortgage payment. Of course, the remaining $450 is deductible from federal and most state income taxes, another factor that makes borrowing money for a house more reasonable than borrowing for other purposes. The house can also be the basis for a loan, using the house equity for collateral. And the interest on that kind of loan, unlike store or credit card interest, is tax deductible. If a person needs to borrow money for a car or other major purchase, the home loan is often the lowest cost. Many consumer advisors urge those who are paying mortgages to make the equivalent of an extra monthly payment each year. That will help pay off the mortgage much more rapidly with a much lower expenditure on interest.

4. Save money. When it is possible at all, most people find it wise to build some savings. Even small monthly dollar amounts of ten percent of after-tax income can make a difference in financial security. It is especially reassuring to have a month's or six month's, or a year's income in savings. That becomes a cushion on which to rely in difficult times. It can also be the basis for an investment account and a broker's services. Savings need not be in bank savings accounts or certificates of deposit.

There are often advantages to other kinds of savings. Tax-sheltered annuities, available from stock brokers and insurance companies, allow savings with dollars that are not taxed until the annuities are cashed in at an advanced age. There are penalties for cashing them in early, unless the money is withdrawn in small increments over a period of years. Mutual funds, which are combinations of stocks, can be purchased a little at a time over a period of years after a small initial purchase. Generally, sound stocks that are held for long periods pay better than bank savings account interest. Of course, saving money is a good way to avoid interest, by purchasing needed items for cash rather than with interest payments.

Some of the above suggestions are simply mechanisms for living within individual means—the essence of smart personal budgeting and economics. Smart personal finances can make a great difference in your career and life. They are worth considering a high priority.

Conclusion

The following are basic suggestions that summarize some of the content in this chapter:

1. Stay on the job for as long as it makes sense. Unless an offer of a new job is for much better work in an area that is especially exciting, that pays more, and that offers significant career advancement, it is usually best to keep a job for at least two, and preferably three years. It takes months to learn how to do a job and a person is only productive after learning the basics. It also looks much better on a resumé for someone to have several years on a job rather than only a few months or just a year.

2. Learn to do the job well. If that means extra preparation and training or help from friends or colleagues or family members, or investing in a course of study, use whatever is necessary to perform as well as is possible.

3. Watch and listen but be careful about judging the behavior of others in the organization. It is especially important to avoid conflict, whistle blowing, and carrying tales until it is known what the organization's norms and standards are and until it is understood what the organization has tolerated and is willing to tolerate from its employees.

4. Get along with the supervisor or boss as best as possible. It is up to the worker to take the initiative to keep the relationship positive by going to meetings, asking for advice, and otherwise trying to maintain positive connections with the boss. It is all right and sometimes advisable to ask for a performance evaluation. The boss is likely to be positive about a worker who cares about performing well.

5. Avoid burnout and avoid becoming a workaholic.

6. Assure yourself that you are covered by malpractice or liability insurance with either your own policy or one provided by the agency.

7. Time is the most valuable asset. Manage it carefully and effectively.

8. Come to work and be available.

9. Keep a good listing—by address book, electronic organizer, or computer—of all those who are important to your work.

10. Stay healthy through proper diet and exercise.

The National Association of Social Workers Code of Ethics

Approved by the 1996 NASW Delegate Assembly and revised by the 1999 NASW Delegate Assembly.

Overview

The *NASW Code of Ethics* is intended to serve as a guide to the everyday professional conduct of social workers. This *Code* includes four sections. The first section, "Preamble," summarizes the social work profession's mission and core values. The second section, "Purpose of the *NASW Code of Ethics*," provides an overview of the *Code*'s main functions and a brief guide for dealing with ethical issues or dilemmas in social work practice. The third section, "Ethical Principles," presents broad ethical principles, based on social work's core values, that inform social work practice. The final section, "Ethical Standards," includes specific ethical standards to guide social workers' conduct and to provide a basis for adjudication.

Preamble

The primary mission of the social work profession is to enhance human well-being and help meet the basic human needs of all people, with particular attention to the needs and empowerment of people who are vulnerable, oppressed, and living in poverty. A historic and defining feature of social work is the profession's focus on individual well-being in a social context and the well-being of society. Fundamental to social work is attention to the environmental forces that create, contribute to, and address problems in living.

Social workers promote social justice and social change with and on behalf of clients. "Clients" is used inclusively to refer to individuals, families, groups, organizations, and communities. Social workers are sensitive to cultural and ethnic diversity and strive to end discrimination, oppression, poverty, and other forms of social injustice. These activities may be in the form of direct practice, community organizing, supervision, consultation, administration, advocacy, social and political action, policy development and implementation, education, and research and evaluation. Social workers seek to enhance the capacity of people to address their own needs. Social workers also seek to promote the responsiveness of organizations, communities, and other social institutions to individuals' needs and social problems.

The mission of the social work profession is rooted in a set of core values. These core values, embraced by social workers throughout the profession's history, are the foundation of social work's unique purpose and perspective:

- service
- social justice
- dignity and worth of the person

- importance of human relationships
- integrity
- competence.

This constellation of core values reflects what is unique to the social work profession. Core values, and the principles that flow from them, must be balanced within the context and complexity of the human experience.

Purpose of the NASW Code of Ethics
Professional ethics are at the core of social work. The profession has an obligation to articulate its basic values, ethical principles, and ethical standards. The *NASW Code of Ethics* sets forth these values, principles, and standards to guide social workers' conduct. The *Code* is relevant to all social workers and social work students, regardless of their professional functions, the settings in which they work, or the populations they serve.

The *NASW Code of Ethics* serves six purposes:

1. The *Code* identifies core values on which social work's mission is based.

2. The *Code* summarizes broad ethical principles that reflect the profession's core values and establishes a set of specific ethical standards that should be used to guide social work practice.

3. The *Code* is designed to help social workers identify relevant considerations when professional obligations conflict or ethical uncertainties arise.

4. The *Code* provides ethical standards to which the general public can hold the social work profession accountable.

5. The *Code* socializes practitioners new to the field to social work's mission, values, ethical principles, and ethical standards.

6. The *Code* articulates standards that the social work profession itself can use to assess whether social workers have engaged in unethical conduct. NASW has formal procedures to adjudicate ethics complaints filed against its members.[1] In subscribing to this *Code,* social workers are required to cooperate in its implementation, participate in NASW adjudication proceedings, and abide

by any NASW disciplinary rulings or sanctions based on it.

The *Code* offers a set of values, principles, and standards to guide decision making and conduct when ethical issues arise. It does not provide a set of rules that prescribe how social workers should act in all situations. Specific applications of the *Code* must take into account the context in which it is being considered and the possibility of conflicts among the *Code*'s values, principles, and standards. Ethical responsibilities flow from all human relationships, from the personal and familial to the social and professional.

Further, the *NASW Code of Ethics* does not specify which values, principles, and standards are most important and ought to outweigh others in instances when they conflict. Reasonable differences of opinion can and do exist among social workers with respect to the ways in which values, ethical principles, and ethical standards should be rank ordered when they conflict. Ethical decision making in a given situation must apply the informed judgment of the individual social worker and should also consider how the issues would be judged in a peer review process where the ethical standards of the profession would be applied.

Ethical decision making is a process. There are many instances in social work where simple answers are not available to resolve complex ethical issues. Social workers should take into consideration all the values, principles, and standards in this *Code* that are relevant to any situation in which ethical judgment is warranted. Social workers' decisions and actions should be consistent with the spirit as well as the letter of this *Code.*

In addition to this *Code,* there are many other sources of information about ethical thinking that may be useful. Social workers should consider ethical theory and principles generally, social work theory and research, laws, regulations, agency policies, and other

---

[1]For information on NASW adjudication procedures, see *NASW Procedures for the Adjudication of Grievances.*

relevant codes of ethics, recognizing that among codes of ethics social workers should consider the *NASW Code of Ethics* as their primary source. Social workers also should be aware of the impact on ethical decision making of their clients' and their own personal values and cultural and religious beliefs and practices. They should be aware of any conflicts between personal and professional values and deal with them responsibly. For additional guidance social workers should consult the relevant literature on professional ethics and ethical decision making and seek appropriate consultation when faced with ethical dilemmas. This may involve consultation with an agency-based or social work organization's ethics committee, a regulatory body, knowledgeable colleagues, supervisors, or legal counsel.

Instances may arise when social workers' ethical obligations conflict with agency policies or relevant laws or regulations. When such conflicts occur, social workers must make a responsible effort to resolve the conflict in a manner that is consistent with the values, principles, and standards expressed in this *Code*. If a reasonable resolution of the conflict does not appear possible, social workers should seek proper consultation before making a decision.

The *NASW Code of Ethics* is to be used by NASW and by individuals, agencies, organizations, and bodies (such as licensing and regulatory boards, professional liability insurance providers, courts of law, agency boards of directors, government agencies, and other professional groups) that choose to adopt it or use it as a frame of reference. Violation of standards in this *Code* does not automatically imply legal liability or violation of the law. Such determination can only be made in the context of legal and judicial proceedings. Alleged violations of the *Code* would be subject to a peer review process. Such processes are generally separate from legal or administrative procedures and insulated from legal review or proceedings to allow the profession to counsel and discipline its own members.

A code of ethics cannot guarantee ethical behavior. Moreover, a code of ethics cannot resolve all ethical issues or disputes or capture the richness and complexity involved in striving to make responsible choices within a moral community. Rather, a code of ethics sets forth values, ethical principles, and ethical standards to which professionals aspire and by which their actions can be judged. Social workers' ethical behavior should result from their personal commitment to engage in ethical practice. The *NASW Code of Ethics* reflects the commitment of all social workers to uphold the profession's values and to act ethically. Principles and standards must be applied by individuals of good character who discern moral questions and, in good faith, seek to make reliable ethical judgments.

Ethical Principles
The following broad ethical principles are based on social work's core values of service, social justice, dignity and worth of the person, importance of human relationships, integrity, and competence. These principles set forth ideals to which all social workers should aspire.

Value: *Service*
Ethical Principle: *Social workers' primary goal is to help people in need and to address social problems.*

Social workers elevate service to others above self-interest. Social workers draw on their knowledge, values, and skills to help people in need and to address social problems. Social workers are encouraged to volunteer some portion of their professional skills with no expectation of significant financial return (pro bono service).

Value: *Social Justice*
Ethical Principle: *Social workers challenge social injustice.*

Social workers pursue social change, particularly with and on behalf of vulnerable and oppressed individuals and groups of people. Social workers' social change efforts are focused primarily on issues of poverty, unemployment, discrimination, and other forms of social injustice. These activities seek to promote sensitivity to and knowledge about oppression and cultural and ethnic diversity. Social workers strive to ensure access to needed information, services, and resources; equality of opportunity; and meaningful participation in decision making for all people.

Value: *Dignity and Worth of the Person*
Ethical Principle: *Social workers respect the inherent dignity and worth of the person.*

Social workers treat each person in a caring and respectful fashion, mindful of individual differences and cultural and ethnic diversity. Social workers promote clients' socially responsible self-determination. Social workers seek to enhance clients' capacity and opportunity to change and to address their own needs. Social workers are cognizant of their dual responsibility to clients and to the broader society. They seek to resolve conflicts between clients' interest and the broader society's interests in a socially responsible manner consistent with the values, ethical principles, and ethical standards of the profession.

Value: *Importance of Human Relationships*
Ethical Principle: *Social workers recognize the central importance of human relationships.*

Social workers understand that relationships between and among people are an important vehicle for change. Social workers engage people as partners in the helping process. Social workers seek to strengthen relationships among people in a purposeful effort to promote, restore, maintain, and enhance the well-being of individuals, families, social groups, organizations, and communities.

Value: *Integrity*
Ethical Principle: *Social workers behave in a trustworthy manner.*

Social workers are continually aware of the profession's mission, values, ethical principles, and ethical standards and practice in a manner consistent with them. Social workers act honestly and responsibly and promote ethical practices on the part of the organizations with which they are affiliated.

Value: *Competence*
Ethical Principle: *Social workers practice within their areas of competence and develop and enhance their professional expertise.*

Social workers continually strive to increase their professional knowledge and skills and to apply them in practice. Social workers should aspire to contribute to the knowledge base of the profession.

Ethical Standards
The following ethical standards are relevant to the professional activities of all social workers. These standards concern (1) social workers' ethical responsibilities to clients, (2) social workers' ethical responsibilities to colleagues, (3) social workers' ethical responsibilities in practice settings, (4) social workers' ethical responsibilities as professionals, (5) social workers' ethical responsibilities to the social work profession, and (6) social workers' ethical responsibilities to the broader society.

Some of the standards that follow are enforceable guidelines for professional conduct, and some are aspirational. The extent to which each standard is enforceable is a matter of professional judgment to be exercised by those responsible for reviewing alleged violations of ethical standards.

1. Social Workers' Ethical Responsibilities to Clients

1.01 Commitment to Clients
Social workers' primary responsibility is to promote the well-being of clients. In general, clients' interests are primary. However, social workers' responsibility to the larger society or specific legal obligations may on limited occasions supersede the loyalty owed clients, and clients should be so advised. (Examples include when a social worker is required by law to report that a client has abused a child or has threatened to harm self or others.)

1.02 Self-Determination
Social workers respect and promote the right of clients to self-determination and assist clients in their efforts to identify and clarify their goals. Social workers may limit clients' right to self-determination when, in the social workers' professional judgment, clients' actions or potential actions pose a serious, foreseeable, and imminent risk to themselves or others.

1.03 Informed Consent

(a) Social workers should provide services to clients only in the context of a professional relationship based, when appropriate, on valid informed consent. Social workers should use clear and understandable language to inform clients of the purpose of the services, risks related to the services, limits to services because of the requirements of a third-party payer, relevant costs, reasonable alternatives, clients' right to refuse or withdraw consent, and the time frame covered by the consent. Social workers should provide clients with an opportunity to ask questions.

(b) In instances when clients are not literate or have difficulty understanding the primary language used in the practice setting, social workers should take steps to ensure clients' comprehension. This may include providing clients with a detailed verbal explanation or arranging for a qualified interpreter or translator whenever possible.

(c) In instances when clients lack the capacity to provide informed consent, social workers should protect clients' interests by seeking permission from an appropriate third party, informing clients consistent with the clients' level of understanding. In such instances social workers should seek to ensure that the third party acts in a manner consistent with clients' wishes and interests. Social workers should take reasonable steps to enhance such clients' ability to give informed consent.

(d) In instances when clients are receiving services involuntarily, social workers should provide information about the nature and extent of services and about the extent of clients' right to refuse service.

(e) Social workers who provide services via electronic media (such as computer, telephone, radio, and television) should inform recipients of the limitations and risks associated with such services.

(f) Social workers should obtain clients' informed consent before audiotaping or videotaping clients or permitting observation of services to clients by a third party.

1.04 Competence

(a) Social workers should provide services and represent themselves as competent only within the boundaries of their education, training, license, certification, consultation received, supervised experience, or other relevant professional experience.

(b) Social workers should provide services in substantive areas or use intervention techniques or approaches that are new to them only after engaging in appropriate study, training, consultation, and supervision from people who are competent in those interventions or techniques.

(c) When generally recognized standards do not exist with respect to an emerging area of practice, social workers should exercise careful judgment and take responsible steps (including appropriate education, research, training, consultation, and supervision) to ensure the competence of their work and to protect clients from harm.

1.05 Cultural Competence and Social Diversity

(a) Social workers should understand culture and its function in human behavior and society, recognizing the strengths that exist in all cultures.

(b) Social workers should have a knowledge base of their clients' cultures and be able to demonstrate competence in the provision of services that are sensitive to clients' cultures and to differences among people and cultural groups.

(c) Social workers should obtain education about and seek to understand the nature of social diversity and oppression with respect to race, ethnicity, national origin, color, sex, sexual orientation, age, marital status, political belief, religion, and mental or physical disability.

1.06 Conflicts of Interest

(a) Social workers should be alert to and avoid conflicts of interest that interfere with the exercise of professional discretion and impartial judgment. Social workers should inform clients when a real or potential conflict of interest arises and take reasonable steps to resolve the issue in a manner that makes the clients' interests primary and protects clients' interests to the greatest extent possible. In some cases, protecting clients' interests may require termination of the professional relationship with proper referral of the client.

(b) Social workers should not take unfair advantage of any professional relationship or exploit others to further their personal, religious, political, or business interests.

(c) Social workers should not engage in dual or multiple relationships with clients or former clients in which there is a risk of exploitation or potential harm to the client. In instances when dual or multiple relationships are unavoidable, social workers should take steps to protect clients and are responsible for setting clear, appropriate, and culturally sensitive boundaries. (Dual or multiple relationships occur when social workers relate to clients in more than one relationship, whether professional, social, or business. Dual or multiple relationships can occur simultaneously or consecutively.)

(d) When social workers provide services to two or more people who have a relationship with each other (for example, couples, family members), social workers should clarify with all parties which individuals will be considered clients and the nature of social workers' professional obligations to the various individuals who are receiving services. Social workers who anticipate a conflict of interest among the individuals receiving services or who anticipate having to perform in potentially conflicting roles (for example, when a social worker is asked to testify in a child custody dispute or divorce proceedings involving clients) should clarify their role with the parties involved and take appropriate action to minimize any conflict of interest.

1.07 Privacy and Confidentiality

(a) Social workers should respect clients' right to privacy. Social workers should not solicit private information from clients unless it is essential to providing services or conducting social work evaluation or research. Once private information is shared, standards of confidentiality apply.

(b) Social workers may disclose confidential information when appropriate with valid consent from a client or a person legally authorized to consent on behalf of a client.

(c) Social workers should protect the confidentiality of all information obtained in the course of professional service, except for compelling professional reasons. The general expectation that social workers will keep information confidential does not apply when disclosure is necessary to prevent serious, foreseeable, and imminent harm to a client or other identifiable person. In all instances, social workers should disclose the least amount of confidential information necessary to achieve the desired purpose; only information that is directly relevant to the purpose for which the disclosure is made should be revealed.

(d) Social workers should inform clients, to the extent possible, about the disclosure of confidential information and the potential consequences, when feasible before the disclosure is made. This applies whether social workers disclose confidential information on the basis of a legal requirement or client consent.

(e) Social workers should discuss with clients and other interested parties the nature of confidentiality and limitations of clients' right to confidentiality. Social workers should review with clients circumstances where confidential information may be requested and where disclosure of confidential information may be legally required. This discussion should occur as soon as possible in the social worker–client relationship and as needed throughout the course of the relationship.

(f) When social workers provide counseling services to families, couples, or groups, social workers should seek agreement among the parties involved concerning each individual's right to confidentiality and obligation to preserve the confidentiality of information shared by others. Social workers should inform participants in family, couples, or group counseling that social workers cannot guarantee that all participants will honor such agreements.

(g) Social workers should inform clients involved in family, couples, marital, or group counseling of the social worker's, employer's, and agency's policy concerning the social worker's disclosure of confidential information among the parties involved in the counseling.

(h) Social workers should not disclose confidential information to third-party payers unless clients have authorized such disclosure.

(i) Social workers should not discuss confidential information in any setting unless privacy can be ensured. Social workers should not discuss confidential information in public or semipublic areas such as hallways, waiting rooms, elevators, and restaurants.

(j) Social workers should protect the confidentiality of clients during legal proceedings to the extent permitted by law. When a court of law or other legally authorized body orders social workers to disclose confidential or privileged information without a client's consent and such disclosure could cause harm to the client, social workers should request that the court withdraw or limit the order as narrowly as possible or maintain the records under seal, unavailable for public inspection.

(k) Social workers should protect the confidentiality of clients when responding to requests from members of the media.

(l) Social workers should protect the confidentiality of clients' written and electronic records and other sensitive information. Social workers should take reasonable steps to ensure that clients' records are stored in a secure location and that clients' records are not available to others who are not authorized to have access.

(m) Social workers should take precautions to ensure and maintain the confidentiality of information transmitted to other parties through the use of computers, electronic mail, facsimile machines, telephones and telephone answering machines, and other electronic or computer technology. Disclosure of identifying information should be avoided whenever possible.

(n) Social workers should transfer or dispose of clients' records in a manner that protects clients' confidentiality and is consistent with state statutes governing records and social work licensure.

(o) Social workers should take reasonable precautions to protect client confidentiality in the event of the social worker's termination of practice, incapacitation, or death.

(p) Social workers should not disclose identifying information when discussing clients for teaching or training purposes unless the client has consented to disclosure of confidential information.

(q) Social workers should not disclose identifying information when discussing clients with consultants unless the client has consented to disclosure of confidential information or there is a compelling need for such disclosure.

(r) Social workers should protect the confidentiality of deceased clients consistent with the preceding standards.

1.08 Access to Records

(a) Social workers should provide clients with reasonable access to records concerning the clients. Social workers who are concerned that clients' access to their records could cause serious misunderstanding or harm to the client should provide assistance in interpreting the records and consultation with the client regarding the records. Social workers should limit clients' access to their records, or portions of their records, only in exceptional circumstances when there is compelling evidence that such access would cause serious harm to the client. Both clients' requests and the rationale for withholding some or all of the record should be documented in clients' files.

(b) When providing clients with access to their records, social workers should take steps to protect the confidentiality of other individuals identified or discussed in such records.

1.09 Sexual Relationships

(a) Social workers should under no circumstances engage in sexual activities or sexual contact with current clients, whether such contact is consensual or forced.

(b) Social workers should not engage in sexual activities or sexual contact with clients' relatives or other individuals with whom clients maintain a close personal relationship when there is a risk of exploitation or potential harm to the client. Sexual activity or sexual contact with clients' relatives or other individuals with whom clients maintain a personal relationship has the potential to be harmful to the client and may make it difficult for the social worker and client to maintain appropriate professional boundaries. Social workers—not their clients, their clients' relatives, or other individuals with whom the client maintains a personal relationship—assume the full burden for setting clear, appropriate, and culturally sensitive boundaries.

(c) Social workers should not engage in sexual activities or sexual contact with former clients because of the potential for harm to the client. If social workers engage in conduct contrary to this prohibition or claim that an exception to this prohibition is warranted due to extraordinary circumstances, it is social workers—not their clients—who assume the full burden of demonstrating that the former client has not been exploited, coerced, or manipulated, intentionally or unintentionally.

(d) Social workers should not provide clinical services to individuals with whom they have had a prior sexual relationship. Providing clinical services to a former sexual partner has the potential to be harmful to the individual and is likely to make it difficult for the social worker and individual to maintain appropriate professional boundaries.

1.10 Physical Contact

Social workers should not engage in physical contact with clients when there is a possibility of psychological harm to the client as a result of the contact (such as cradling or caressing clients). Social workers who engage in appropriate physical contact with clients are responsible for setting clear, appropriate, and culturally sensitive boundaries that govern such physical contact.

1.11 Sexual Harassment

Social workers should not sexually harass clients. Sexual harassment includes sexual advances, sexual solicitation, requests for sexual favors, and other verbal or physical conduct of a sexual nature.

1.12 Derogatory Language

Social workers should not use derogatory language in their written or verbal communications to or about clients. Social workers should use accurate and respectful language in all communications to and about clients.

1.13 Payment for Services

(a) When setting fees, social workers should ensure that the fees are fair, reasonable, and commensurate with the services performed. Consideration should be given to clients' ability to pay.

(b) Social workers should avoid accepting goods or services from clients as payment for professional services. Bartering arrangements, particularly involving services, create the potential for conflicts of interest, exploitation, and inappropriate boundaries in social workers' relationships with clients. Social workers should explore and may participate in bartering only in very limited circumstances when it can be demonstrated that such arrangements are an accepted practice among professionals in the local community, considered to be essential for the provision of services, negotiated without coercion, and entered into at the client's initiative and with the client's informed consent. Social workers who accept goods or services from clients as payment for professional services assume the full burden of demonstrating that this arrangement will not be detrimental to the client or the professional relationship.

(c) Social workers should not solicit a private fee or other remuneration for providing services to clients who are entitled to such available services through the social workers' employer or agency.

1.14 Clients Who Lack Decision-Making Capacity

When social workers act on behalf of clients who lack the capacity to make informed decisions, social workers should take reasonable steps to safeguard the interests and rights of those clients.

1.15 Interruption of Services

Social workers should make reasonable efforts to ensure continuity of services in the event that services are interrupted by factors such as unavailability, relocation, illness, disability, or death.

1.16 Termination of Services

(a) Social workers should terminate services to clients and professional relationships with them when such services and relationships are no longer required or no longer serve the clients' needs or interests.

(b) Social workers should take reasonable steps to avoid abandoning clients who are still in need of services. Social workers should withdraw services precipitously only under unusual circumstances, giving careful consideration to all factors in the situation and taking care to minimize possible adverse effects. Social workers should assist in making appropriate arrangements for continuation of services when necessary.

(c) Social workers in fee-for-service settings may terminate services to clients who are not paying an overdue balance if the financial contractual arrangements have been made clear to the client, if the client does not pose an imminent danger to self or others, and if the clinical and other consequences of the current nonpayment have been addressed and discussed with the client.

(d) Social workers should not terminate services to pursue a social, financial, or sexual relationship with a client.

(e) Social workers who anticipate the termination or interruption of services to clients should notify clients promptly and seek the transfer, referral, or continuation of services in relation to the clients' needs and preferences.

(f) Social workers who are leaving an employment setting should inform clients of appropriate options for the continuation of services and of the benefits and risks of the options.

2. Social Workers' Ethical Responsibilities to Colleagues

2.01 Respect
(a) Social workers should treat colleagues with respect and should represent accurately and fairly the qualifications, views, and obligations of colleagues.

(b) Social workers should avoid unwarranted negative criticism of colleagues in communications with clients or with other professionals. Unwarranted negative criticism may include demeaning comments that refer to colleagues' level of competence or to individuals' attributes such as race, ethnicity, national origin, color, sex, sexual orientation, age, marital status, political belief, religion, and mental or physical disability.

(c) Social workers should cooperate with social work colleagues and with colleagues of other professions when such cooperation serves the well-being of clients.

2.02 Confidentiality
Social workers should respect confidential information shared by colleagues in the course of their professional relationships and transactions. Social workers should ensure that such colleagues understand social workers' obligation to respect confidentiality and any exceptions related to it.

2.03 Interdisciplinary Collaboration
(a) Social workers who are members of an interdisciplinary team should participate in and contribute to decisions that affect the well-being of clients by drawing on the perspectives, values, and experiences of the social work profession. Professional and ethical obligations of the interdisciplinary team as a whole and of its individual members should be clearly established.

(b) Social workers for whom a team decision raises ethical concerns should attempt to resolve the disagreement through appropriate channels. If the disagreement cannot be resolved, social workers should pursue other avenues to address their concerns consistent with client well-being.

2.04 Disputes Involving Colleagues
(a) Social workers should not take advantage of a dispute between a colleague and employer to obtain a position or otherwise advance the social workers' own interests.

(b) Social workers should not exploit clients in disputes with colleagues or engage clients in any inappropriate discussion of conflicts between social workers and their colleagues.

2.05 Consultation
(a) Social workers should seek the advice and counsel of colleagues whenever such consultation is in the best interests of clients.

(b) Social workers should keep themselves informed about colleagues' areas of expertise and competencies. Social workers should seek consultation only from colleagues who have demonstrated knowledge, expertise, and competence related to the subject of the consultation.

(c) When consulting with colleagues about clients, social workers should disclose the least amount of information necessary to achieve the purposes of the consultation.

2.06 Referral for Services

(a) Social workers should refer clients to other professionals when the other professionals' specialized knowledge or expertise is needed to serve clients fully or when social workers believe that they are not being effective or making reasonable progress with clients and that additional service is required.

(b) Social workers who refer clients to other professionals should take appropriate steps to facilitate an orderly transfer of responsibility. Social workers who refer clients to other professionals should disclose, with clients' consent, all pertinent information to the new service providers.

(c) Social workers are prohibited from giving or receiving payment for a referral when no professional service is provided by the referring social worker.

2.07 Sexual Relationships

(a) Social workers who function as supervisors or educators should not engage in sexual activities or contact with supervisees, students, trainees, or other colleagues over whom they exercise professional authority.

(b) Social workers should avoid engaging in sexual relationships with colleagues when there is potential for a conflict of interest. Social workers who become involved in, or anticipate becoming involved in, a sexual relationship with a colleague have a duty to transfer professional responsibilities, when necessary, to avoid a conflict of interest.

2.08 Sexual Harassment

Social workers should not sexually harass supervisees, students, trainees, or colleagues. Sexual harassment includes sexual advances, sexual solicitation, requests for sexual favors, and other verbal or physical conduct of a sexual nature.

2.09 Impairment of Colleagues

(a) Social workers who have direct knowledge of a social work colleague's impairment that is due to personal problems, psychosocial distress, substance abuse, or mental health difficulties and that interferes with practice effectiveness should consult with that colleague when feasible and assist the colleague in taking remedial action.

(b) Social workers who believe that a social work colleague's impairment interferes with practice effectiveness and that the colleague has not taken adequate steps to address the impairment should take action through appropriate channels established by employers, agencies, NASW, licensing and regulatory bodies, and other professional organizations.

2.10 Incompetence of Colleagues

(a) Social workers who have direct knowledge of a social work colleague's incompetence should consult with that colleague when feasible and assist the colleague in taking remedial action.

(b) Social workers who believe that a social work colleague is incompetent and has not taken adequate steps to address the incompetence should take action through appropriate channels established by employers, agencies, NASW, licensing and regulatory bodies, and other professional organizations.

2.11 Unethical Conduct of Colleagues

(a) Social workers should take adequate measures to discourage, prevent, expose, and correct the unethical conduct of colleagues.

(b) Social workers should be knowledgeable about established policies and procedures for handling concerns about colleagues' unethical behavior. Social workers should be familiar with national, state, and local procedures for handling ethics complaints. These include policies and procedures created by NASW, licensing and regulatory bodies, employers, agencies, and other professional organizations.

(c) Social workers who believe that a colleague has acted unethically should seek resolution by discussing their concerns with the colleague when feasible and when such discussion is likely to be productive.

(d) When necessary, social workers who believe that a colleague has acted unethically should take action through appropiate formal channels (such as contacting a state licensing board or regulatory body, an NASW committee on inquiry, or other professional ethics committees).

(e) Social workers should defend and assist colleagues who are unjustly charged with unethical conduct.

3. Social Workers' Ethical Responsibilities in Practice Settings

3.01 Supervision and Consultation

(a) Social workers who provide supervision or consultation should have the necessary knowledge and skill to supervise or consult appropriately and should do so only within their areas of knowledge and competence.

(b) Social workers who provide supervision or consultation are responsible for setting clear, appropriate, and culturally sensitive boundaries.

(c) Social workers should not engage in any dual or multiple relationships with supervisees in which there is a risk of exploitation of or potential harm to the supervisee.

(d) Social workers who provide supervision should evaluate supervisees' performance in a manner that is fair and respectful.

3.02 Education and Training

(a) Social workers who function as educators, field instructors for students, or trainers should provide instruction only within their areas of knowledge and competence and should provide instruction based on the most current information and knowledge available in the profession.

(b) Social workers who function as educators or field instructors for students should evaluate students' performance in a manner that is fair and respectful.

(c) Social workers who function as educators or field instructors for students should take reasonable steps to ensure that clients are routinely informed when services are being provided by students.

(d) Social workers who function as educators or field instructors for students should not engage in any dual or multiple relationships with students in which there is a risk of exploitation or potential harm to the student. Social work educators and field instructors are responsible for setting clear, appropriate, and culturally sensitive boundaries.

3.03 Performance Evaluation

Social workers who have responsibility for evaluating the performance of others should fulfill such responsibility in a fair and considerate manner and on the basis of clearly stated criteria.

3.04 Client Records

(a) Social workers should take reasonable steps to ensure that documentation in records is accurate and reflects the services provided.

(b) Social workers should include sufficient and timely documentation in records to facilitate the delivery of services and to ensure continuity of services provided to clients in the future.

(c) Social workers' documentation should protect clients' privacy to the extent that is possible and appropriate and should include only information that is directly relevant to the delivery of services.

(d) Social workers should store records following the termination of services to ensure reasonable future access. Records should be maintained for the number of years required by state statutes or relevant contracts.

3.05 Billing

Social workers should establish and maintain billing practices that accurately reflect the nature and extent of services provided and that identify who provided the service in the practice setting.

3.06 Client Transfer

(a) When an individual who is receiving services from another agency or colleague contacts a social worker for services, the social worker should carefully consider the client's needs before agreeing to provide services. To minimize possible confusion and conflict, social workers should discuss with potential clients the nature of the clients' current relationship with other service providers and the implications, including possible benefits or risks, of entering into a relationship with a new service provider.

(b) If a new client has been served by another agency or colleague, social workers should discuss with the client whether consultation with the previous service provider is in the client's best interest.

3.07 Administration

(a) Social work administrators should advocate within and outside their agencies for adequate resources to meet clients' needs.

(b) Social workers should advocate for resource allocation procedures that are open and fair. When not all clients' needs can be met, an allocation procedure should be developed that is nondiscriminatory and based on appropriate and consistently applied principles.

(c) Social workers who are administrators should take reasonable steps to ensure that adequate agency or organizational resources are available to provide appropriate staff supervision.

(d) Social work administrators should take reasonable steps to ensure that the working environment for which they are responsible is consistent with and encourages compliance with the *NASW Code of Ethics.* Social work administrators should take reasonable steps to eliminate any conditions in their organizations that violate, interfere with, or discourage compliance with the *Code.*

3.08 Continuing Education and Staff Development

Social work administrators and supervisors should take reasonable steps to provide or arrange for continuing education and staff development for all staff for whom they are responsible. Continuing education and staff development should address current knowledge and emerging developments related to social work practice and ethics.

3.09 Commitments to Employers

(a) Social workers generally should adhere to commitments made to employers and employing organizations.

(b) Social workers should work to improve employing agencies' policies and procedures and the efficiency and effectiveness of their services.

(c) Social workers should take reasonable steps to ensure that employers are aware of social workers' ethical obligations as set forth in the *NASW Code of Ethics* and of the implications of those obligations for social work practice.

(d) Social workers should not allow an employing organization's policies, procedures, regulations, or administrative orders to interfere with their ethical practice of social work. Social workers should take reasonable steps to ensure that their employing organizations' practices are consistent with the *NASW Code of Ethics.*

(e) Social workers should act to prevent and eliminate discrimination in the employing organization's work assignments and in its employment policies and practices.

(f) Social workers should accept employment or arrange student field placements only in organizations that exercise fair personnel practices.

(g) Social workers should be diligent stewards of the resources of their employing organizations, wisely conserving funds where appropriate and never misappropriating funds or using them for unintended purposes.

3.10 Labor–Management Disputes

(a) Social workers may engage in organized action, including the formation of and participation in labor unions, to improve services to clients and working conditions.

(b) The actions of social workers who are involved in labor–management disputes, job actions, or labor strikes should be guided by the profession's values, ethical principles, and ethical standards. Reasonable differences of opinion exist among social workers concerning their primary obligation as professionals during an actual or threatened labor strike or job action. Social workers should carefully examine relevant issues and their possible impact on clients before deciding on a course of action.

4. Social Workers' Ethical Responsibilities as Professionals

4.01 Competence

(a) Social workers should accept responsibility or employment only on the basis of existing competence or the intention to acquire the necessary competence.

(b) Social workers should strive to become and remain proficient in professional practice and the performance of professional functions. Social workers should critically examine and keep current with emerging knowledge relevant to social work. Social workers should routinely review the professional literature and participate in continuing education relevant to social work practice and social work ethics.

(c) Social workers should base practice on recognized knowledge, including empirically based knowledge, relevant to social work and social work ethics.

4.02 Discrimination

Social workers should not practice, condone, facilitate, or collaborate with any form of discrimination on the basis of race, ethnicity, national origin, color, sex, sexual orientation, age, marital status, political belief, religion, or mental or physical disability.

4.03 Private Conduct

Social workers should not permit their private conduct to interfere with their ability to fulfill their professional responsibilities.

4.04 Dishonesty, Fraud, and Deception

Social workers should not participate in, condone, or be associated with dishonesty, fraud, or deception.

4.05 Impairment

(a) Social workers should not allow their own personal problems, psychosocial distress, legal problems, substance abuse, or mental health difficulties to interfere with their professional judgment and performance or to

jeopardize the best interests of people for whom they have a professional responsibility.

(b) Social workers whose personal problems, psychosocial distress, legal problems, substance abuse, or mental health difficulties interfere with their professional judgment and performance should immediately seek consultation and take appropriate remedial action by seeking professional help, making adjustments in workload, terminating practice, or taking any other steps necessary to protect clients and others.

4.06 Misrepresentation

(a) Social workers should make clear distinctions between statements made and actions engaged in as a private individual and as a representative of the social work profession, a professional social work organization, or the social worker's employing agency.

(b) Social workers who speak on behalf of professional social work organizations should accurately represent the official and authorized positions of the organizations.

(c) Social workers should ensure that their representations to clients, agencies, and the public of professional qualifications, credentials, education, competence, affiliations, services provided, or results to be achieved are accurate. Social workers should claim only those relevant professional credentials they actually possess and take steps to correct any inaccuracies or misrepresentations of their credentials by others.

4.07 Solicitations

(a) Social workers should not engage in uninvited solicitation of potential clients who, because of their circumstances, are vulnerable to undue influence, manipulation, or coercion.

(b) Social workers should not engage in solicitation of testimonial endorsements (including solicitation of consent to use a client's prior statement as a testimonial endorsement) from current clients or from other people who, because of their particular circumstances, are vulnerable to undue influence.

4.08 Acknowledging Credit

(a) Social workers should take responsibility and credit, including authorship credit, only for work they have actually performed and to which they have contributed.

(b) Social workers should honestly acknowledge the work of and the contributions made by others.

5. Social Workers' Ethical Responsibilities to the Social Work Profession

5.01 Integrity of the Profession

(a) Social workers should work toward the maintenance and promotion of high standards of practice.

(b) Social workers should uphold and advance the values, ethics, knowledge, and mission of the profession. Social workers should protect, enhance, and improve the integrity of the profession through appropriate study and research, active discussion, and responsible criticism of the profession.

(c) Social workers should contribute time and professional expertise to activities that promote respect for the value, integrity, and competence of the social work profession. These activities may include teaching, research, consultation, service, legislative testimony, presentations in the community, and participation in their professional organizations.

(d) Social workers should contribute to the knowledge base of social work and share with colleagues their knowledge related to practice, research, and ethics. Social workers should seek to contribute to the profession's literature and to share their knowledge at professional meetings and conferences.

(e) Social workers should act to prevent the unauthorized and unqualified practice of social work.

5.02 Evaluation and Research

(a) Social workers should monitor and evaluate policies, the implementation of programs, and practice interventions.

(b) Social workers should promote and facilitate evaluation and research to contribute to the development of knowledge.

(c) Social workers should critically examine and keep current with emerging knowledge relevant to social work and fully use evaluation and research evidence in their professional practice.

(d) Social workers engaged in evaluation or research should carefully consider possible consequences and should follow guidelines developed for the protection of evaluation and research participants. Appropriate institutional review boards should be consulted.

(e) Social workers engaged in evaluation or research should obtain voluntary and written informed consent from participants, when appropriate, without any implied or actual deprivation or penalty for refusal to participate; without undue inducement to participate; and with due regard for participants' well-being, privacy, and dignity. Informed consent should include information about the nature, extent, and duration of the participation requested and disclosure of the risks and benefits of participation in the research.

(f) When evaluation or research participants are incapable of giving informed consent, social workers should provide an appropriate explanation to the participants, obtain the participants' assent to the extent they are able, and obtain written consent from an appropriate proxy.

(g) Social workers should never design or conduct evaluation or research that does not use consent procedures, such as certain forms of naturalistic observation and archival research, unless rigorous and responsible review of the research has found it to be justified because of its prospective scientific, educational, or applied value and unless equally effective alternative procedures that do not involve waiver of consent are not feasible.

(h) Social workers should inform participants of their right to withdraw from evaluation and research at any time without penalty.

(i) Social workers should take appropriate steps to ensure that participants in evaluation and research have access to appropriate supportive services.

(j) Social workers engaged in evaluation for research should protect participants from unwarranted physical or mental distress, harm, danger, or deprivation.

(k) Social workers engaged in the evaluation of services should discuss collected information only for professional purposes and only with people professionally concerned with this information.

(l) Social workers engaged in evaluation or research should ensure the anonymity or confidentiality of participants and of the data obtained from them. Social workers should inform participants of any limits of confidentiality, the measures that will be taken to ensure confidentiality, and when any records containing research data will be destroyed.

(m) Social workers who report evaluation and research results should protect participants' confidentiality by omitting identifying information unless proper consent has been obtained authorizing disclosure.

(n) Social workers should report evaluation and research findings accurately. They should not fabricate or falsify results and should take steps to correct any errors later found in published data using standard publication methods.

(o) Social workers engaged in evaluation or research should be alert to and avoid conflicts of interest and dual relationships with participants, should inform participants when a real or potential conflict of interest arises, and should take steps to resolve the issue in a manner that makes participants' interests primary.

(p) Social workers should educate themselves, their students, and their colleagues about responsible research practices.

6. Social Workers' Ethical Responsibilities to the Broader Society

6.01 Social Welfare

Social workers should promote the general welfare of society, from local to global levels, and the development of people, their communities, and their environments. Social workers should advocate for living conditions conducive to the fulfillment of basic human needs and should promote social, economic, political, and cultural values and institutions that are compatible with the realization of social justice.

6.02 Public Participation

Social workers should facilitate informed participation by the public in shaping social policies and institutions.

6.03 Public Emergencies

Social workers should provide appropriate professional services in public emergencies to the greatest extent possible.

6.04 Social and Political Action

(a) Social workers should engage in social and political action that seeks to ensure that all people have equal access to the resources, employment, services, and opportunities they require to meet their basic human needs and to develop fully. Social workers should be aware of the impact of the political arena on practice and should advocate for changes in policy and legislation to improve social conditions in order to meet basic human needs and promote social justice.

(b) Social workers should act to expand choice and opportunity for all people, with special regard for vulnerable, disadvantaged, oppressed, and exploited people and groups.

(c) Social workers should promote conditions that encourage respect for cultural and social diversity within the United States and globally. Social workers should promote policies and practices that demonstrate respect for difference, support the expansion of cultural knowledge and resources, advocate for programs and institutions that demonstrate cultural competence, and promote policies that safeguard the rights of and confirm equity and social justice for all people.

(d) Social workers should act to prevent and eliminate domination of, exploitation of, and discrimination against any person, group, or class on the basis of race, ethnicity, national origin, color, sex, sexual orientation, age, marital status, political belief, religion, or mental or physical disability.

Appendix 2

Accredited Master's and Baccalaureate Social Work Programs, Programs in Candidacy for Accreditation, and Doctoral Programs

Accredited Master's Social Work Programs
August 1, 1999

Alabama
Alabama A&M University
University of Alabama

Alaska
University of Alaska

Arizona
Arizona State University

Arkansas
University of Arkansas

California
California State University, Fresno
California State University, Long
  Beach
California State University,
  Sacramento
California State University, San
  Bernardino
California State University,
  Stanislaus
Loma Linda University
San Diego State University
San Francisco State University
San Jose University
University of California at
  Berkeley
University of California at Los
  Angeles

University of Southern
  California

Colorado
Colorado State University
University of Denver

Connecticut
Southern Connecticut State
  University
University of Connecticut

Delaware
Delaware State University

District of Columbia
Catholic University of
  America
Gallaudet University
Howard University

Florida
Barry University
Florida International
  University
Florida State University
University of Central Florida
University of South Florida

Georgia
Clark Atlanta University

University of Georgia
Valdosta State University

Hawaii
University of Hawaii
  at Manoa

Idaho
Boise State University

Illinois
Aurora University
Loyola University of
  Chicago
Southern Illinois University at
  Carbondale
University of Chicago
University of Illinois
  at Chicago
University of Illinois at
  Urbana-Champaign

Indiana
Indiana University/Purdue
  University at Indianapolis
  Branches:
    Indiana University:
      Northwest Campus
    Indiana University: South
      Bend Campus
University of Southern Indiana

Iowa
University of Iowa

Kansas
University of Kansas
Washburn University

Kentucky
University of Kentucky
University of Louisville

Louisiana
Louisiana State University
Southern University at New
  Orleans
Tulane University

Maine
University of Maine
University of New England

Maryland
University of Maryland
  at Baltimore

Massachusetts
Boston College
Boston University
Salem State College
Simmons College
Smith College
Springfield College

Michigan
Andrews University
Eastern Michigan University
Grand Valley State University
Michigan State University
University of Michigan
Wayne State University
Western Michigan University

Minnesota
Augsburg College
College of St. Catherine/
  University of St. Thomas
University of Minnesota-
  Duluth
University of Minnesota-
  Twin Cities

Mississippi
Jackson State University
University of Southern
  Mississippi

Missouri
Saint Louis University

Southwest Missouri State
  University
University of Missouri-
  Columbia
Washington University

Nebraska
University of Nebraska at Omaha

Nevada
University of Nevada,
  Las Vegas
University of Nevada, Reno

New Hampshire
University of New Hampshire

New Jersey
Kean University
Rutgers-The State University of
  New Jersey

New Mexico
New Mexico Highlands
  University
New Mexico State University

New York
Adelphi University
Columbia University
Fordham University
Hunter College of the City
  University of New York
New York University
Roberts Wesleyan College
State University of New York,
  Albany
State University of New York,
  Buffalo
State University of New York,
  Stony Brook
Syracuse University
Yeshiva University

North Carolina
East Carolina University
University of North Carolina at
  Chapel Hill

North Dakota
University of North Dakota

Ohio
Case Western Reserve
Cleveland State University
Ohio State University
University of Akron
University of Cincinnati

Oklahoma
University of Oklahoma

Oregon
Portland State University

Pennsylvania
Marywood College
Temple University
University of Pennsylvania
University of Pittsburgh
Widener University

Puerto Rico
University of Puerto Rico, Rio
  Piedras Campus

Rhode Island
Rhode Island College

South Carolina
University of South Carolina

Tennessee
University of Tennessee
  Branches:
    Knoxville
    Memphis
    Nashville

Texas
Our Lady of the Lake
  University
University of Houston
The University of Texas at
  Arlington
The University of Texas
  at Austin

Utah
Brigham Young University
University of Utah

Vermont
University of Vermont

Virginia
Norfolk State University
Radford University
Virginia Commonwealth
  University

Washington
Eastern Washington University
University of Washington
Walla Walla College

West Virginia
West Virginia University

Wisconsin
University of Wisconsin-
Madison
University of Wisconsin-
Milwaukee

Master's Programs in Candidacy

California
California State University,
Los Angeles

Georgia
Georgia State University
Savannah State College

Illinois
Southern Illinois University
at Edwardsville

Iowa
St. Ambrose University

Kansas
Newman University
Witchita State University

Kentucky
Spalding University

Louisiana
Grambling State University

Missouri
University of Missouri-St. Louis

New Jersey
Monmouth University

North Carolina
University of North Carolina at
Greensboro/A&T State
University

Ohio
Ohio University

Pennsylvania
West Chester University

Puerto Rico
Universidad Interamericana de
Puerto Rico, Recinto de
Metropolitano

Texas
Baylor University
Southwest Texas State University
Stephen F. Austin State University
University of Texas-Pan American

Wyoming
University of Wyoming

Accredited Baccalaureate Social Work Programs

Alabama
Alabama A&M University
Alabama State University
Auburn University
Jacksonville State University
Miles College of Social Work
Oakwood College of Social Work
Talladega College of Social Work
Troy State University
Tuskegee University
University of Alabama
University of Alabama at
Birmingham
University of Montevallo
University of North Alabama

Alaska
University of Alaska, Anchorage

University of Alaska, Fairbanks

Arizona
Arizona State University
Arizona State University-West
Northern Arizona University

Arkansas
Arkansas State University
Harding University
University of Arkansas at
Fayetteville
University of Arkansas at Pine
Bluff

California
Azusa Pacific University
California State University, Chico

California State University,
Fresno
California State University, Long
Beach
California State University, Los
Angeles
California State University,
Sacramento
Humboldt State University
La Sierra University
Pacific Union College
San Diego State University
San Francisco State University
San Jose State University
Whittier College

Colorado
Colorado State University

Metropolitan State College of
  Denver
University of Southern Colorado

Connecticut
Central Connecticut State
  University
Sacred Heart University
Saint Joseph College
Southern Connecticut State
  University
Western Connecticut State
  University

Delaware
Delaware State University

District of Columbia
Catholic University of America
Gallaudet University
University of the District
  of Columbia

Florida
Florida Agriculture and
  Mechanical University
Florida Atlantic University
Florida International University
Florida State University
Saint Leo College
University of Central Florida
University of South Florida
University of West Florida

Georgia
Clark Atlanta University
Georgia State University
Savannah State University
University of Georgia

Hawaii
Brigham Young University,
  Hawaii Campus
University of Hawaii at Manoa

Idaho
Boise State University
Idaho State University
Lewis-Clark State College
Northwest Nazarene College

Illinois
Aurora University
Governors State University
Illinois State University
Loyola University of Chicago
MacMurray College
Northeastern Illinois University
Olivet Nazarene University

Southern Illinois University
Southern Illinois University at
  Edwardsville
University of Illinois at Chicago
University of Saint Francis
Western Illinois University

Indiana
Anderson University
Ball State University
Goshen College
Indiana State University
Indiana University
Indiana Wesleyan University
Manchester College
Saint Francis College
Saint Mary's College
Taylor University
University of Indianapolis
University of Southern Indiana
Valparaiso University

Iowa
Briar Cliff College
Buena Vista University
Clarke College
Dordt College
Loras College
Luther College
Marycrest International University
Mount Mercy College
Northwestern College
University of Iowa
University of Northern Iowa
Wartburg College

Kansas
Bethany College
Bethel College
Fort Hays State University
Kansas State University
Pittsburg State University
University of Kansas
Washburn University
Wichita State University

Kentucky
Eastern Kentucky University
Kentucky Christian College
Kentucky State University
Morehead State University
Murray State University
Northern Kentucky University
Spalding University
University of Kentucky
Western Kentucky University

Louisiana
Grambling State University

Louisiana College
Northeast Louisiana University
Northwestern State University
Southeastern Louisiana
  University
Southern University of A&M
  College
Southern University at New
  Orleans

Maine
University of Maine
University of Southern Maine

Maryland
Bowie State University
Coppin State College
Frostburg State University
Hood College
Morgan State University
Salisbury State University
University of Maryland-
  Baltimore County
Western Maryland College

Massachusetts
Anna Maria College
Atlantic Union College
Bridgewater State College
Eastern Nazarene College
Gordon College
Our Lady of the Elms College
Regis College
Salem State College
Western New England College
Wheelock College

Michigan
Andrews University
Calvin College
Eastern Michigan University
Ferris State University
Grand Valley State University
Hope College
Madonna University
Marygrove College
Michigan State University
Northern Michigan University
Saginaw Valley State University
Spring Arbor College
University of Detroit Mercy
University of Michigan–Flint
Wayne State University
Western Michigan University

Minnesota
Augsburg College
Bemidji State University
Bethel College

College of St. Benedict
College of St. Catherine
College of St. Scholastica
Concordia College
Metropolitan State University
Minnesota State University-
    Mankato
Moorhead State University
Southwest State Univeristy
St. Cloud State University
St. John's University
St. Olaf College
University of St. Thomas
Winona State University

Mississippi
Delta State University
Jackson State University
Mississippi College
Mississippi State University
Mississippi Valley State
    University
University of Mississippi
University of Southern
    Mississippi

Missouri
Avila College
Central Missouri State
    University
Columbia College
Evangel University
Missouri Western State College
Saint Louis University
Southeast Missouri State
    University
Southwest Missouri State
    University
University of Missouri-Columbia
University of Missouri-St. Louis
William Woods College

Montana
Carroll College
University of Montana

Nebraska
Chadron State College
Creighton University
Dana College
Nebraska Wesleyan University
Union College
University of Nebraska at
    Kearney
University of Nebraska at Omaha

Nevada
University of Nevada,
    Las Vegas

University of Nevada, Reno

New Hampshire
Plymouth State College
University of New Hampshire

New Jersey
Georgian Court College
Kean University
Monmouth University
Ramapo College of New Jersey
Richard Stockton College of New
    Jersey
Rutgers-The State University of
    New Jersey
Seton Hall University

New Mexico
New Mexico Highlands University
New Mexico State University
Western New Mexico University

New York
Adelphi University
Buffalo State College
College of New Rochelle
Concordia College
Cornell University
Daemen College
Dominican College of Blauvet
D'Youville College
Herbert H. Lehman College
Iona College
Keuka College
Marist College
Marymount College
Mercy College
Molloy College
Nazareth College of Rochester
New York University
Niagara University
Roberts Wesleyan College
Rochester Institute of Technology
Siena College
Skidmore College
State University of New York at
    Albany
State University of New York at
    Brockport
State University of New York at
    Stony Brook
Syracuse University
York College of the City,
    University of New York

North Carolina
Appalachian State University
Barton College
Bennett College

Campbell University
East Carolina University
Livingstone College
Mars Hill College
Meredith College
Methodist College
North Carolina A&T University
North Carolina Central University
North Carolina State University
University of North Carolina at
    Charlotte
University of North Carolina at
    Greensboro
University of North Carolina at
    Pembroke
Warren Wilson College
Western Carolina University

North Dakota
Minot State University
University of Mary
University of North Dakota

Ohio
Ashland University
Bluffton College
Bowling Green State University
Capital University
Cedarville College
Cleveland State University
College of Mount St. Joseph
Defiance College
Lourdes College
Malone College
Miami University
Ohio State University
Ohio University
University of Akron
University of Cincinnati
University of Findlay
University of Rio Grande
University of Toledo
Ursuline College
Wright State University
Xavier University
Youngstown State University

Oklahoma
East Central University
Northeastern State University
Oral Roberts University
University of Oklahoma

Pennsylvania
Alvernia College
Bloomsburg University
Cabrinir College
California University of
    Pennsylvania

Cedar Crest College
College Misericordia
Eastern College
Edinboro University
Elizabethtown College
Gannon University
Juniata College
Kutztown University
La Salle University
Lock Haven University of
    Pennsylvania
Mansfield University of
    Pennsylvania
Marywood University
Mercyhurst College
Messiah College
Millersville University of
    Pennsylvania
Philadelphia College
    of Bible
Saint Francis College
Shippensburg University
Slippery Rock University
Temple University
University of Pittsburgh
West Chester University
Widener University

Puerto Rico
Pontificia Universidad Catolica
    de Puerto Rico
Universidad Interamericana de
    Puerto Rico, Recinto de
    Arecibo
Universidad Interamericana de
    Puerto Rico, Recinto de
    Metropolitano
University of Puerto Rico
University of Puerto Rico-
    Humacao University College
University of the Sacred Heart

Rhode Island
Providence College
Rhode Island College
Salve Regina University

South Carolina
Benedict College
Columbia College
South Carolina State University
Winthrop University

South Dakota
Augustana College
Presentation College
University of Sioux Falls
University of South Dakota

Tennessee
Austin Peay State University
Belmont University

David Lipscomb University
East Tennessee State
    University
Freed-Hardeman University
Middle Tennessee State
    University
South Adventist University
Tennessee State University
University of Memphis
University of Tennessee at
    Chattanooga
University of Tennessee at
    Knoxville
University of Tennessee
    at Martin

Texas
Abilene Christian University
Baylor University
Hardin-Simmons University
Lamar University
Lubbock Christian University
Midwestern State University
Our Lady of the Lake
    University
Prairie View A & M University
Southwestern Adventist
    College
Southwest Texas State
    University
St. Edward's University
Stephen F. Austin State
    University
Tarleton State University
Texas A & M University-
    Commerce
Texas Christian University
Texas Lutheran University
Texas Southern University
Texas Tech University
Texas Woman's University
University of Central Texas
University of Mary Hardin-
    Baylor
University of North Texas
University of Texas at Arlington
University of Texas at Austin
University of Texas at El Paso
University of Texas-Pan
    American
West Texas A & M University

Utah
Brigham Young University
Utah State University
Weber State University

Vermont
Castleton State College
Trinity College
University of Vermont

Virginia
Christopher Newport University
Eastern Mennonite College
Ferrum College
George Mason University
James Madison University
Longwood College
Norfolk State University
Radford University
Virginia Commonwealth
    University
Virginia Intermont College
Virginia State University
Virginia Union University

Washington
Eastern Washington University
Heritage College
Pacific Lutheran University
University of Washington
Walla Walla College

West Virginia
Bethany College
Concord College
Marshall University
Shepherd College
West Virginia State College
West Virginia University

Wisconsin
Carroll College
Carthage College
Concordia University
Marian College
Marquette University
Mount Mary College
Mount Senario College
University of Wisconsin-
    Eau Claire
University of Wisconsin-
    Green Bay
University of Wisconsin-
    Madison
University of Wisconsin-
    Milwaukee
University of Wisconsin-
    Oshkosh
University of Wisconsin-
    River Falls
University of Wisconsin-
    Superior
University of Wisconsin-
    Whitewater

Wyoming
University of Wyoming

Baccalaureate Programs in Candidacy

Arkansas
Philander Smith College
Southern Arkansas University
University of Arkansas at
    Little Rock
University of Arkansas at
    Monticello

Connecticut
Eastern Connecticut State
    University

Georgia
Albany State College
Thomas College

Hawaii
Hawaii Pacific University

Illinois
Bradley University
University of Illinois at
    Springfield

Kentucky
Brescia University
Campbellsville University

Maine
University of Maine at
    Presque Isle

Massachusetts
Westfield State College

Mississippi
Mississippi State University-
    Meridian
Rust College

New York
College of Saint Rose
College of Staten Island
Fordham University
Long Island University-
    Brooklyn Campus
Long Island University-
    C.W. Post
State University of
    New York at Plattsburgh
State University of
    New York College
    at Fredonia

North Carolina
Johnson C. Smith University
University of North Carolina
    at Wilmington

Oklahoma
Southwestern Oklahoma State
    University

Oregon
George Fox University

Pennsylvania
Carlow College
Seton Hill College

South Carolina
Limestone College

Tennessee
Lincoln Memorial University
Union University

West Virginia
College of West Virginia

1999 Doctoral Social Work Programs

U.S. Members

Adelphi University
Garden City, NY

Arizona State University
Tempe, AZ

Barry University
Miami Shores, FL

Boston College
Chestnut Hill, MA

Boston University
Boston, MA

Brandeis University
Waltham, MA

Bryn Mawr College
Bryn Mawr, PA

Case Western Reserve University
Cleveland, OH

Catholic University of American
Washington, DC

Clark Atlanta University
Atlanta, GA

Columbia University
New York, NY

Florida International University
N. Miami, FL

Florida State University
Tallahasee, FL

Fordham University
New York, NY

Howard University
Washington, DC

Hunter College-CUNY
New York, NY

Indiana University
Indianapolis, IN

Jackson State University
Jackson, MS

Louisiana State University
Baton Rouge, LA

Loyola University of Chicago
Chicago, IL

Michigan State University
E. Lansing, MI

New York University
New York, NY

Norfolk State University
Norfolk, VA

Ohio State University
Columbus, OH

Portland State University
Portland, OR

Rutgers University
New Brunswick, NJ

Simmons College
Boston, MA

Smith College
Northampton, MA

SUNY-Albany
Albany, NY

SUNY-Buffalo
Buffalo, NY

SUNY-Stony Brook
Stony Brook, NY

Tulane University
New Orleans, LA

University of Alabama
Tuscaloosa, AL

University of California at
    Berkeley
Berkeley, CA

University of California at Los
    Angeles
Los Angeles, California

University of Chicago
Chicago, IL

University of Denver
Denver, CO

University of Georgia
Athens, GA

University of Hawaii at Manoa
Honolulu, HI

University of Houston
Houston, TX

University of Illinois-Chicago
Chicago, IL

University of Illinois-Urbana
Urbana, IL

University of Iowa
Iowa City, IA

University of Kansas
Lawrence, KS

University of Kentucky
Lexington, KY

University of Louisville
Louisville, KY

University of Maryland at
    Baltimore
Baltimore, MD

University of Michigan
Ann Arbor, MI

University of Minnesota
St. Paul, MN

University of North Carolina
Chapel Hill, NC

University of Pennsylvania
Philadelphia, PA

University of Pittsburgh
Pittsburgh, PA

University of South Carolina
Columbia, SC

University of Southern
    California
Los Angeles, CA

University of Tennessee
Knoxville, TN

University of Texas-Arlington
Arlington, TX

University of Texas-Austin
Austin, TX

University of Utah
Salt Lake City, UT

University of Washington
Seattle, WA

University of Wisconsin-Madison
Madison, WI

Virginia Commonwealth
    University
Richmond, VA

Washington University
St. Louis, MO

Yeshiva University
New York, NY

International Programs

Bar-Ilan University
Ramat-Gan, Israel

Memorial University of
    Newfoundland
St. John's Newfoundland,
    Canada

University of Calgary
Calgary, Alberta

Universite Laval
Sainte Foy, Quebec

University of Toronto
Toronto, Ontario

Wilfrid Laurier University
Waterloo, Ontario

Developing Programs

University of Connecticut
West Hartford, CT

University of Missouri-
    Columbia
Columbia, MO

University of Oklahoma
Norman, OK

Source: Adapted from *Directory of Colleges and Universities with Accredited Social Work Degree Programs,* by the Council on Social Work Education, 1999, Washington, DC. Copyright © 1999 by the Council on Social Work Education. Reprinted with permission.

Appendix 3

Example of State Government Application Form

SOUTH CAROLINA DEPARTMENT OF SOCIAL SERVICES
APPLICATION PROCESS EFFECTIVE APRIL 1, 1998

Effective April 1, 1998, the Human Resources Management Employment Unit will administer the hiring and recruiting services for the Department of Social Services. The Employment Unit will be responsible for recruiting, advertising vacancies and collecting employment applications. The unit will also provide assistance and counseling to applicants, employees and managers regarding the hiring process. Below is important information about the unit:

UNIT NAME:	Human Resources Management Employment Unit
LOCATION:	1001 Harden Street (Five Points area in Columbia, SC)
OFFICE HOURS:	8:30 am to 5:00 pm
MAILING ADDRESS:	1001 Harden Street, Suite 225 Columbia, SC 29205
PHONE NUMBER:	(803) 253-6318
TDD:	(803) 253-4133
FAX:	(803) 253-7557
CAREER LINE:	(803) 898-7636
INTERNET:	http://www.state.sc.us/jobs

HOW TO APPLY FOR PERMANENT POSITIONS

You must complete a State Job Application for *each* posted position that you wish to apply for. State Applications are available at the Employment Unit, by mail, by fax or at various DSS county locations. Photocopies are accepted.

You must include the internal position title, position number, and location of the job on your application. This information can be found on the vacancy announcement.

The application must be received in the Employment Unit *by the closing date* of the announcement. You may mail, fax or hand deliver the application.

Select clerical positions require taking a performance typing test with 35 wpm as the passing score. The vacancy announcement will indicate whether a test is required. Final candidates will be contacted to schedule testing.

Current written test will be discontinued.

WHAT HAPPENS NEXT

Once received, your application is evaluated to determine if you meet the agency's training and experience requirements. If you meet the requirements, your application will be forwarded to the appointing authority. You will be notified if you did not meet the requirements.

Once the application has been forwarded, any questions about the job should be addressed to the hiring county or division.

HOW TO APPLY FOR TEMPORARY GRANT POSITIONS
You must follow instructions provided on the vacancy announcement for temporary and temporary grant positions.

SOUTH CAROLINA DEPARTMENT OF SOCIAL SERVICES
CONTINUOUS RECRUITING APPLICATION PROCESS

Effective May 3, 1999, the Human Resources Management Employment Unit will begin implementing the Continuous Recruiting Process for selected county offices that have frequent and recurring vacancies for specific positions. Continuous vacancy announcements for these positions will be posted for an extended period of time up to six months. These vacancies are available for review at the following locations:

- DSS Employment Unit at 1001 Harden Street (Five Points area in Columbia)
- DSS Regional/County Offices
- DSS State Office Locations
- DSS Career Line (803) 898-7636
- Internet at http://www.state.sc.us/jobs
- State Career Center
- Job Service

HOW TO APPLY FOR A CONTINUOUS VACANCY
You must complete a State Job Application for *each* posted position that you wish to apply for. State Applications are available at the Employment Unit, via mail, by calling (803) 253-6318 or TDD (803) 253-4133, by fax or at various DSS county locations. Photocopies are accepted.

You must include the internal position title, position number, and location of the job on your application. This information can be found on the continuous vacancy announcement.

Applications must be received in the Employment Unit *by the closing date* of the continuous announcement. Applications may be hand delivered or mailed to the DSS Employment Unit at 1001 Harden Street, Suite 225, Columbia, S.C. 29205 or faxed to (803) 253-7557.

Applicants need to only apply *once* for each vacancy posting during this continuous announcement period unless pertinent information should change on their employment application such as work history, address, phone number, etc.

WHAT HAPPENS NEXT
Once received, your application is evaluated to determine if you meet the agency's training and experience requirements. You will notified if you do not meet the requirements. If you meet the requirements, your application will be forwarded to the appointing authority. All forwarded applications will be maintained by the hiring county for consideration during the continuous announcement period. Once the application has been forwarded, any questions about the continuous announcement should be addressed to the hiring county.

STATE OF SOUTH CAROLINA

EMPLOYMENT APPLICATION

RETURN TO:

1. APPLYING FOR

Job Title _____

Position Number _____ Location _____

2. HOW DO WE CONTACT YOU?

Social Security Number _____ ‒ _____ ‒ _____ Your Name _____

Mailing Address _____

City _____ County _____ State _____ Zip Code _____

Home Phone ( ) _____ Business Phone ( ) _____

Fax Number ( ) _____ E-mail Address _____

3. TELL US ABOUT YOUR EDUCATION

High School (Name) _____ (Location) _____

Diploma ☐   Other(Specify) ☐ _____ Highest Grade Completed _____

College Graduate? Yes ☐   No ☐   If no, give total credit received _____ Your Name If Different While Attending School _____

Give name & address of school, major course of study, and degree received.

Undergraduate College / University		Graduate School	
Degree	Year Degree Obtained	Degree	Year Degree Obtained
Pertinent Undergraduate Courses	Credits	Pertinent Graduate Courses	Credits

Job-Related Training and Course Work

List any skills, licenses, and certificates which are related to the job you seek (including words per minute typing speed and computer software proficiency).

STATE OF SOUTH CAROLINA - AN EQUAL OPPORTUNITY EMPLOYER

PD- 1 DID (REVISED 6/98)

4. TELL US ABOUT YOUR WORK EXPERIENCE:

Describe your work experience in detail, beginning with your current or most recent job. Include military service (indicate rank) and job related volunteer work, if applicable. Provide an explanation for any gaps in employment. **All information in this section must be complete. A résumé may be attached, but not substituted for completing this section.**

1. Name of Present or Last Employer _____

Address _____ Phone ( ) _____

Job Title _____

Number Supervised _____ Supervisor's Name _____

From _____ / _____ / _____ To _____ / _____ / _____ Hours Per Week _____ Salary _____

May we contact this employer? ☐ Yes ☐ No

Job Duties (give details)

Reason for Leaving

2. Your Next Most Recent Employer _____

Address _____ Phone ( ) _____

Job Title _____

Number Supervised _____ Supervisor's Name _____

From _____ / _____ / _____ To _____ / _____ / _____ Hours Per Week _____ Salary _____

May we contact this employer?   Yes   No

Job Duties (give details)

Reason for Leaving

3. Your Next Most Recent Employer _____

Address _____ Phone ( ) _____

Job Title _____

Number Supervised _____ Supervisor's Name _____

From _____ / _____ / _____ To _____ / _____ / _____ Hours Per Week _____ Salary _____

Job Duties (give details)

Reason for Leaving

Do you possess a valid driver's license? ☐ Yes ☐ No _____ If yes, provide

(State)

Number _____ Expiration Date _____ Class: (check one) ☐ A ☐ B ☐ C ☐ D ☐ E ☐ F ☐ M ☐ G

Do you have any relatives employed with the State of South Carolina? If yes, please provide names below:

Name _____ Relation _____ Agency _____

Name _____ Relation _____ Agency _____

Have you ever been convicted of a criminal offense? ☐ Yes ☐ No

Note: Omit minor vehicle violations and any offense committed before your 17th birthday, which was finally adjudicated in juvenile court or under a youthful offender law. Conviction of a criminal offense is not a bar to employment in all cases. Each conviction is evaluated individually.

If yes, please list charge(s) _____

Where Convicted Date Disposition/Status

Have you ever been terminated or forced to resign from any job? ☐ Yes ☐ No _____
If yes, explain
Are you legally authorized to work in the United States? ☐ Yes ☐ No

Give the names of two people, not relatives, who are familiar with your work.

Name _____ Address _____ Phone _____

Name _____ Address _____ Phone _____

PLEASE CAREFULLY READ THE FOLLOWING STATEMENTS

Student Loan: State law (59-111-50) prohibits employment with the State to people who have defaulted on certain student loans, unless they can prove that satisfactory arrangements have been made for repayment. By my signature, I certify that I am not currently in default on a student loan.

Signature _____ Date _____

Authority to Release Information: By my signature, I consent to the release of information to authorized officers, agents, and/or employees of the State of South Carolina which may include but not be limited to information concerning my past and present work; including my official personnel files; attendance records; evaluations; educational records including transcripts; military service; law enforcement records; and/or any personnel record deemed necessary. In addition, I consent to authorize appropriate officers, agents, and/or employees of the State of South Carolina to make inquiries of third parties such as credit bureaus. I further release the organization, educational entity, present and former employers, law enforcement organization, and all third parties from any and all claims of whatever nature that I may have as a result of any inquiry or response given to such inquiries made in connection with my application for employment.

Signature _____ Date _____

Certification of Applicant: By my signature, I affirm, agree, and understand that all statements on this form are true and accurate. Any misrepresentation, falsification, or material omission of information or data on this application may result in exclusion from further consideration or, if hired, termination of employment. If I have requested herein that my present employer not be contacted, an offer of employment may be conditioned upon acceptable information and verification from such employer prior to beginning work.

Signature _____ Date _____

5. EEO DATA REPORTING FORM:

The federal government requires the following information to be collected for statistical reporting as a part of the Affirmative Action Program. Refusal to answer will not result in adverse treatment of any applicant. This information is not used in the employment process nor released in a manner which identifies the individual. This form will be removed prior to being forwarded to the hiring authority.

Today's Date _____ / _____ / _____

Social Security Number _____ – _____ – _____

Last Name _____

First Name _____ **Middle** _____

Position for which you are applying _____
                                                        Title

Position Number _____

Sex (Check appropriate box)   ☐ Male   ☐ Female

Date of Birth _____ / _____ / _____

Race (Check appropriate box)   ☐ 1. American Indian / Alaskan Native

                                            ☐ 2. Asian / Pacific Islanders

                                            ☐ 3. Black / Non Hispanic

                                            ☐ 4. Hispanic

                                            ☐ 5. White / Non Hispanic

Will you need reasonable accommodations to participate in the selection procedures (e.g., interview, written tests, or job demonstration)?

☐ Yes   ☐ No

If yes, please notify the Personnel Office or Human Resources Office at the state agency which has the job vacancy.

State agencies are actively supporting the Family Independence Act by hiring welfare and food stamp recipients for certain jobs. Are you currently receiving AFDC benefits or food stamps?

☐ Yes   ☐ No

Source: Authorized form of the Office of Human Resources, State of South Carolina. Reprinted with permission.

Examples of Federal Government Application Forms

Standard Form 171 — Application for Federal Employment

Read The Following Instructions Carefully Before You Complete This Application

- DO NOT SUBMIT A RESUME INSTEAD OF THIS APPLICATION.
- TYPE OR PRINT CLEARLY IN DARK INK.
- IF YOU NEED MORE SPACE for an answer, use a sheet of paper the same size as this page. On **each** sheet write your name, Social Security Number, the announcement number or job title, and the item number. Attach all additional forms and sheets to this application at the top of page 3.
- If you do not answer **all** questions fully and correctly, you may delay the review of your application and lose job opportunities.
- Unless you are asked for additional material in the announcement or qualification information, **do not attach** any materials, such as: official position descriptions, performance evaluations, letters of recommendation, certificates of training, publications, etc. Any materials you attach which were not asked for may be removed from your application and will **not** be returned to you.
- We suggest that you **keep a copy** of this application for your use. If you plan to make copies of your application, we suggest you leave items **1, 48** and **49** blank. Complete these blank items each time you apply. **YOU MUST SIGN AND DATE, IN INK, EACH COPY YOU SUBMIT.**
- To apply for a specific **Federal civil service examination** (whether or not a written test is required) **or a specific vacancy in an Federal agency:**
  - Read the announcement and other materials provided.
  - Make sure that your work experience and/or education meet the qualification requirements described.
  - Make sure the announcement is open for the job and location you are interested in. Announcements may be closed to receipt of applications for some types of jobs, grades, or geographic locations.
  - Make sure that you are allowed to apply. Some jobs are limited to veterans, or to people who work for the Federal Government or have worked for the Federal Government in the past.
  - Follow any directions on "How to Apply", If a written test is required, bring any material you are instructed to bring to the test session. For example, you may be instructed to "Bring a completed SF 171 to the test." If a written test is not required, mail this application and all other forms required by the announcement to the address specified in the announcement.

Work Experience *(Item 24)*

- Carefully complete each experience block you need to describe your work experience. Unless you qualify based on education alone, **your rating will depend on your description of previous jobs. Do not leave out any jobs you held during the last ten years.**
- Under **Description of Work**, write a **clear and brief**, but **complete** description of your **major** duties and responsibilities for each job. Include any supervisory duties, special assignments, and your accomplishments in the job. We may verify your description with your former employers.
- If you had a major change of duties or responsibilities while you worked for the same employer, describe each major change as a separate job.

Veteran Preference in Hiring *(Item 22)*

- **DO NOT LEAVE Item 22 BLANK.** If you do **not** claim veteran preference, place an **"X"** in the box next to **"NO PREFERENCE"**.
- You **cannot** receive veteran preference if you are retired or plan to retire at or above the rank of major or lieutenant commander, **unless** you are disabled or retired from the active military Reserve.
- To receive veteran preference your separation from active duty must have been under honorable conditions. This includes honorable and general discharges. A clemency discharge does not meet the requirements of the Veteran Preference Act.
- Active duty for training in the military Reserve and National Guard programs is not considered active duty for purposes of veteran preference.
- To qualify for preference you must meet **ONE** of the following conditions:
  1. Served on active duty anytime between December 7, 1941, and July 1, 1955; (If you were a Reservist called to active duty between February 1, 1955 and July 1, 1955, you must meet condition **2**, below.)

     or
  2. Served on active duty any part of which was between July 2, 1955 and October 14, 1976 or a Reservist called to active duty between February 1, 1955 and October 14, 1976 and who served for more than 180 days;

     or
  3. Entered on active duty between October 15, 1976 and September 7, 1980 or a Reservist who entered on active duty between October 15, 1976 and October 13, 1982 **and** received a Campaign Badge or Expeditionary Medal **or** are a disabled veteran;

     or
  4. Enlisted in the Armed Forces after September 7, 1980 or entered active duty other than by enlistment on or after October 14, 1982 **and:**
     a. completed 24 months of continuous active duty or the full period called or ordered to active duty, or were discharged under 10 U.S.C. 1171 or for hardship under 10 U.S.C. 1173 **and** received or were entitled to receive a Campaign Badge or Expeditionary Medal; **or**
     b. are a disabled veteran.
- If you meet one of the four conditions above, you qualify for 5-point preference. If you want to claim 5-point preference **and** do not meet the requirements for 10-point preference, discussed below, place an **"X"** in the box next to **"5-POINT PREFERENCE"**.
- If you think you qualify for 10-Point Preference, review the requirements described in the Standard Form (SF) 15, Application for 10-Point Veteran Preference. The SF 15 is available from any Federal Job Information Center. The 10-point preference groups are:
  - Non-Compensably Disabled or Purple Heart Recipient.
  - Compensably Disabled (less than 30%).
  - Compensably Disabled (30% or more).
  - Spouse, Widow(er) or Mother of a deceased or disabled veteran.
- If you claim 10-point preference, place an **"X"** in the box next to the group that applies to you. To receive **10-point** preference you must attach a completed **SF 15** to this application together with the proof requested in the SF 15.

DETACH THIS PAGE—NOTE SF 171-A ON BACK

Standard Form 171-A— *Continuation Sheet for SF 171*

Form Approved:
OMB No. 3206-0012

● Attach all SF 171-A's to your application at the top of page 3.

1. Name *(Last, First, Middle Initial)*	2. Social Security Number

3. Job Title or Announcement Number You Are Applying For	4. Date Completed

ADDITIONAL WORK EXPERIENCE BLOCKS

Name and address of employer's organization *(include ZIP Code, if known)*	Dates employed *(give month, day and year)*	Average number of hours per week	Number of employees you supervised
	From: To:		
	Salary or earnings	Your reason for leaving	
	Starting $ per		
	Ending $ per		

Your immediate supervisor			Exact title of your job	If Federal employment *(civilian or military)* list series, grade or rank, and, if promoted in this job, the date of your last promotion
Name	Area Code	Telephone No.		

Description of work: Describe your specific duties, responsibilities and accomplishments in this job, **including** the job title(s) of any employees you supervised.   *If you describe more than one type of work (for example, carpentry and painting, or personnel and budget), write the approximate percentage of time you spent doing each.*

For Agency Use (skill codes, etc.)

Name and address of employer's organization *(include ZIP Code, if known)*	Dates employed *(give month, day and year)*	Average number of hours per week	Number of employees you supervised
	From: To:		
	Salary or earnings	Your reason for leaving	
	Starting $ per		
	Ending $ per		

Your immediate supervisor			Exact title of your job	If Federal employment *(civilian or military)* list series, grade or rank, and, if promoted in this job, the date of your last promotion
Name	Area Code	Telephone No.		

Description of work: Describe your specific duties, responsibilities and accomplishments in this job, **including** the job title(s) of any employees you supervised.   *If you describe more than one type of work (for example, carpentry and painting, or personnel and budget), write the approximate percentage of time you spent doing each.*

For Agency Use (skill codes, etc.)

THE FEDERAL GOVERNMENT IS AN EQUAL OPPORTUNITY EMPLOYER
PREVIOUS EDITION USABLE

Standard Form **171-A** (Rev. 6-88)
U.S. Office of Personnel Management
FPM Chapter 295

Application for Federal Employment—SF 171

Read the instructions before you complete this application. *Type or print clearly in dark ink.*

Form Approved.
OMB No. 3206-0012

GENERAL INFORMATION

1 What kind of job are you applying for? *Give title and announcement no. (if any)*

2 Social Security Number

3 Sex
☐ Male   ☐ Female

4 Birth date *(Month, Day, Year)*

5 Birthplace *(City and State or Country)*

6 Name *(Last, First, Middle)*

Mailing address *(include apartment number, if any)*

City   State   ZIP Code

7 Other names ever used *(e.g., maiden name, nickname, etc.)*

8 Home Phone
Area Code | Number

9 Work Phone
Area Code | Number   Extension

10 Were you ever employed as a civilian by the Federal Government? If **"NO"**, go to **Item 11.** If **"YES"**, mark each type of job you held with an **"X"**.

☐ Temporary   ☐ Career-Conditional   ☐ Career   ☐ Excepted

What is your **highest** grade, classification series and job title?

Dates at **highest** grade: FROM   TO

FOR USE OF EXAMINING OFFICE ONLY

Date entered register

Form reviewed:
Form approved:

Option	Grade	Earned Rating	Veteran Preference	Augmented Rating

☐ No Preference Claimed
☐ 5 Points *(Tentative)*
☐ 10 Pts. *(30% Or More Comp. Dis.)*
☐ 10 Pts. *(Less Than 30% Comp. Dis.)*
☐ Other 10 Points

Initials and Date

☐ Disallowed   ☐ Being Investigated

FOR USE OF APPOINTING OFFICE ONLY

Preference has been verified through proof that the separation was under honorable conditions, and other proof as required.

☐ 5-Point   ☐ 10-Point—30% or More Compensable Disability   ☐ 10-Point—Less Than 30% Compensable Disability   ☐ 10-Point—Other

Signature and Title

Agency   Date

AVAILABILITY

11 When can you start work? *(Month and Year)*

12 What is the **lowest** pay you will accept? *(You will not be considered for jobs which pay less than you indicate.)*
Pay $ ____ per ____ OR Grade ____

13 In what geographic area(s) are you willing to work?

14 Are you willing to work:

	YES	NO
A. 40 hours per week *(full-time)?*		
B. 25-32 hours per week *(part-time)?*		
C. 17-24 hours per week *(part-time)?*		
D. 16 or fewer hours per week *(part-time)?*		
E. An intermittent job *(on-call/seasonal)?*		
F. Weekends, shifts, or rotating shifts?		

15 Are you willing to take a temporary job lasting:

A. 5 to 12 months *(sometimes longer)?*
B. 1 to 4 months?
C. Less than 1 month?

16 Are you willing to travel away from home for:

A. 1 to 5 nights each month?
B. 6 to 10 nights each month?
C. 11 or more nights each month?

MILITARY SERVICE AND VETERAN PREFERENCE

17 Have you served in the United States Military Service? *If your only active duty was training in the Reserves or National Guard, answer "NO".* If **"NO"**, go to item 22.

YES	NO

18 Did you or will you retire at or above the rank of major or lieutenant commander?

MILITARY SERVICE AND VETERAN PREFERENCE *(Cont.)*

19 Were you discharged from the military service under honorable conditions? *(If your discharge was changed to "honorable" or "general" by a Discharge Review Board, answer "YES". If you received a clemency discharge, answer "NO".)* If **"NO"**, provide below the date and type of discharge you received.

YES	NO

Discharge Date *(Month, Day, Year)*   Type of Discharge

20 List the dates *(Month, Day, Year)*, and branch for all **active duty** military service.

From	To	Branch of Service

21 If all your active military duty was after October 14, 1976, list the full names and dates of all campaign badges or expeditionary medals you received or were entitled to receive.

22 Read the instructions that came with this form before completing this item. When you have determined your eligibility for veteran preference from the instructions, place an **"X"** in the box next to your veteran preference claim.

☐ NO PREFERENCE

☐ 5-POINT PREFERENCE -- You must show proof when you are hired.

10-POINT PREFERENCE -- If you claim 10-point preference, place an **"X"** in the box below next to the basis for your claim. **To receive 10-point preference you must also complete a Standard Form 15, Application for 10-Point Veteran Preference, which is available from any Federal Job Information Center. ATTACH THE COMPLETED SF 15 AND REQUESTED PROOF TO THIS APPLICATION.**

☐ Non-compensably disabled or Purple Heart recipient.
☐ Compensably disabled, less than 30 percent.
☐ Spouse, widow(er), or mother of a deceased or disabled veteran.
☐ Compensably disabled, 30 percent or more.

THE FEDERAL GOVERNMENT IS AN EQUAL OPPORTUNITY EMPLOYER
PREVIOUS EDITION USABLE UNTIL 12-31-90

NSN 7540-00-935-7150   171-110   Standard Form **171** (Rev. 6-88)
U.S. Office of Personnel Management
FPM Chapter 295

Page 1

WORK EXPERIENCE *If you have no work experience, write "NONE" in A below and go to 25 on page 3.*

23 May we ask your present employer about your character, qualifications, and work record? *A "NO" will not affect our review of your qualifications. If you answer "NO" and we need to contact your present employer before we can offer you a job, we will contact you first.* . . . . . | **YES** | **NO** |

24 READ **WORK EXPERIENCE** IN THE INSTRUCTIONS BEFORE YOU BEGIN.

- Describe your current or most recent job in Block **A** and work backwards, describing each job you held **during the past 10 years.** If you were **unemployed** for longer than **3 months** within the past 10 years, list the dates and your address(es) in an experience block.

- You may sum up in one block work that you did **more than 10 years ago.** But if that work **is related** to the type of job you are applying for, describe each related job in a separate block.

- INCLUDE VOLUNTEER WORK *(non-paid work)*--**If the work** *(or a part of the work)* **is like the job you are applying for,** complete **all** parts of the experience block just as you would for a paying job. You may receive credit for work experience with religious, community, welfare, service, and other organizations.

- INCLUDE MILITARY SERVICE--You should complete **all** parts of the experience block just as you would for a non-military job, including **all** supervisory experience. Describe each major change of duties or responsibilities in a separate experience block.

- IF YOU NEED MORE SPACE TO DESCRIBE A JOB--Use sheets of paper the same size as this page (be sure to include **all** information we ask for in **A** and **B** below). On **each** sheet show your name, Social Security Number, and the announcement number or job title.

- IF YOU NEED MORE EXPERIENCE BLOCKS, use the SF 171-A or a sheet of paper.

- IF YOU NEED TO UPDATE (ADD MORE RECENT JOBS), use the SF 172 or a sheet of paper as described above.

A | Name and address of employer's organization *(include ZIP Code, if known)* | Dates employed *(give month, day and year)* | Average number of hours per week | Number of employees you supervise |

From: To:

Salary or earnings | Your reason for wanting to leave

Starting $ per

Ending $ per

Your immediate supervisor | Exact title of your job | If Federal employment *(civilian or military)* list series, grade or rank, and, if promoted in this job, the date of your last promotion

Name | Area Code | Telephone No.

Description of work: Describe your specific duties, responsibilities and accomplishments in this job, **including** the job title(s) of any employees you supervise. *If you describe more than one type of work (for example, carpentry and painting, or personnel and budget), write the approximate percentage of time you spent doing each.*

For Agency Use (skill codes, etc.)

B | Name and address of employer's organization *(include ZIP Code, if known)* | Dates employed *(give month, day and year)* | Average number of hours per week | Number of employees you supervised |

From: To:

Salary or earnings | Your reason for leaving

Starting $ per

Ending $ per

Your immediate supervisor | Exact title of your job | If Federal employment *(civilian or military)* list series, grade or rank, and, if promoted in this job, the date of your last promotion

Name | Area Code | Telephone No.

Description of work: Describe your specific duties, responsibilities and accomplishments in this job, **including** the job title(s) of any employees you supervised. *If you describe more than one type of work (for example, carpentry and painting, or personnel and budget), write the approximate percentage of time you spent doing each.*

For Agency Use (skill codes, etc.)

Page 2   IF YOU NEED MORE EXPERIENCE BLOCKS, USE SF 171-A *(SEE BACK OF INSTRUCTION PAGE).*

← ──────── **ATTACH ANY ADDITIONAL FORMS AND SHEETS HERE**

EDUCATION

25 Did you graduate from high school? *If you have a GED high school equivalency or will graduate within the next nine months, answer* **"YES"**.

YES ⎤ If **"YES"**, give month and year graduated or received GED equivalency: . . . .
NO ⎦ If **"NO"**, give the highest grade you completed: .

26 Write the name and location *(city and state)* of the last high school you attended or where you obtained your GED high school equivalency.

27 Have you ever attended college or graduate school? **YES** **NO**   If **"YES"**, continue with **28**. If **NO"**, go to **31**.

28 NAME AND LOCATION *(city, state and ZIP Code)* OF COLLEGE OR UNIVERSITY.. *If you expect to graduate within nine months, give the* **month** *and* **year** *you expect to receive your degree:*

	Name	City	State	ZIP Code	MONTH AND YEAR ATTENDED From	To	NUMBER OF CREDIT HOURS COMPLETED Semester	Quarter	TYPE OF DEGREE *(e.g. B.A., M.A.)*	MONTH AND YEAR OF DEGREE
1)										
2)										
3)										

29

CHIEF UNDERGRADUATE SUBJECTS *Show major on the first line*	NUMBER OF CREDIT HOURS COMPLETED Semester	Quarter
1)		
2)		
3)		

30

CHIEF GRADUATE SUBJECTS *Show major on the first line*	NUMBER OF CREDIT HOURS COMPLETED Semester	Quarter
1)		
2)		
3)		

31 If you have completed any **other courses or training related to the kind of jobs you are applying for** *(trade, vocational, Armed Forces, business)* give information below.

NAME AND LOCATION *(city, state and ZIP Code)* OF SCHOOL	MONTH AND YEAR ATTENDED From	To	CLASS-ROOM HOURS	SUBJECT(S)	TRAINING COMPLETED YES	NO
School Name 1) City State ZIP Code						
School Name 2) City State ZIP Code						

SPECIAL SKILLS, ACCOMPLISHMENTS AND AWARDS

32 Give the title and year of any honors, awards or fellowships you have received. List your special qualifications, skills or accomplishments that may help you get a job. *Some examples are: skills with computers or other machines; most important publications (do not submit copies); public speaking and writing experience; membership in professional or scientific societies; patents or inventions; etc.*

33 How many words per minute can you: TYPE? TAKE DICTATION?

Agencies may test your skills before hiring you.

34 List **job-related** licenses or certificates that you have, such as: *registered nurse; lawyer; radio operator; driver's; pilot's; etc.*

	LICENSE OR CERTIFICATE	DATE OF LATEST LICENSE OR CERTIFICATE	STATE OR OTHER LICENSING AGENCY
1)			
2)			

35 Do you speak or read a language other than English *(include sign language)?* **Applicants for jobs that require a language other than English may be given an interview conducted solely in that language.** **YES** **NO**   If **"YES"**, list each language and place an **"X"** in each column that applies to you. If **"NO"**, go to **36**.

LANGUAGE(S)	CAN PREPARE AND GIVE LECTURES Fluently	With Difficulty	CAN SPEAK AND UNDERSTAND Fluently	Passably	CAN TRANSLATE ARTICLES Into English	From English	CAN READ ARTICLES FOR OWN USE Easily	With Difficulty
1)								
2)								

REFERENCES

36 List three people who are not related to you and are not supervisors you listed under **24** who know your qualifications and fitness for the kind of job for which you are applying. At least **one** should know you well on a personal basis.

FULL NAME OF REFERENCE	TELEPHONE NUMBER(S) *(Include Area Code)*	PRESENT BUSINESS OR HOME ADDRESS *(Number, street and city)*	STATE	ZIP CODE
1)				
2)				
3)				

Page 3

BACKGROUND INFORMATION--*You must answer each question in this section before we can process your application.*

		YES	NO
37	Are you a citizen of the United States? *(In most cases you must be a U.S. citizen to be hired. You will be required to submit proof of identity and citizenship at the time you are hired.)* If **"NO"**, give the country or countries you are a citizen of:_____		

> **NOTE:** It is important that you give complete and truthful answers to questions 38 through 44. If you answer **"YES"** to any of them, provide your explanation(s) in **Item 45.** Include convictions resulting from a plea of nolo contendere *(no contest)*. Omit: 1) traffic fines of $100.00 or less; 2) any violation of law committed before your 16th birthday; 3) any violation of law committed before your 18th birthday, if finally decided in juvenile court or under a Youth Offender law; 4) any conviction set aside under the Federal Youth Corrections Act or similar State law; 5) any conviction whose record was expunged under Federal or State law. We will consider the date, facts, and circumstances of each event you list. In most cases you can still be considered for Federal jobs. However, **if you fail to tell the truth or fail to list all relevant** events or circumstances, this may be grounds for not hiring you, for firing you after you begin work, or for criminal prosecution (18 USC 1001).

		YES	NO
38	During the last **10 years**, were you **fired from any job** for any reason, did you **quit after being told that you would be fired**, or did you leave by mutual agreement because of specific problems?..........................		
39	Have you **ever** been convicted of, or forfeited collateral for **any felony violation?** *(Generally, a felony is defined as any violation of law punishable by imprisonment of longer than one year, except for violations called misdemeanors under State law which are punishable by imprisonment of two years or less.)*..........................		
40	Have you **ever** been convicted of, or forfeited collateral for **any firearms or explosives violation?**................		
41	Are you **now** under charges for **any** violation of law?..........................		
42	During the **last 10 years** have you forfeited collateral, been convicted, been imprisoned, been on probation, or been on parole? Do **not** include violations reported in 39, 40, or 41, above..........................		
43	Have you **ever** been convicted by a military **court-martial?** If no military service, answer **"NO"**..........................		
44	Are you **delinquent** on any Federal debt? *(Include delinquencies arising from Federal taxes, loans, overpayment of benefits, and other debts to the U.S. Government **plus** defaults on Federally guaranteed or insured loans such as student and home mortgage loans.)*........		

45 If **"YES"** in: **38** - Explain for each job the problem(s) and your reason(s) for leaving. Give the employer's name and address.
                      39 through 43 - Explain each violation. Give place of occurrence and name/address of police or court involved.
                      44 - Explain the type, length and amount of the delinquency or default, and steps you are taking to correct errors or repay the debt. Give any identification number associated with the debt and the address of the Federal agency involved.
     NOTE: If you need more space, use a sheet of paper, and include the item number.

Item No.	Date (Mo./Yr.)	Explanation	Mailing Address
			Name of Employer, Police, Court, or Federal Agency
			City State ZIP Code
			Name of Employer, Police, Court, or Federal Agency
			City State ZIP Code

		YES	NO
46	Do you receive, or have you ever applied for retirement pay, pension, or other pay based on military, Federal civilian, or District of Columbia Government service?..........................		
47	Do any of your relatives work for the United States Government or the United States Armed Forces? Include: *father; mother; husband; wife; son; daughter; brother; sister; uncle; aunt; first cousin; nephew; niece; father-in-law; mother-in-law; son-in-law; daughter-in-law; brother-in-law; sister-in-law; stepfather; stepmother; stepson; stepdaughter; stepbrother; stepsister; half brother; and half sister.*........		

If **"YES"**, provide details below. If you need more space, use a sheet of paper.

Name	Relationship	Department, Agency or Branch of Armed Forces

SIGNATURE, CERTIFICATION, AND RELEASE OF INFORMATION

YOU MUST SIGN THIS APPLICATION. Read the following carefully before you sign.

- A false statement on any part of your application may be grounds for not hiring you, or for firing you after you begin work. Also, you may be punished by fine or imprisonment (U.S. Code, title 18, section 1001).
- If you are a male born after December 31, 1959 you must be registered with the Selective Service System or have a valid exemption in order to be eligible for Federal employment. You will be required to certify as to your status at the time of appointment.
- I **understand** that any information I give may be investigated as allowed by law or Presidential order.
- I **consent** to the release of information about my ability and fitness for Federal employment **by** *employers, schools, law enforcement agencies and other individuals and organizations,* **to** *investigators, personnel staffing specialists, and other authorized employees of the Federal Government.*
- I **certify** that, to the best of my knowledge and belief, **all** of my statements are true, correct, complete, and made in good faith.

48 SIGNATURE *(Sign each application in dark ink)*	**49** DATE SIGNED *(Month, day, year)*

*U.S. Government Printing Office: 1994 — 300-892/60191

OPTIONAL APPLICATION FOR FEDERAL EMPLOYMENT
(OF 612 – Form Approved: OMB No. 3206-021)

You may apply for most jobs with a resume, this form, or other written format. If your resume or application does not provide all the information requested on this form and in the job vacancy announcement, you may lose consideration for a job.

1. JOB TITLE IN ANNOUNCEMENT: _____

2. GRADE(S) APPLYING FOR: _____

3. ANNOUNCEMENT NUMBER: _____

4. LAST NAME: _____ FIRST, MIDDLE: _____

5. SOCIAL SECURITY NUMBER: _____-____-_____

6. MAILING ADDRESS: _____

   CITY/STATE/ZIP: _____

7. PHONE NUMBERS (include area code)   DAYTIME: _____

                                       EVENING: _____

8. WORK EXPERIENCE: Describe your paid and nonpaid work experience related to the job for which you are applying. (Do not attach job descriptions)

1) JOB TITLE (If Federal,
   include series and grade): _____

   FROM (MM/YY): _____ TO (MM/YY): _____

   SALARY: $_____ per _____ HOURS PER WEEK: _____

   EMPLOYER'S NAME: _____

   AND ADDRESS: _____

   SUPERVISOR'S NAME: _____

   AND PHONE: _____

   DESCRIBE YOUR DUTIES AND ACCOMPLISHMENTS:

DUTIES AND ACCOMPLISHMENTS: (CONTINUED)

2) JOB TITLE (If Federal,
    include series and grade): _____

    FROM (MM/YY): _____   TO (MM/YY): _____

    SALARY: $_____ per _____ HOURS PER WEEK: _____

    EMPLOYER'S NAME: _____

    AND ADDRESS: _____

    SUPERVISOR'S NAME: _____

    AND PHONE: _____

    DESCRIBE YOUR DUTIES AND ACCOMPLISHMENTS:

9. MAY WE CONTACT YOUR CURRENT SUPERVISOR?   YES [   ]
    (If we need to contact your current supervisor
    before making an offer, we will contact you first.)   NO [   ]

EDUCATION

                                   Some HS   [   ]   Bachelor [   ]
10. MARK HIGHEST LEVEL COMPLETED: HS/GED   [   ]   Master   [   ]
                                   Associate [   ]   Doctoral [   ]

11. LAST HIGH SCHOOL or GED SCHOOL: _____

    CITY/STATE/ZIP (if ZIP known): _____

    YEAR DIPLOMA or GED RECEIVED: _____

12. COLLEGES AND UNIVERSITIES ATTENDED (Do not attach a copy of your transcript unless requested.)

1) NAME: _____

CITY/STATE/ZIP: _____

SEMESTER CREDITS EARNED: _____   MAJOR(S): _____
   (or)
QUARTER CREDITS EARNED: _____   _____

DEGREE (If any): _____   YEAR RECEIVED: _____

2) NAME: _____

CITY/STATE/ZIP: _____

SEMESTER CREDITS EARNED: _____   MAJOR(S): _____
   (or)
QUARTER CREDITS EARNED: _____   _____

DEGREE (If any): _____   YEAR RECEIVED: _____

3) NAME: _____

CITY/STATE/ZIP: _____

SEMESTER CREDITS EARNED: _____   MAJOR(S): _____
   (or)
QUARTER CREDITS EARNED: _____   _____

DEGREE (If any): _____   YEAR RECEIVED: _____

OTHER QUALIFICATIONS

13. Job-related training courses (give title and year). Job-related skills (other languages, computer software/hardware, tools, machinery, typing speed, etc.). Job-related certificates and licenses (current only). Job-related honors, awards, and special accomplishments (publications, memberships in professional/honor societies, leadership activities, public speaking, and performance awards). Give dates, but do not send documents unless requested.

OTHER QUALIFICATIONS (CONTINUED)

GENERAL:

14. ARE YOU A U.S. CITIZEN?...................... YES [　]　　NO [　]

    If NO, give the country of your citizenship:

15. DO YOU CLAIM VETERANS' PREFERENCE?........ YES [　]　　NO [　]

    If YES, mark your claim of 5 or 10 points below:

    5 POINTS [　]　—　Attach your DD 214 or other proof.

    10 POINTS [　]　—　Attach an Application for 10-Point Veterans'
    　　　　　　　　　　　Preference (SF 15) and proof required.

16. WERE YOU EVER A FEDERAL
    CIVILIAN EMPLOYEE?.......................... YES [　]　　NO [　]

    If YES, for Highest Civilian Grade give:

    SERIES: _____ GRADE: _____ FROM (MM/YY): _____ TO (MM/YY): _____

17. ARE YOU ELIGIBLE FOR REINSTATEMENT
    BASED ON CAREER OR CAREER-CONDITIONAL
    FEDERAL STATUS? .... YES [　]　NO [　]

    If requested, attach SF 50 proof.

APPLICANT CERTIFICATION

18. I certify that, to the best of my knowledge and belief, all of the information on and attached to this application is true, correct, complete and made in good faith. I understand that false or fraudulent information on or attached to this application may be grounds for not hiring me or for firing me after I begin work, and may be punishable by fine or imprisonment. I understand that any information I give may be investigated.

    SIGNATURE: _____ DATE SIGNED: _____

GENERAL INFORMATION

- You may apply for most Federal jobs with a resume, this Optional Application for Federal Employment or other written format. If your resume or application does not provide all the information requested on this form and in the job vacancy announcement, you may lose consideration for a job. Type or print clearly in dark ink. Help speed the selection process by keeping your application brief and sending only the requested information. If essential to attach additional pages, include your name and Social Security Number on each page.
- For information on Federal employment, including job lists, alternative formats for persons with disabilities, and veterans' preference, call the U.S. Office of Personnel

Management at 912-757-3000, TDD 912-744-2299, by computer modem 912-757-3100, or via the Internet (Telnet only) at FJOB.MAIL.OPM.GOV.

- If you served on active duty in the United States Military and were separated under honorable conditions, you may be eligible for veterans' preference. To receive preference if your service began after October 15, 1976, you must have a Campaign Badge, Expeditionary Medal, or a service-connected disability. Veterans preference is not a factor for Senior Executive Service jobs or when competition is limited to status candidates (current or former career or career-conditional Federal employees).
- Most Federal jobs require United States citizenship and also that males over age 18 born after December 31, 1959, be registered with the Selective Service System or have an exemption.
- The law prohibits public official from appointing, promoting, or recommending their relatives.
- Federal annuitants (military and civilian) may have their salaries or annuities reduced. All employees must pay any valid delinquent debts or the agency may garnish their salary.
- Send your application to the office announcing the vacancy. If you have questions, contact that office.

THE FEDERAL GOVERNMENT IS AN EQUAL OPPORTUNITY EMPLOYER.

PRIVACY ACT AND PUBLIC BURDEN STATEMENTS

The Office of Personnel Management and other Federal agencies rate applicants for Federal jobs under the authority of sections 1104, 1302, 3301, 3304, 3320, 3361, 3393, and 3394 of title 5 of the United States Code. We need the information requested in this form and in the associated vacancy announcements to evaluate your qualifications. Other laws require us to ask about citizenship, military service, etc.

We request your Social Security Number (SSN) under the authority of Executive Order 9397 in order to keep your records straight; other people may have the same name. As allowed by law or Presidential directive, we use your SSN to seek information about you from employers, schools, banks, and others who know you. Your SSN may also be used in studies and computer matching with other Government files, for example, files on unpaid student loans.

If you do not give us your SSN or any other information requested, we cannot process your application, which is the first step in getting a job. Also, incomplete addresses and ZIP Codes will slow processing.

We may give information from your records to: training facilities; organizations deciding claims for retirement, insurance, unemployment or health benefits; officials in litigation or administrative proceedings where the Government is a party; law enforcement agencies concerning violations of law or regulation; Federal agencies for statistical reports and studies; officials of labor organizations recognized by law in connection with representing employees; Federal agencies or other sources requesting information for Federal agencies in connection with hiring or retaining, security clearances, security or suitability investigations, classifying jobs, contracting, or issuing licenses, grants, or other benefits; public and private organizations including news media that grant or publicize employee recognition and awards; and the Merit Systems Protection Board, the Office of Special Counsel, the Equal Employment Opportunity Commission, the Federal Labor Relations Authority, the National Archives, the Federal Acquisition Institute, and congressional offices in connection with their official functions.

We may also give information from your records to: prospective nonfederal employers concerning tenure of employment, civil service status, length of service, and date and nature of action for separation as shown on personnel action forms of specifically identified individuals; requesting organizations or individuals concerning the home address and other relevant information on those who might have contracted an illness or been exposed to a health hazard; authorized Federal and nonfederal agencies for use in computer matching; spouses or dependent children asking whether the employee has changed from self-and-family to self-only health benefits enrollment; individuals working on a contract, service, grant, cooperative agreement or job for the Federal Government; non-agency members of an agency's performance or other panel; and agency-appointed representatives of employees concerning information issued to the employee about fitness-for-duty or agency-filed disability retirement procedures.

We estimate the public reporting burden for the employment information will vary from 20 to 240 minutes with an average of 40 minutes per response, including time for reviewing instructions, searching existing data sources, gathering data, and completing and reviewing the information. You may send comments regarding the burden estimate or any other aspect of the collection of information, including suggestions for reducing this burden, to U.S. Office of Personnel Management, Reports and Forms Management Officer, Washington, DC 20415-0001.

Send your application to the agency announcing the vacancy.

Board Structure/Statutory Provisions (A State Comparison Study)

State	Board Members		Type	Practice or Title Protection	Groups Exempted
	Total	SWs			
Alabama State Board of Social Work Examiners Folsom Administrative Building 64 North Union Street, Suite 129 Montgomery, AL 36130 (334) 242-5860	7	7	Independent Licensure	Practice	Qualified other professionals; supervised students; other groups licensed under state law.

Alaska
 Bd. of Clinical Social
   Work Examiners
 Division of Occupational
   Licensing
 Dept. of Commerce & Econ.
   Develop.
 P.O. Box 110806
 Juneau, AK 99811-0806
 (907) 465-2551
	5	4	Independent Licensure	Practice	Qualified other professionals; federal, state, and local government employees; private nonprofit organizations exempt from federal income tax.

Arizona Bd. of Behavioral Health Examiners 1400 West Washington, #350 Phoenix, AZ 85007 (602) 542-1882	12	2	Composite Certification	Title Protection	Qualified other professionals; supervised students; licensed behavioral health agency employees; nonstate residents (consultant status).
Arkansas Social Work Licensing Board 2020 West Third, Suite 503 P.O. Box 250381 Little Rock, AR 72225 (501) 372-5071	9	6	Independent Licensure	Practice	Qualified other professionals; supervised students; employees of licensed hospitals; family and social service workers employed by state agencies and departments.

California Bd. of Behavioral Science Examiners 400 R Street, Suite 3150 Sacramento, CA 95814-6240 (916) 445-4933	11	2	Composite Licensure	Practice	Qualified other professionals; employees of federal, state, county or municipal governmental organizations or non-profit organizations; education institutions engaged in the training of graduate students or social work interns; nonstate residents (consultant status).
Colorado Board of Social Work Examiners 1560 Broadway, Suite 1340 Denver, CO 80202 (303) 894-7766	7	5	Independent Licensure	Practice	Qualified other professionals; rehabilitation counselors; community mental health center employees; department of social service employees; public school employees.
Connecticut Department of Public Health Social Work Regulation 410 Capitol Avenue, MS #12 App. Hartford, CT 06314-0308 (806) 509-7567	—	—	Composite Licensure	Practice	Qualified other professionals and supervised students.
Delaware Board of Social Work Examiners Cannon Building, Suite 203 861 Silverlake Blvd. Dover, DE 19904-2467 (302) 739-4522 × 220	7	4	Independent Licensure	Practice	No exemptions.
District of Columbia Board of Social Work DC Department of Health Office of Professional Licensing, Room 2204 Washington, DC 20001 (202) 442-9200	5	4	Independent Licensure	Practice	Qualified other professionals and supervised students.

Florida
Board of Clinical Social Work,
  Marriage and Family Therapy,
  and Mental Health Counseling
202 Capital Circle, SE,
  BIN #C08
Tallahassee, FL 32399-3258
(850) 488-0595
	9	2	Composite
			Licensure
				Practice	Qualified other professionals; government agency employees; employees of private non-profit organizations; supervised students; nonstate residents (consultant status).

Georgia
Composite Bd. of PC, Social
  Workers and Marriage &
  Family Therapists
237 Coliseum Drive
Macon, GA 31217-3858
(912) 207-1670
	10	3	Composite
			Licensure
				Title
				Protection
					Qualified other profes-
					sionals; government
					agency employees; em-
					ployees of licensed hospi-
					tals and long term care
					facilities; supervised stu-
					dents; school counselors;
					rehabilitation and addic-
					tion counselors.

Hawaii *(No Board)* Department of Commercial Consumer Affairs Social Work Program P.O. Box 3469 Honolulu, HI 96813 (808) 586-3000	—	—	No Board Licensure	Title Protection	Qualified other profes- sionals; supervised stu- dents; employees of federal, state, or county governmental agencies.

Idaho
State Board of Social
  Work Examiners
Bureau of Occupational
  Licensing
Owyhee Plaza/1109 Main St.,
  Ste 220
Boise, ID 83702
(208) 334-3233
	5	5	Independent
			Licensure
				Practice
				Title
				Protection
					Qualified other profes-
					sionals and supervised
					students.

Illinois
SW Examining &
  Disciplinary Board
Dept. of Professional Regulation
320 West Washington Street,
  3rd Floor
Springfield, IL 62786
(217) 785-0800
	9	7	Independent
			Licensure
				Practice
				Title
				Protection
					Qualified other profes-
					sionals; government
					agency employees; vol-
					unteers; persons em-
					ployed by a hospital,
					clinic, or health care
					facility.

Indiana
SW Certification and Marriage
  & Family Therapists
  Credentialing Board
Health Professions Bureau
Indiana Government Center
402 West Washington St.,
  Room 041
Indianapolis, IN 46204
(317) 233-4422
	9	3	Composite
			Licensure
				Title
				Protection
				Practice
					Qualified other profes-
					sionals; supervised stu-
					dents; employees or
					volunteers of a nonprofit
					corporation; nonstate res-
					idents (consultant
					status).

Iowa Board of Social Work Examiners IA Department of Public Health Bureau of Professional Licensure Lucas State Office Building 321 E. 12th Street Des Moines, IA 50319-0075 (515) 281-4422	7	5	Independent Licensure	Title Protection Practice	Qualified other profes- sionals; supervised students.

Kansas Behavioral Sciences Regulatory Board 712 S. Kansas Avenue Topeka, KS 66603-3817 (785) 296-3240	7	2	Composite Licensure	Practice Title Protection	Qualified other professionals.
Kentucky Board of Examiners of Social Work Berry Hill Annex Louisville Road, Box 456 Frankfort, KY 40602 (502) 564-3296	7	6	Independent Licensure	Practice Title Protection	Qualified other profes- sionals; state education employees; government employees.
Louisiana State Board of Board Certified Social Work Examiners 11930 Perkins Rd., Suite B Baton Rouge, LA 70810 (225) 763-5470	5	5	Independent Licensure	Practice Title Protection	Qualified other profes- sionals; government em- ployees; supervised students; state agency or institution employees; employees of nonprofit organizations.
Maine State Board of Social Work Licensure 35 State House Station Augusta, ME 04333 (207) 624-8603	7	5	Independent Licensure	Practice Title Protection	No exemptions.

Maryland
State Board of Social
  Work Examiners
Dept. of Health &
  Mental Hygiene
4201 Patterson Avenue
Baltimore, MD 21215-2299
(410) 764-4788
	7	5	Independent
			Licensure
				Practice
				Title
				Protection
					Federal government em-
					ployees and supervised
					students; qualified other
					professionals.

Massachusetts Commonwealth of Mass., Division of Registration 239 Causeway St. Boston, MA 02114 (617) 727-3073	7	4	Independent Licensure	Practice	Qualified other profes- sionals; supervised stu- dents; employees of state, county, or municipal gov- ernmental agencies.
Michigan Board of Examiners of Social Work P.O. Box 30246 Lansing, MI 48909 (517) 241-9245	9	6	Independent Registration	Title Protection	No exemptions.

Minnesota Board of Social Work Examiners 2829 University Ave., SE, Suite 340 Minneapolis, MN 55414-3239 (612) 617-2100	15	10	Independent Licensure	Practice Title Protection	Qualified other professionals; supervised students; geographic waiver; city, county and state agency social workers; federally recognized tribes and private nonprofit agencies with a minority focus; hospital and nursing home social workers.
Mississippi Board of Examiners for Social Workers and MFT P.O. Box 4508 Jackson, MS 39215-4508 (601) 987-6806	7	6	Independent Licensure	Practice Title Protection	Qualified other professionals; employees of any office, officer, or agency of the United States; supervised students.
Missouri State Committee for Licensed Social Workers Division of Professional Registration P.O. Box 1335 Jefferson City, MO 65102-0085 (573) 751-0885	7	6	Independent Licensure	Practice Title Protection	Qualified other professionals; employees of any agency or departments of the state of Missouri.
Montana Board of Social Work Examiners 111 North Jackson, Arcade Building P.O Box 200513 Helena, MT 59620-0407 (406) 444-4285	5	4	Composite Licensure	Title Protection	Qualified other professionals; employees of federal, state, county, or municipal agencies, educational, research or charitable institution, or a licensed health care facility; nonstate residents (consultant status).
Nebraska Bureau of Examining Boards 301 Centennial Mall South P.O. Box 94986 Lincoln, NE 68509-4986 (402) 471-2115	4	3	Composite Certification	Practice	Qualified other professionals and supervised students.
Nevada Board of Examiners for Social Workers 4600 Kietzke Lane, Suite C121 Reno, NV 89502 (775) 688-2555	5	4	Independent Licensure	Practice	Qualified other professionals; government employees; supervised students.

New Hampshire Board of Examiners of Psychology and Mental Health Practice 105 Pleasant Street, Box 457 Concord, NH 03301 (603) 271-6762	11	2	Composite Certification	Title Protection	Qualified other professionals; supervised students; employees of federal, state, county or municipal agencies, other political subdivisions, or duly chartered educational institutions; persons providing mental health serves as an employee or consultant to an institution, facility, or nonprofit institution or agency.
New Jersey State Board of Social Work Examiners P.O. Box 45033 Newark, NJ 07101 (973) 504-6495	9	6	Independent Licensure	Practice Title Protection	Qualified other professionals; supervised students; employees of the state or other political subdivision; volunteers or employees of a nonprofit organization.
New Mexico Board of Social Work Examiners 2055 S. Pachoco Street P.O. Box 25101 Santa Fe, NM 87504 (505) 476-7100	10	5	Independent Licensure	Practice Title Protection	No exemptions.
New York State Board for Social Work NY State Education Department Cultural Education Center, Rm #3041 Albany, NY 12230 (518) 474-4974	7	7	Independent Certification	Title Protection	No exemptions.
North Carolina NC Social Work Board 130 South Church Street P.O. Box 1043 Asheboro, NC 27204 (336) 625-1679	7	4	Independent Certification	Practice Title Protection	Employees engaged in clinical social work practice exclusively for either the state, a political subdivision of the state, local government, or a hospital or health care facility licensed by the state (effective until January 1, 1999).

North Dakota Board of Social Work Examiners P.O. Box 914 Bismarck, ND 58506-0914 (701) 222-0255	6	4	Independent Licensure	Practice Title Protection	Qualified other professionals; supervised students; employees of nonprofit agencies or organizations; employees of hospitals, intermediate care facilities or nursing homes.
Ohio Social Work Board 77 South High Street, 16th Floor Columbus, OH 43266-0340 (614) 466-0912	11	4	Composite Licensure	Practice Title Protection	Qualified other professionals; persons certified by the state board of education; supervised students; civil service employees; members of the profession of alcoholism training and drug abuse training; employees of the American Red Cross; members of labor organizations with union counselor certificates; employees of hospitals and nursing homes.
Oklahoma Board of Licensed Social Workers 3535 NW 58th, Suite 765 Oklahoma City, OK 73112 (405) 946-7230	7	6	Independent Licensure	Practice	Qualified other professionals and state agency employees.
Oregon State Board of Licensed Clinical SWs 3218 Pringle Road, SE, Suite 140 Salem, OR 97302-6310 (503) 378-5735	7	4	Independent Licensure	Title Protection	No exemptions.
Pennsylvania State Board of Social Work Examiners P.O. Box 2649 Harrisburg, PA 17105-2649 (717) 783-1389	7	4	Independent Licensure	Title Protection	No exemptions.
Puerto Rico *(No Board)* c/o NASW, Puerto Rico Chapter 271 Ramon Ramos Urb. Roosevelt Hata Rey, PR 00918 (809) 758-3588	7 (not in effect)	7 (not in effect)	Independent Licensure	Practice	No exemptions.

Rhode Island Division of Professional Regulation RI Department of Health 3 Capitol Hill, Room 104 Providence, RI 02908-5097 (401) 277-2827	7	6	Independent Licensure	Practice Title Protection	Qualified other profes- sionals; supervised stu- dents; state employees.
South Carolina Board of Social Work Examiners P.O. Box 11329 Columbia, SC 29211-1329 (803) 896-4665	7	6	Independent Licensure	Title Protection	Qualified other profes- sionals; employees of li- censed hospitals; supervised students.
South Dakota Board of Social Work Examiners 135 East Illinois, Suite 214 Spearfish, SD 57783 (605) 642-1600	5	4	Independent Licensure	Practice Title Protection	Qualified other profes- sionals and supervised students.
Tennessee Board of SW Certification & Licensure Cordell Hull Building 426 5th Ave. N Nashville, TN 37247-1010 (615) 532-5132	5	4	Independent Licensure	Practice Title Protection	No exemptions.
Texas State Board of Social Work Examiners 1100 W. 49th Street Austin, TX 78756-3183 (512) 719-3521	9	6	Independent Licensure	Title Protection	Qualified other profes- sionals; supervised stu- dents; nonstate residents (consultant status).
Utah Social Work Licensing Board Occupational & Professional Licensing 160 East 300 South P.O. Box 146741 Salt Lake City, UT 84145-0805 (801) 530-6163	5	4	Independent Licensure	Practice Title Protection	Qualified other profes- sionals; supervised stu- dents; persons serving in the U.S. armed forces or other federal agencies; nonstate residents (con- sultant status).
Vermont *(No Board)* Office of the Secretary of State Licensing & Registration Division 109 State Street Montpelier, VT 05609-1106 (802) 828-2390	—	2 (on adv. comm.)	Independent Licensure	Practice Title Protection	Qualified other profes- sionals; supervised stu- dents; employees of schools.

Virginia Board of Social Work 6606 West Broad Street, 4th Floor Richmond, VA 23230-1717 (804) 662-9914	7	5	Independent Licensure	Practice Title Protection	Qualified other profes- sionals; supervised stu- dents; private personnel managers; employees of the federal government, the Commonwealth, a lo- cality, or of any agency established or funded by any such governmental entity or of a private, non- profit organization or agency.
Virgin Islands Board of Social Work Licensure No. 1 Subbase, 2nd Floor, Room 205 St. Thomas, VI 00802 (809) 774-3130	5	4	Independent Licensure	Practice Title Protection	Qualified other profes- sionals and supervised students.

Washington
Mental Health Q. Assurance
    Council
Dept. of Health Counselors
    Section
P.O. Box 47869
Olympia, WA 98504-7869
(360) 236-4900
	7	1	Composite
			Certification
				Practice
				Title
				Protection
					Qualified other profes-
					sionals; employees or
					trainees of the federal
					government; practice of
					counseling by persons in
					public and private non-
					profit organizations; non-
					state residents (consultant
					status).

West Virginia Board of Social Work Examiners P.O. Box 5459 Charleston, WV 25361 (304) 558-8816	7	6	Independent Licensure	Practice Title Protection	Qualified other profes- sionals and supervised students.

Wisconsin
Board of Social Workers, MFTs,
    and Professional Counselors
Department of Regulation
    & Licensing
P.O. Box 8935
Madison, WI 53708-8935
(608) 267-7212
	13	4	Composite
			Certification
				Title
				Protection
					School social workers
					and school counselors.

Wyoming
Prof. Counselors, MFTs, SWs,
    & Chemical Dependency
    Licensing Board
2020 Carey Ave., Suite 201
Cheyenne, WY 82002
(307) 777-7788
	6	1	Composite
			Licensure
				Practice
				Title
				Protection
					Qualified other professionals; employees of any agency of the federal, state, or any political subdivision, or public or private educational institution; supervised students; persons offering volunteer services in public or private nonprofit organizations; nonstate residents (consultant status).

Source: Adapted from *Social Work Laws and Board Regulations: A State Comparison Study,* by the American Association of State Social Work Boards, 1998, Culpeper, VA. Copyright © 1998 by the American Association of State Social Work Boards. Reprinted with permission. Updated from web site www.aswb.org.

Note: An independent board only regulates the social work profession. A composite board is multidisciplinary and regulates more than one profession, usually all mental health related. State laws use three terms for legal regulation—licensing, certification, and, in Michigan, registration. Practice acts set forth criteria for authorization to practice a profession with a defined scope. They determine who can perform the professional activities defined by the law as social work. A title protection act specifies who may use the title of social worker.

Levels of Practice Regulated (A State Comparison Study)

State	Title	Initials	Education	Experience	Exam Required	Board Approval
Alabama	Private Independent Practice	PIP	DSW/MSW	2 yrs POST	N/R	YES
	Licensed Certified Social Worker	LCSW	DSW/MSW	2 yrs POST	Clinical/ Advanced	
	Licensed Graduate Social Worker	LGSW	DSW/MSW	0	Intermediate	
	Licensed Bachelor Social Worker	LBSW	BSW	0	Basic	
Alaska	Licensed Master Social Worker	LMSW	DSW/MSW	0	Intermediate	YES
	Licensed Baccalaureate Social Worker	LBSW	BSW	0	Basic	
Arizona	Certified Independent Social Worker	CISW	DSW/MSW	2 yrs POST	Clin/Adv	YES
	Certified Master Social Worker	CMSW	DSW/MSW	0	Intermediate	
	Certified Baccalaureate Social Worker	CBSW	BSW	0	Basic	
Arkansas	Licensed Certified Social Worker	LCSW	MSW	2 yrs POST	Clin/Adv	YES
	Licensed Master Social Worker	LMSW	MSW	0	Intermediate	
	Licensed Social Worker	LSW	BSW	0	Basic	
California	Licensed Clinical Social Worker	LCSW	MSW	2 yrs POST	Clinical*	YES
	Associate Clinical Social Worker	ASW	MSW	0	N/R	
Colorado	Licensed Independent Social Worker	LISW	DSW/MSW	1 yr POST 2 yrs POST	Clin/Adv Clin/Adv	NO
	Licensed Social Worker	LSW	MSW	0	Intermediate	
	Registered Social Worker	RSW	BSW	0	Basic	

*Oral exam

Connecticut	Licensed Clinical Social Worker	LCSW	DSW/MSW	3000 hrs POST	Clin/Adv	YES
Delaware	Licensed Clinical Social Worker	LCSW	DSW/MSW	2 yrs POST	Clinical	YES
District of Columbia	Licensed Independent Clinical Social Worker	LICSW	DSW/MSW	3000 hrs POST	Clinical	NO
	Licensed Independent Social Worker	LISW	DSW/MSW	3000 hrs POST	Advanced	
	Licensed Graduate Social Worker	LGSW	DSW/MSW	0	Intermediate	
	Licensed Social Work Associate	LSWA	BSW	0	Basic	
Florida	Licensed Clinical Social Worker	LCSW	DSW/MSW	3 yrs (2 yrs POST)	Clinical*	YES
	Certified Master Social Worker	CMSW	MSW	3 yrs (2 yrs POST)	Intermediate*	
Georgia	Licensed Clinical Social Worker	LCSW	MSW	3 yrs POST	Clinical/ Advanced	YES
	Licensed Master Social Worker	LMSW	MSW	0	Intermediate	
Hawaii	Licensed Social Worker	LSW	DSW/MSW	0	Intermediate	YES
Idaho	Independent Practice Certified Social Worker	CSWP	DSW/MSW	2 yrs POST	Intermediate	YES
		CSW	DSW/MSW	0	Intermediate	
	Social Worker	SW	BSW	0	Basic	
Illinois	Licensed Clinical Social Worker	LCSW	DSW or MSW	2000 hrs POST 3000 hrs POST	Clinical Clinical	NO
	Licensed Social Worker	LSW	MSW or BSW	0 3 yrs POST	Intermediate Intermediate	
Indiana	Licensed Clinical Social Worker	LCSW	MSW	2000 hrs POST	Clinical	YES
	Licensed Social Worker	LSW	MSW or BSW	0 2 yrs POST	Intermediate Intermediate	
Iowa	Licensed Independent Social Worker	LISW	DSW/MSW	2 yrs POST	Clinical	YES
	Licensed Master Social Worker	LMSW	DSW/MSW	0	Intermediate	
	Licensed Bachelor Social Worker	LBSW	BSW	0	Basic	
Kansas	Specialist Clinical Social Worker	LSCSW	DSW/MSW	2 yrs POST	Clinical	YES
	Master Social Worker	MSW	MSW	0	Intermediate	
	Baccalaureate Social Worker	BSW	BSW	0	Basic	

*Laws/rules exam

State	License	Abbr.	Degree	Experience	Level	Exam
Kentucky	Licensed Independent Practice	LCSW	DSW/MSW	2 yrs POST	Clinical	YES
	Certified Social Worker	CSW	DSW/MSW	0	Intermediate	
	Licensed Social Worker	LSW	BSW or BA	0 / 2 yrs	Basic / Basic	
Louisiana	Board Certified Social Worker	BCSW	MSW	2 yrs POST	Clin/Adv	YES
Maine	Licensed Clinical Social Worker	LCSW	DSW/MSW	2 yrs POST	Clinical	NO
	Licensed Master Social Worker	LMSW	DSW/MSW	0	Intermediate	
	Licensed Social Worker	LSW	BSW or BA/BS	0 / 3200 hrs	Basic / Basic	
Maryland	Licensed Cert. Social Worker—Clinical	LCSW/C	DSW/MSW	2 yrs POST	Clinical	YES
	Licensed Certified Social Worker	LCSW	DSW/MSW	2 yrs POST	Advanced	
	Licensed Graduate Social Worker	LGSW	DSW/MSW	0	Intermediate	
	Licensed Social Work Associate	LSWA	BSW	0	Basic	
Massachusetts	Licensed Independent Clinical Social Worker	LICSW	DSW/MSW	3 yrs	Clinical	NO
	Licensed Certified Social Worker	LCSW	DSW/MSW	0	Intermediate	
	Licensed Social Worker	LSW	BSW or BA or 1 yr college or HS	0 / 2 yrs / 1 yr / 8 yrs	Basic / Basic / Basic / Basic	
	Licensed Social Work Associate	LSWA	AA/BA	0	Associate	
Michigan	Certified Social Worker	CSW	MSW	2 yrs POST	N/R	NO
	Social Worker	SW	MSW or BA	0 / 2 yrs POST	N/R / N/R	
	Social Work Technician	SWT	2 yrs college or 1 yr exp	0 / 1 yr exp	N/R / N/R	
Minnesota	Licensed Independent Clinical Social Worker	LCSW	DSW/MSW	2 yrs POST	Clinical	YES
	Licensed Independent Social Worker	LISW	DSW/MSW	2 yrs POST	Advanced	
	Licensed Graduate Social Worker	LGSW	MSW	0	Intermediate	
	Licensed Social Worker	LSW	BSW	0	Basic	

Mississippi	Licensed Certified Social Worker	LCSW	DSW/MSW	2 yrs POST	Clin/Adv	YES
	Licensed Master Social Worker	LMSW	DSW/MSW	0	Intermediate	
	Licensed Social Worker	LSW	BSW	0	Basic	
Missouri	Licensed Clinical Social Worker	LCSW	DSW/MSW	2 yrs POST	Clin/Adv	NO
Montana	Licensed Social Worker	LSW	DSW/MSW	2 yrs POST	Advanced	YES
Nebraska	Certified Master Social Worker	CMSW	DSW/MSW	3000 hrs POST	Clin/Adv	YES
	Licensed Independent Social Worker	LMHP	DSW/MSW	3000 hrs POST	Clinical	
	Certified Social Worker	CSW	MSW/BSW	0	N/R	
Nevada	Licensed Clinical Social Worker	LCSW	DSW/MSW	3000 hrs POST	Clinical	YES
	Licensed Independent Social Worker	LISW	DSW/MSW	3000 hrs POST	Adv/Interm	
	Licensed Social Worker	LSW	MSW/BSW or MA/BA	0 3000 hrs POST	Basic/Interm Basic	
New Hampshire	Certified Clinical Social Worker	CCSW	DSW/MSW	2 yrs POST	Clinical	NO
New Jersey	Licensed Clinical Social Worker	LCSW	DSW/MSW	2 yrs	Clinical	NO
	Licensed Social Worker	LSW	DSW/MSW	0	Intermediate	
	Certified Social Worker	CSW	BSW or BA (prior to 4/6/95)	0 1 yr	N/R N/R	
New Mexico	Licensed Independent Social Worker	LISW	MSW	2 yrs POST	Clin/Adv*	YES
	Licensed Master Social Worker	LMSW	MSW	0	Intermediate*	
	Licensed Baccalaureate Social Worker	LBSW	BSW	0	Basic*	
New York	Certified Social Worker	CSW	MSW	0	Clin/Adv/ Intermediate	NO

*Cultural awareness exam required

State	License	Abbr	Degree	Experience	Level	Exam
North Carolina	Certified Clinical Social Worker	CCSW	DSW/MSW	2 yrs POST	Clinical	YES
	Certified Social Work Manager	CSWM	DSW/MSW	2 yrs POST	Advanced	
	Certified Master Social Worker	CMSW	DSW/MSW/ BSW	0	Intermediate	
	Certified Social Worker	CSW	BSW	0	Basic	
North Dakota	Licensed Indep. Clincal Social Worker	LICSW	DSW/MSW	4 yrs POST	Clinical	YES
					Intermediate	
	Licensed Certified Social Worker	LCSW	DSW/MSW	0		
					Basic	
	Licensed Social Worker	LSW	BSW	0		
Ohio	Licensed Independent Social Worker	LISW	DSW/MSW	2 yrs POST	Clin/Adv	NO
	Licensed Social Worker	LSW	DSW/MSW/ BSW	0	Basic	
	Registered Social Work Assistant	SWA	AA	0	N/R	
Oklahoma	Licensed for Private Practice	LSW	DSW/MSW	2 yrs POST	Clinical	YES
	Licensed Social Worker	LSW	DSW/MSW	2 yrs POST	Advanced	
	Licensed Social Work Associate	LSWA	BSW	2 yrs POST	Inter/Basic	
Oregon	Licensed Clinical Social Worker	LCSW	MSW	2 yrs POST	Clinical	YES
	Clinical Social Work Associate	CSWA	MSW	0	N/R	
Pennsylvania	Licensed Social Worker	LSW	DSW/MSW	0	Intermediate	NO
Puerto Rico	Licensed Social Worker	LSW	BSW	2 yrs POST	N/R	NO
Rhode Island	Licensed Independent Clinical Social Worker	LICSW	DSW/MSW	2 yrs POST	Clinical	YES
	Licensed Clinical Social Worker	LCSW	MSW	0	Intermediate	
South Carolina	Licensed Independent Social Worker	LISW	DSW/MSW	2 yrs POST	Clin/Adv	YES
	Licensed Master Social Worker	LMSW	DSW/MSW	0	Intermediate	
	Licensed Baccalaureate Social Worker	LBSW	BSW	0	Basic	

State	Title	Abbr.	Degree	Experience	Level	Exam
South Dakota	Independent Practice	CSW-PIP	DSW/MSW	2 yrs	Advanced	YES
	Certified Social Worker	CSW	DSW/MSW	0	Intermediate	
	Social Worker	SW	BSW or BA	0 / 2 yrs	Basic / Basic	
	Social Work Associate	SWA	AA/BA	0	Associate	
Tennessee	Independent Practitioner	LCSW	DSW/MSW	2 yrs POST	Clinical	YES
	Certified Master Social Worker	CMSW	DSW/MSW	0	N/R	
Texas	Advanced Clinical Practitioner	LMSW-ACP	DSW/MSW	3 yrs POST	Clinical	YES
	Advanced Practice	LMSW-AP	DSW/MSW	3 yrs POST	Advanced	
	Licensed Master Social Worker	LMSW	DSW/MSW	0	Intermediate	
	Licensed Social Worker	LSW	BSW	0	Basic	
	Social Work Associate	SWA	BA/AA	1 yr/3 yrs	Associate	
Utah	Clinical Social Worker	CSW	DSW/MSW	2 yrs POST	Clinical*	NO
	Certified Social Worker	CSW	DSW/MSW	0	Intermediate*	
	Social Service Worker	SSW	MSW/BSW or BA	0 / 1 yr POST	Basic* / Basic*	
Vermont	Licensed Indep. Clinical Social Worker	LICSW	DSW/MSW	2 yrs POST	Clinical	NO
Virginia	Licensed Clinical Social Worker	LCSW	MSW	2 yrs POST	Clinical	YES
	Licensed Social Worker	LSW	MSW or BSW	0 / 2 yrs POST	Basic / Basic	
Virgin Islands	Certified Independent Social Worker	CISW	DSW/MSW	2 yrs POST	Clin/Adv	YES
	Certified Social Worker	CSW	DSW/MSW	0	Intermediate	
	Social Worker	SW	BSW or BA	0 / 2 yrs POST	Basic / Basic	
	Social Work Associate	SWA	AA/BA	0	Basic	
Washington	Certified Social Worker	CSW	DSW/MSW	2 yrs POST	Clin/Adv	YES

*Laws/rules exam

West Virginia	Licensed Independent Clinical Social Worker	LICSW	DSW/MSW	2 yrs POST	Clinical	YES
	Licensed Certified Social Worker	LCSW	DSW/MSW	2 yrs POST	Advanced	
	Licensed Graduate Social Worker	LGSW	MSW	0	Intermediate	
	Licensed Social Worker	LSW	BSW	0	Basic	
Wisconsin	Certified Independent Clinical Social Worker	CICSW	DSW/MSW	2 yrs POST	Clinical*	YES
	Certified Independent Social Worker	CISW	DSW/MSW	2 yrs POST	Advanced*	
	Certified Adv. Practice Social Worker	CAPSW	DSW/MSW	0	Intermediate*	
	Certified Social Worker	CSW	MSW/BSW	0	Basic*	
Wyoming	Licensed Clinical Social Worker	LCSW	DSW/MSW	2 yrs POST	Clin/Adv	YES

Source: Adapted from *Social Work Laws and Board Regulations: A State Comparison Study,* by the American Association of State Social Work Boards, 1998, Culpeper, VA. Copyright © 1998 by the American Association of State Social Work Boards. Reprinted with permission.

Note: The terms refer to the number of years of experience required for the credential after earning the degree. The exams required are the four that are provided by the ASWB. Michigan does not require an examination and Puerto Rico does not use the ASWB exams. All other states require at least one of the exams. Board approval refers to the state requirements to approve the candidates before they take the exam. The states that don't require board approval allow candidates to take the exam; the results are reported to the board.

*Laws/rules exam

References

Academy of Certified Social Workers, National Association of Social Workers. (undated). *Academy of certified social workers (ACSW) credential.* Washington, DC: Author.

Allen, G. F. (1995). Probation and Parole. In R. L. Edwards et al. (Eds.), *Encyclopedia of social work* (19th ed.). (pp. 1910–1916). Washington, DC: NASW Press.

Alexander, C. A. (1995). Distinctive dates in social welfare history. In R. L. Edwards et al. (Eds.), *Encyclopedia of social work* (19th ed.). (pp. 2631–2647). Washington, DC: NASW Press.

Alinsky, S. D. (1969). *Reveille for radicals.* New York: Vintage books.

American Association of State Social Work Boards. (1997). *The exam "blue book."* Culpeper, VA: Author.

American Association of State Social Work Boards. (1996). *Social work job analysis in support of the American Association of State Social Work Boards examination program.* Culpeper, VA: Author.

Andrews, A. B. (1990). Interdisciplinary and interorganizational collaboration. In L. Ginsberg et al. (Eds.), *Encyclopedia of social work* (18th ed.), 1990 supplement (pp. 175–188). Silver Spring, MD: NASW Press.

Arches, J. (1991). Social structure, burnout, and job satisfaction. *Social Work, 36,* 203–207.

Axinn, J. & Levin, H. (1999). *Social welfare: A history of the American response to need* (4th ed.). Boston: Allyn and Bacon.

Barker, R. (1999). *Social work dictionary* (4th ed.). Washington, DC: NASW Press.

Begun, B. (2000, January 1). USA: The way we'll live then. *Newsweek, 34–35.*

Bernstein, P. and Ma, C. (Eds.). (1996). *The practical guide to practically everything.* New York: Almanac, Inc.

Bloom, M., Fischer, J., & Orme, J. G. (1999). *Evaluating practice: Guidelines for the accountable professional.* Boston: Allyn and Bacon.

Bly, R. W. (2000). Job burnout. Dumont, NJ: Center for Technical Communication.

Bonczar, T. P. & Glaze, L. E. (1999, August). *Probation and parole in the United States, 1998.* Washington, DC: U.S. Department of Justice, Bureau of Justice Statistics.

Brilliant, E. L. (1990). *The United Way: Dilemmas of organized charity.* New York: Columbia University Press.

Brown, J. M. & Langan, P. A. (1999, July). *Felony sentences in the United States, 1996.* Washington, DC: U.S. Department of Justice, Bureau of Justice Statistics.

Brown, J. M, Langan, P. A., & Levin, D. J. (1999, July). *Felony sentences in state courts, 1996.* Washington, DC: U.S. Department of Justice, Bureau of Justice Statistics.

Bureau of Justice Statistics. (1996). *Correctional populations in the United States, 1994.* Washington, DC: U.S. Department of Justice, Bureau of Justice Statistics.

Bureau of Labor Statistics. (1998, January 15). *1998–99 occupational outlook handbook: Counselors.* Washington, DC: Author.

Bureau of Labor Statistics. (1999a, September 15). *1998–99 occupational outlook handbook: Social Workers.* Washington, DC: Author.

Bureau of Labor Statistics. (1999b, September 15). *1998–99 occupational outlook handbook: Social and human service assistants.* Washington, DC: Author.

Constable, R. T., Flynn, J. P., & McDonald, S. (Eds.). (1991). *School Social Work: Practice and research perspectives.* Chicago: Lyceum.

Council on Social Work Education. (1994). *Curriculum policy statements for baccalaureate and master's social work education.* Alexandria, VA: Author.

Council on Social Work Education. (1996). *Summary information on master of social work programs.* Alexandria, VA: Author.

Covey, S. R. (1990). *The seven habits of highly effective people: Restoring the character ethic.* New York: Simon and Schuster.

Cunningham, P. (1996). *Peace Corps today.* Washington, DC: Peace Corps.

Day, P. J. (2000). *A new history of social welfare* (3rd ed.). Boston: Allyn and Bacon.

Educational Testing Service. (1997). *GRE: Practice general test.* Princeton, NJ: Author.

Educational Testing Service. (1999). *Graduate Record Examinations: 1999–2000, Guide to the use of scores.* Princeton, NJ: Author.

Edwards, R. L. et al. (Eds.). (1995). *Encyclopedia of social work* (19th ed.). Washington, DC: NASW Press.

Edwards, R. L. et al. (Eds.). (1997). *Encyclopedia of social work: 1997 supplement.* Washington, DC: NASW Press.

Gabor, P. A. & Grinnell, Jr., R. M. (1994). *Evaluation and quality improvement in the human services.* Boston: Allyn and Bacon.

Gibelman, M. (1995). *What social workers do.* Washington, DC: NASW Press.

Gibelman, M. & Schervish, P. H. (1993a). *Who we are.* Washington, DC: NASW Press.

Gibelman, M. & Schervish, P. H. (1993b). *What we earn.* Washington, DC: NASW Press.

Gibelman, M. & Schervish, P. H. (1996). *Who we are: A second look.* Washington, DC: NASW Press.

Gill, M. S. (2000, January). Look who's cheating. *Details,* 46–49.

Gilliard, D. K. & Beck, A. J. (1996, August). *Prison and jail inmates, 1995.* Washington, DC: U.S. Department of Justice, Office of Justice Programs, Bureau of Justice Statistics.

Ginsberg, L. (1983). *The practice of social work in public welfare.* New York: Free Press.

Ginsberg, L. (1995). *Social work almanac* (2nd ed.). Washington, DC: NASW Press.

Ginsberg, L. (1999a). *Social work in rural communities* (3rd ed.). Alexandria, VA: Council on Social Work Education.

Ginsberg, L. (1999b) *Understanding social welfare problems, policies, and programs* (3rd. ed.). Columbia, SC: USC Press.

Ginsberg, L. (2001). *Social work evaluation: Principles and methods.* Boston: Allyn and Bacon. In press.

Ginsberg, L. & Keys, P. (1995). New management in human services. (2nd ed) Washington, DC: NASW Press.

Harbert, A. & Ginsberg, L. (1990). *Human services for older adults: Concepts and skills.* (2nd ed.). Columbia, SC: University of South Carolina Press.

Kotz, N. & Kotz, M. L. (1977). *A passion for equality: George Wiley and the movement.* New York: W.W. Norton.

Lally, E. M. & Haynes, H. A. (1995). Alaska natives. Edwards, R. L. et al. (Eds.). (1995). *Encyclopedia of social work* (19th ed.). Washington, DC: NASW Press.

Lawrence, L. & Hall, M. J. (1999, August 18). *1997 Summary: National hospital discharge survey.* Hyattsville, MD: U.S. Department of Health and Human Services, Centers for Disease Control and Prevention, National Center for Health Statistics.

Lemann, N. (1999). *The big test: The secret history of the American meritocracy.* New York: Farrar, Straus, and Giroux.

Lennon, T. M. (1999). *Statistics on social work education in the United States:1998.* Alexandria, VA: Council on Social Work Education.

Lewis, R. G. (1995). American Indians. Edwards, R. L. et al. (Eds.). (1995). *Encyclopedia of social work* (19th ed.). Washington, DC: NASW Press.

Lyles, C. D. & Mosley, A. (1996, September 2). Career currents. *The Columbia State.* Moneywise, 10.

Marris, P. & Rein, M. (1967). *Dilemmas of social reform: Poverty and community action in the United States.* New York: Atherton.

McCourt, F. (1996). *Angela's ashes.* New York: Scribner.

McCourt, F. (1999). *'Tis.* New York: Simon and Schuster.

Meadowcroft, P. & Trout, B. (Eds.). (1990). *Troubled youth in treatment homes: A handbook for therapeutic foster care.* Washington, DC: Child Welfare League of America.

Middleman, R. R. (1996). *Study guide for ACSW certification* (4th ed.). Washington, DC: NASW Press.

NASW Register of Clinical Social Workers Credentialing Office. (1999). *Information bulletin and application for new applicants and QCSW's applying for diplomate in clinical social work.* Washington, DC: Author.

National Association of Social Workers. (1999). *Code of ethics.* Washington, DC: Author.

National Association of Social Workers. (undated a). *Academy of Certified Social Workers (ACSW) credential.* Washington, DC: Author.

National Association of Social Workers. (undated b). *Academy of Certified Social Workers information bulletin 1998/1999.* Washington, DC: Author.

National Association of Social Workers. (undated c). *School social work specialist (SSWS) credential: Application packet.* Washington, DC: Author.

Perlmutter, F. D. (1995). Administering alternative social programs. In Ginsberg, L. and Keyes, P. R. *New management in human services* (2nd ed.). Washington, DC: NASW Press.

Peterson, L. (1996, July). Petrified at the podium? *A & E Monthly,* 47–48.

Poole, D. L. (1996, August). Keeping managed care in balance. *Health and Social Work,* 163–166.

Poole, D. L., et al. (1996, August). *Health and Social Work (Special issue on managed care).* Washington, DC: NASW Press.

Royse, D. & Thyer, B. (1996). *Program evaluation: An introduction* (2nd ed.). Chicago: Nelson-Hall.

Sabol, W. J. & McGready, J. (1999, June). *Time served in prison by federal offenders, 1986–87.* Washington, DC: U.S. Department of Justice, Bureau of Justice Statistics.

Sheafor, B. & Morales, A. (1995). *Social work: A profession of many faces* (2nd ed.). Boston: Allyn and Bacon.

South Carolina Board of Social Work Examiners. (1996, July 17). *Supervised experience for LISW licensure.* Columbia, SC: Author.

Task Force on DSM-IV and other committtees and work groups of the American Psychiatric Association (1994). *Diagnostic and statistical manual of mental disorders, fourth edition: DSM-IV.* Washington, DC: American Psychiatric Association.

Tatara, T. (1993). *Summaries of the statistical data on elder abuse in domestic settings for FY 90 and FY 91: A final report.* Washington, DC: National Aging Resource Center on Elder Abuse.

Time. (1996, July 22). Less pain, more gain, 65.

Tirrito, T. (1996). *Elder practice.* Columbia, SC: University of South Carolina Press.

Tripodi, T. (1994). *A primer of single subject design for clinical social workers.* Washington, DC: NASW Press.

U.S. Department of Health and Human Services. (1999). *Mental health: A report of the surgeon general.* Rockville, MD: Author.

U.S. Department of Labor, Bureau of Labor Statistics. (1993, November). *BLS releases new 1992–2005 employment projections.* Washington, DC: Author.

Weinbach, R. (1994). *The social worker as manager.* New York: Longman.

Wild, R., D'Agostino, R., Schulz, B., Dolan, M., & Batistick, M. (2000, January). Have you annoyed your boss today? *Details,* 108–113, 122.

Wilkes-Hull, M. & Crosswait, C. B. (1996). *Professional development: The dynamics of success* (5th ed.). Belmont, CA: Wadsworth.

Winters, W. G. & Easton, F. (1983). *The practice of social work in schools.* New York: Free Press.

Index